NANCY CALLAN

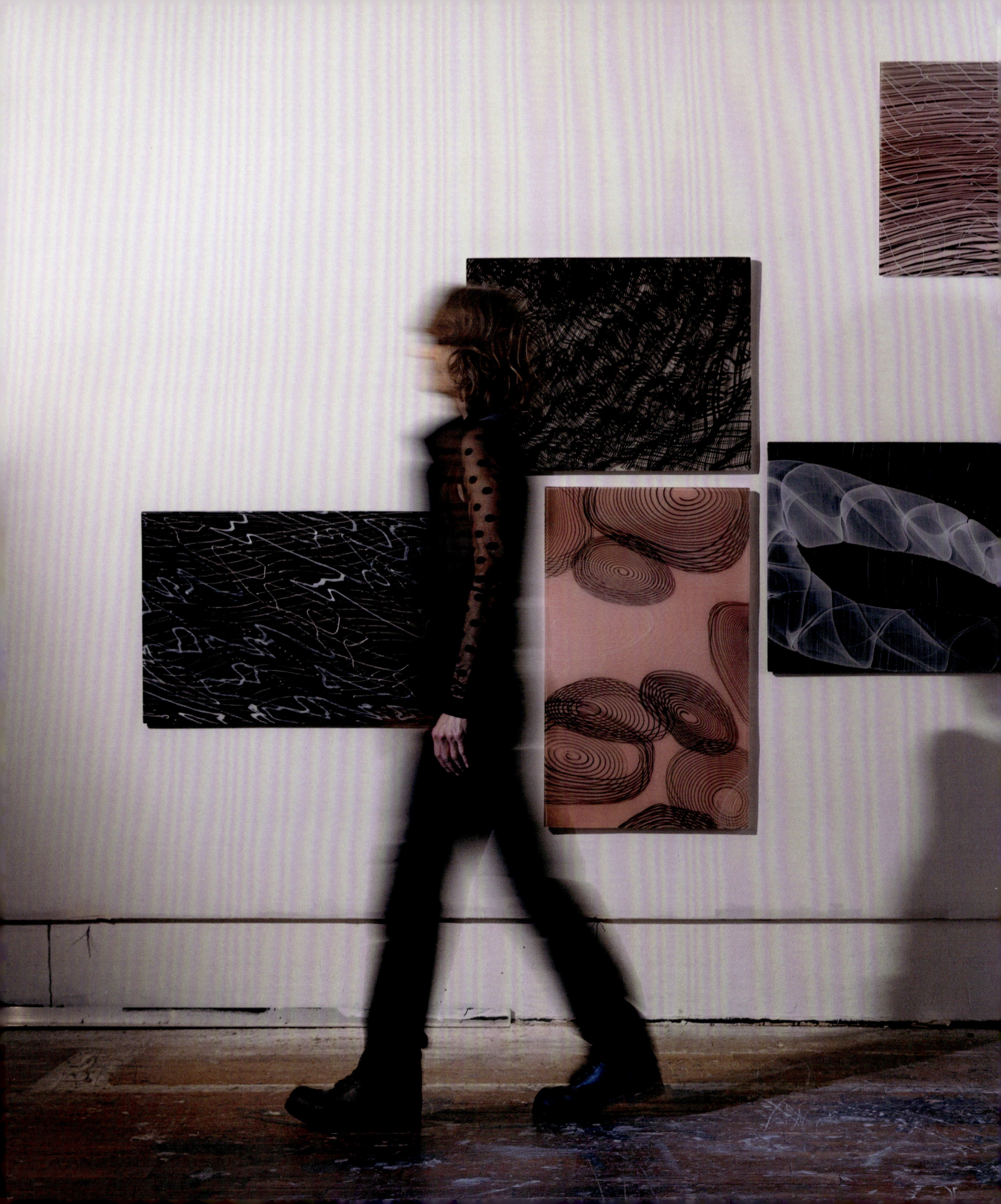

NANCY CALLAN

Contributions by
Katie Buckingham
Gayle Clemans
Kim Harty

Primary photography by
Russell Johnson

Museum of Glass
Tacoma, Washington

FORCES AT PLAY

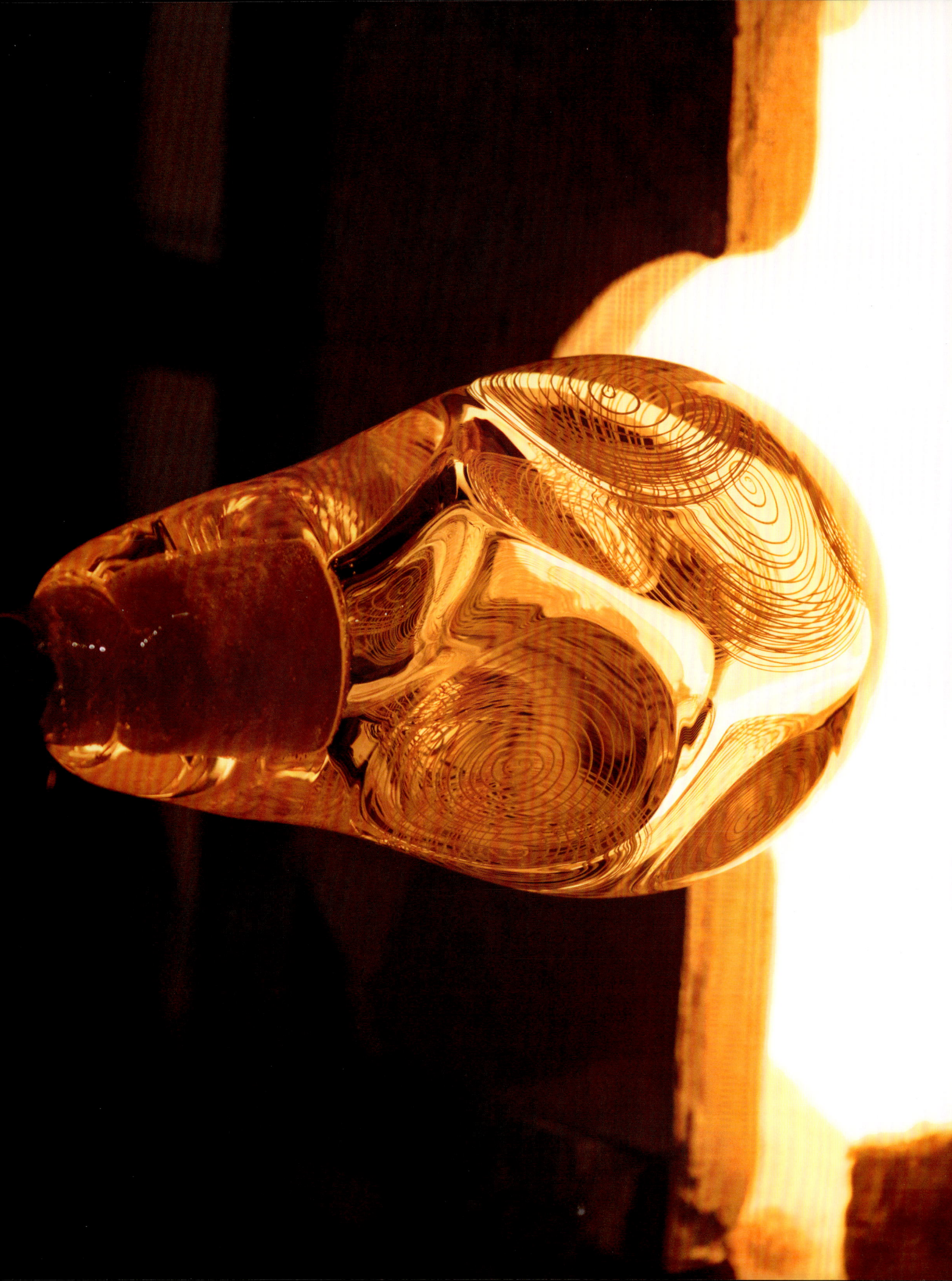

CONTENTS

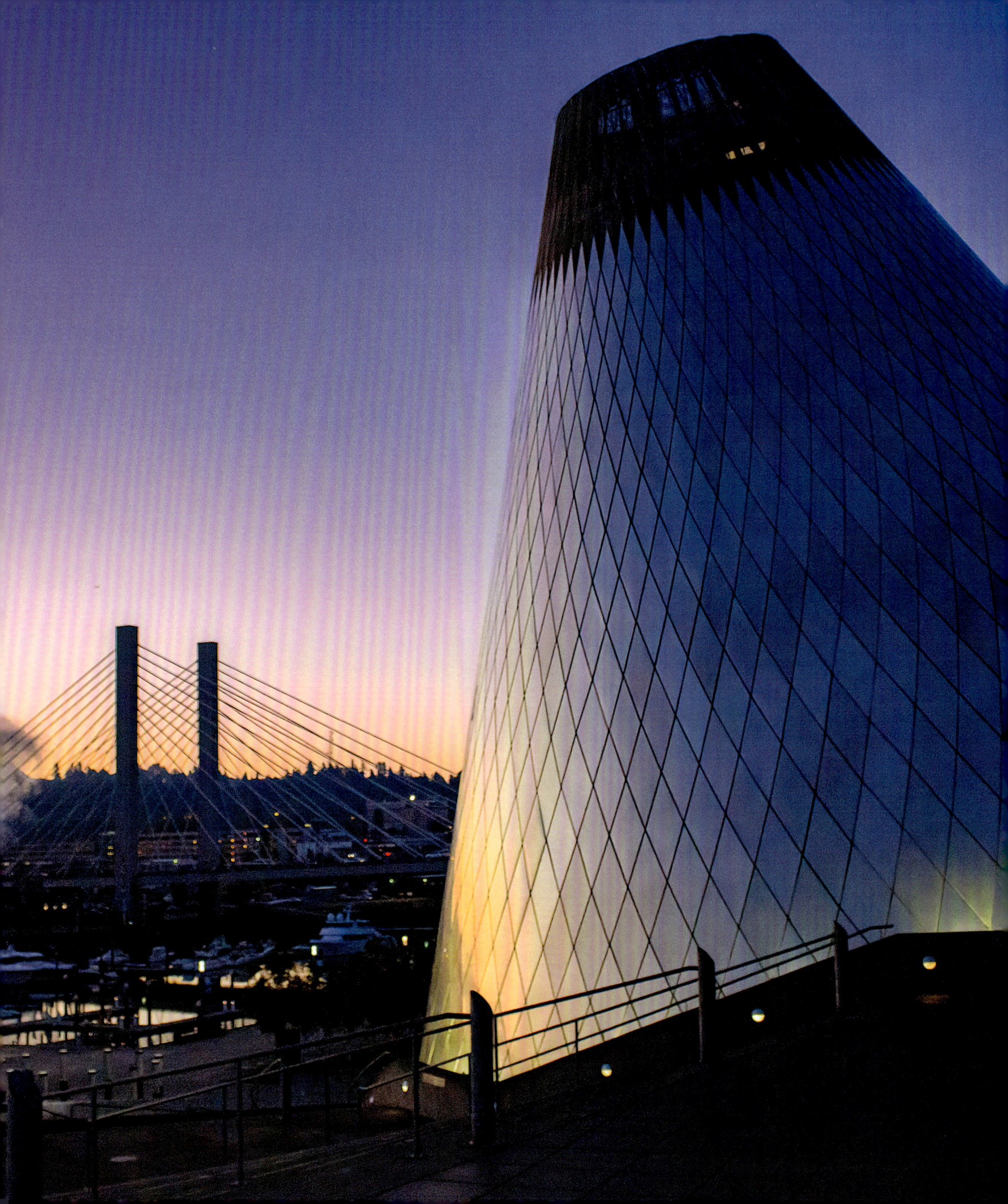

FOREWORD

It is time for Nancy Callan's work to be seen in an in-depth solo exhibition. While she has demonstrated her craft in front of packed crowds in over a dozen Visiting Artist Residencies in the Museum of Glass (MOG) Hot Shop as a solo artist, and her designs have been featured in the Museum's galleries as integral parts of other shows, *Nancy Callan: Forces at Play* puts her alone in the spotlight, where she belongs.

This exhibition allows us to observe the world through Callan's unique perspective, extensive visual vocabulary, and mastery of the artistic process. She is a *maestro* in her own right, and the Museum is thrilled that her work is receiving this platform and recognition.

Callan continues to break barriers in the field. Importantly, *Forces at Play* creates an inclusive historical narrative in glass, featuring a female, LGBTQ+ artist, at the peak of her career, in a solo show and catalog. Additionally, it spotlights a glassblowing team creating works of ambitious scale and sophistication. Museum of Glass strives to present the entire glass community in its exhibitions and Hot Shop—amplifying the voices, experiences, and identities of artists like Callan. Her exhibition is essential to these important discussions about representation, as we aim to broaden the conversation about glass and who makes it. Documenting the evolution of Callan's career through residencies, demonstrations, and lectures has only further enriched the depth of these conversations in the exhibition.

In my tenure as executive director at Museum of Glass, I have come to know Callan well, and therefore have seen that the work presented in this catalog is the result of significant determination and tenacity—qualities in her that I admire. And while Callan's skill is evident in each piece, I have found that what I enjoy the most is perhaps the most basic: her designs bring a smile to my face. I am proud that this publication will commemorate *Forces at Play* and showcase her beautiful creations, while adding a chapter to the important glass story told at the Museum.

There are several individuals, listed in this publication's credits, who provided funding and were instrumental in making this exhibition and publication a reality. We are grateful for their dedication to this artist and to the art form.

Thank you as well to the dedicated staff, volunteers, and board of trustees at Museum of Glass, without whom a project like this would not be possible. I would like to specifically acknowledge our curatorial, development, and education departments, for their vision and creativity, as well as the Museum of Glass Hot Shop team for their direct support of Callan in making much of the art exhibited in *Forces at Play*.

And, most importantly, thank you to Nancy Callan for sharing her artistry and vision with Museum of Glass and the world. We are honored to be entrusted with her legacy story in this solo exhibition.

Deborah Lenk
Executive Director
Museum of Glass

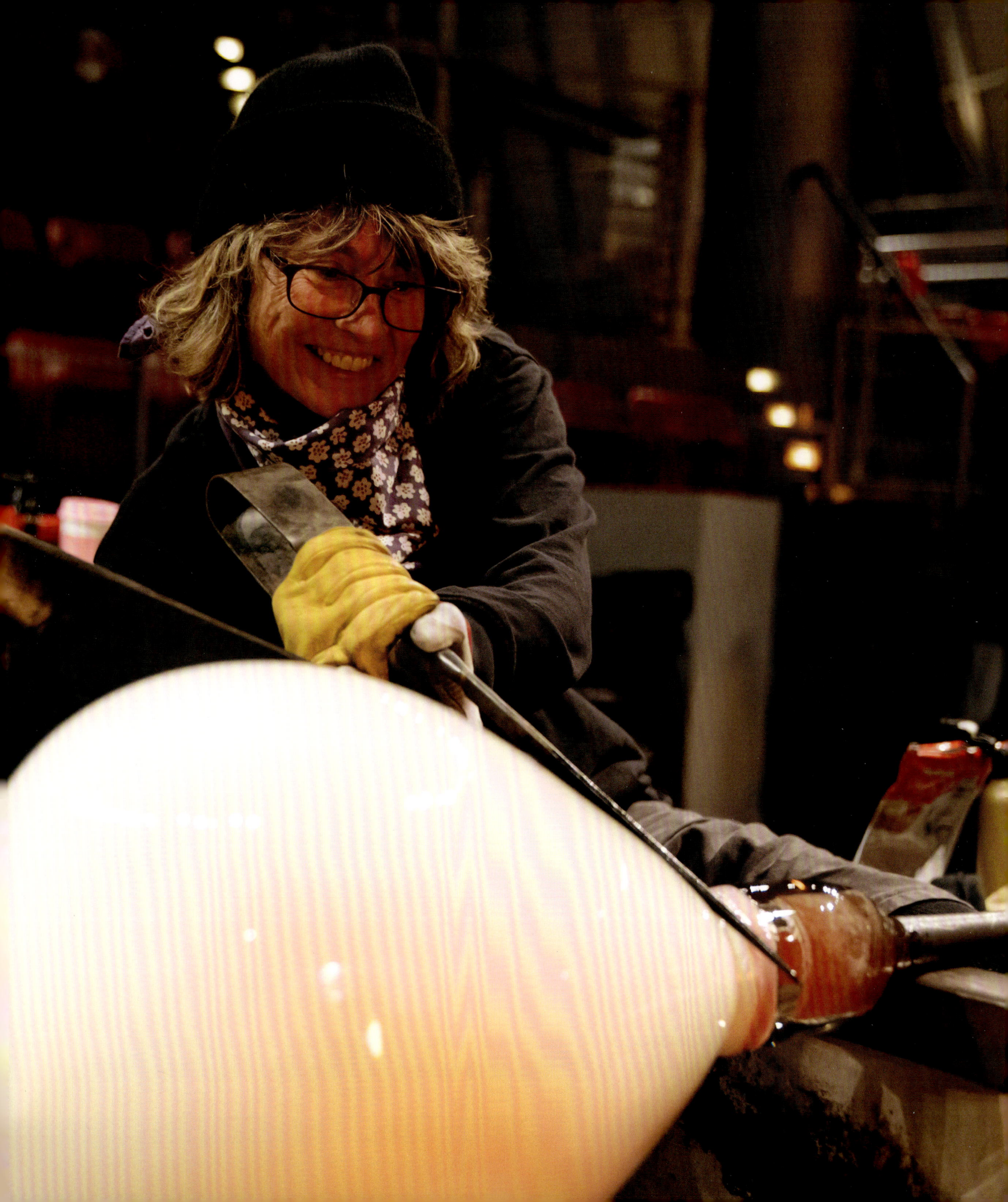

Katie Buckingham

INTRODUCTION

*Art is both a question and an answer. We ask . . .
"What if?" and we answer that question through the
process of making.*
—Nancy Callan

To experience the material of glass through the eyes of Nancy Callan is to see a centuries-long craft tradition through a contemporary lens. Her elegant, playful designs are inspired by a limitless curiosity in the world around us. Each piece is the result of Callan's career-long discipline, executed with extraordinary technical expertise. And, speaking from personal experience, she is incredibly *cool*.

It is truly a privilege to set the stage for *Nancy Callan: Forces at Play*. Museum of Glass (MOG) has been honored to have a front-row seat to major developments in Callan's career. Located in Tacoma, Washington, Museum of Glass is home to one of the largest glassblowing studios on the West Coast. Each year, the Museum's Visiting Artist Residency program invites artists to work with the Hot Shop team, to experiment with new ideas, and to push the boundaries of glass as an art medium. The Hot Shop is surrounded by an amphitheater that offers visitors an unparalleled view of this captivating, molten material, where they witness the successes and failures that are inevitable as the creative process unfolds in real time.

Glass finds itself at a crossroads between its history as a production and studio medium, and how it should continue to evolve in the 21st century. Callan's *oeuvre* is a salient example of this transition: historic Venetian techniques, traditionally used for ornamentation, now translated as a vocabulary to investigate identity, wonder, popular culture, and the large and small worlds found in nature. While glass is ubiquitous in our day-to-day lives, Callan opens the material up to spark wonder and to question the world around us.

Although initially trained as a graphic designer, Callan was immediately captivated by a chance encounter with glassblowing at Massachusetts College of Art. With an eye toward mastering the material, she signed up for a class with Italian glass *maestro* Lino Tagliapietra (Italian, born 1934), regarded as the best glassblower in the world. "I remember the first time I saw Lino blow glass, I knew immediately that I wanted to learn from him. He *was* glass. Passionate and fluid, like a magician. You could see his love and respect for the material in just one moment."[1] With Tagliapietra's referral, Callan moved from the East Coast to Seattle, where she began working at a production studio, Manifesto, making blown-glass lighting. She also joined Tagliapietra's team, starting a 19-year relationship that was essential to her mastery of the specialized techniques that are the foundation of her innovative work with line, pattern, and color (fig. 1).

Forces at Play encapsulates the development of Callan's career by featuring works from some of her earliest series as well as examples of current work, revealing how her innovative approach to contemporary sculpture is grounded in her training in Italian glassblowing techniques. The Museum has been fortunate to facilitate some of the experimentation that has led to the development of many of her signature series, in a prolific succession of residencies that has spanned the Museum's entire history.

Since the Museum opened in 2002, Callan has worked in the Hot Shop 20 times: 10 times to make her own work as a Visiting Artist; five as a member of Lino Tagliapietra's team; and five working with or alongside other artists, including collaborating with Katherine Gray (Canadian-American, born 1965) and Julia Ricketts (American, born 1970), acting as Guest Gaffer for Kids Design Glass with Deborah Czeresko (American, born 1961), and assisting sculptor Anne Wilson (American, born 1959). The first time I had the opportunity to watch her work was when she was a member of Tagliapietra's team in a 2012 MOG residency. One of my first impressions was one of quiet discipline. The team worked together in balletic cadence. While most of the attention focused on the *Maestro*, dramatically sculpting on the Hot Shop's center bench, Callan was already starting the bubble needed for the next piece, in a rhythm that seemed to flow without any need for conversation or

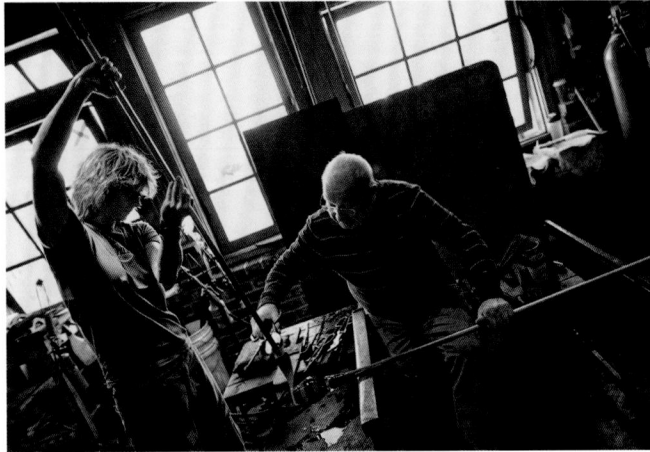

direction. It was a symphony of movement that was magical to behold—clearly forged in trust and leadership.

Perched on the Hot Shop balcony, watching Callan work over a decade later in 2022, it is easy to see the influence of Tagliapietra's rigorous yet seamless cadence on Callan's own style of working. She is calmly, competently everywhere, moving fluidly between shaping a large cylinder (one of the panels for *Comme les Filles*), then using tweezers to sculpt the cane emerging on the molten bubble that will become the next piece, while double-checking the pattern of *murrine* and cane waiting for a future sculpture. Assisted by David Walters (American, born 1968) and Jen Elek (American, born 1972), who also held key roles on the Tagliapietra team, and the Museum's Hot Shop team, led by Benjamin Cobb (American, born 1979), Callan notes that she can "plan and execute complex work with confidence. It makes such a difference having the support of amazing artists like Dave, Jen, and Ben, as well as the entire MOG team (figs. 2, 3). They are all incredibly skilled and understand my work and the standards I bring to it."[2]

Callan describes each Museum of Glass residency as a chance to experiment and to push her extensive knowledge of Italian canework and *murrine*-pattern techniques to new heights. During residencies between 2011–2017, she crafted a series of *Snowmen* whose sheer size and dramatic on-the-pipe assembly delighted the Museum's visitors. *Blueprint for a Snowman I* (Chk. 16, p. 45) stands out as a tour de force of glass-cane design and execution: Callan achieved perfect grids of white lines on three different-sized orbs, scaling each to account for the expansion while blowing the shape, and even extending the grid onto the upturned nose (fig. 3). Other significant series developed at MOG are represented in *Nancy Callan: Forces at Play*, including *Winkles*, *Stingers*, and, most recently, a series of daring panels, *Shadow Realm* (Chk. 47, pp. 21, 28, 119–126), which represents both a pinnacle of Callan's accomplishments in glass and a full-circle return to the two-dimensional origins of her artistic career.

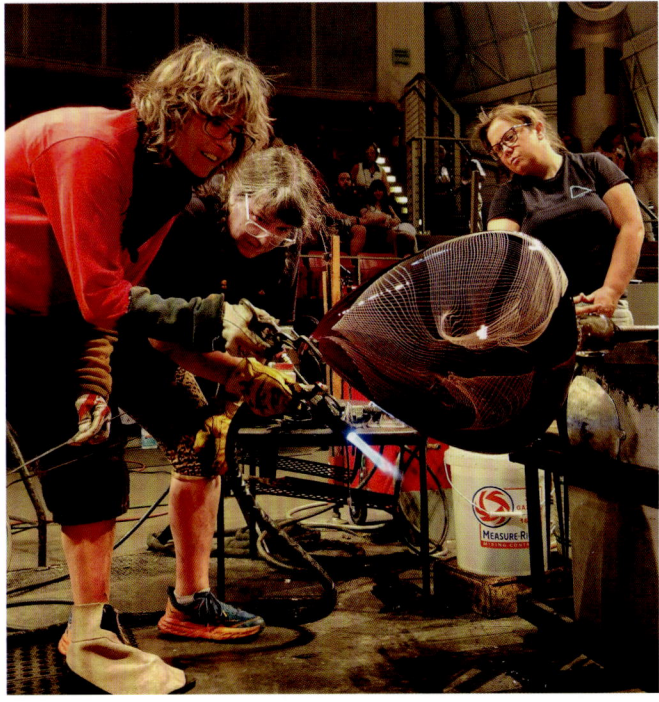

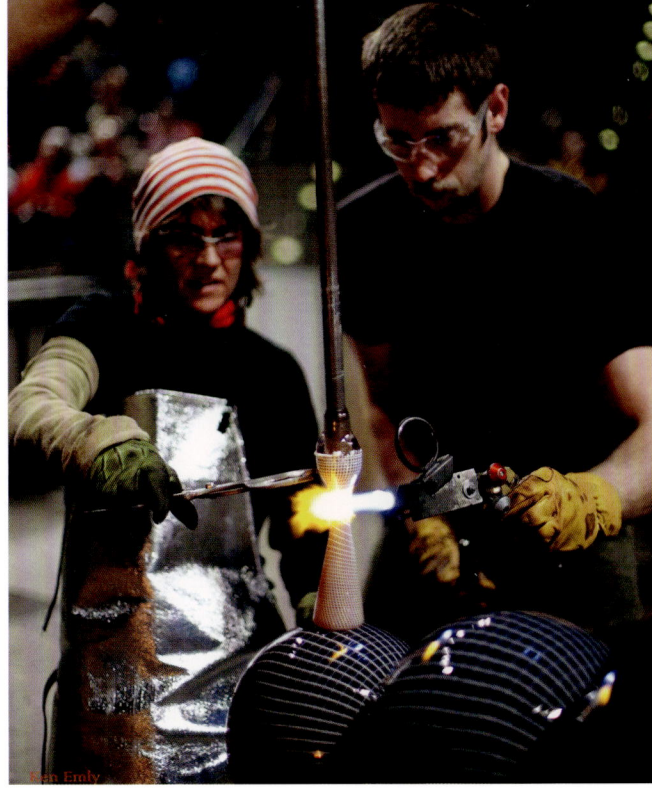

Callan uses the molten fluidity of glass as a canvas to interpret the world around her. She finds inspiration in the everyday as well as the extraordinary, filtering her observations through the material to arrive at startling new patterns and forms. She is intrigued by the transformative aspects of glassworking and the process of abstraction: "I might find a pattern in nature or a piece of fabric fascinating, but the process of making it in glass always leads to something new and unexpected. In this way, my work is less a mirror on the world and more of a filter, in which ideas and images are transformed into something new."[3]

There is something innately human about observation. This is the nut that Artificial Intelligence will be unable to crack, the magic that is inherent to artmaking. At its core, the creative act is about observing something in the world and capturing its emotional resonance. Callan is a keen observer, and the exhibition is full of references to things: fabrics, clouds, snowmen. But the magic happens when Callan adds mystery and depth through her command of glassblowing techniques. This intersection between *what*, *how*, and *why* inspired Callan to become an artist. "It is hard to express thoughts and feelings with words, and that is what drew me to being a visual artist. I did not have to explain myself. I could just be."[4]

In addressing larger issues of identity, wonder, and the order of the universe, Callan's work encourages viewers to step back and commit to the act of observing in their own lives. When you see the world like Nancy Callan, there is no moment too small to be inspirational. It is at this point where the magnetic magic of molten glass intersects with the arresting moments of wonder and questioning of the world around us. By focusing on this intersection, *Forces at Play* takes glass into the 21st century. Rather than positioning the material as "craft" or "art," Callan's work shows us that glass can be both.

Sharing Callan's incredible work through *Forces at Play* is Museum of Glass at its best. Over the past two decades, Callan has not only pushed the boundaries of her own work, but has given our visitors the joy of watching this process in action. By sharing Callan's immense artistic achievements alongside the insight into her creative process, this exhibition invites viewers to appreciate the nuances and rigor of the glassmaking, while it encourages each of us to find the same spark of creativity in our own lives.

Notes

1 Nancy Callan, "Nancy Callan - 21st Century Glassblower," TEDxEast, 2011, www.youtube.com/watch?v=XpWZIr6yDt0, accessed February 15, 2023.

2 Communication between artist and author, October 9, 2023.

3 Communication between artist and author, March 28, 2023.

4 Derek Klein, "Nancy Callan: Vision & Process," May 31, 2009, www.youtube.com/watch?v=epcitNd8uOA, accessed February 15, 2023.

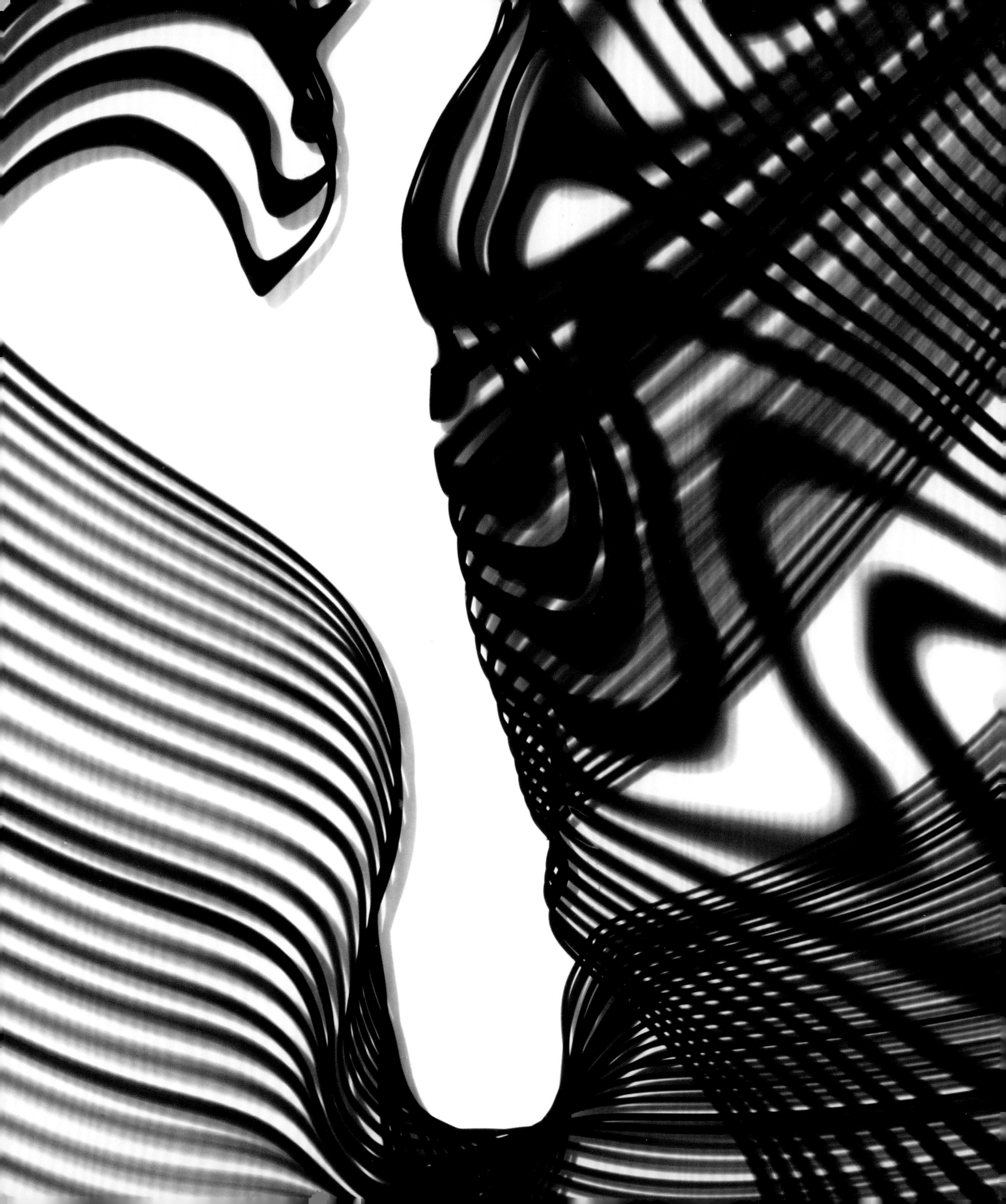

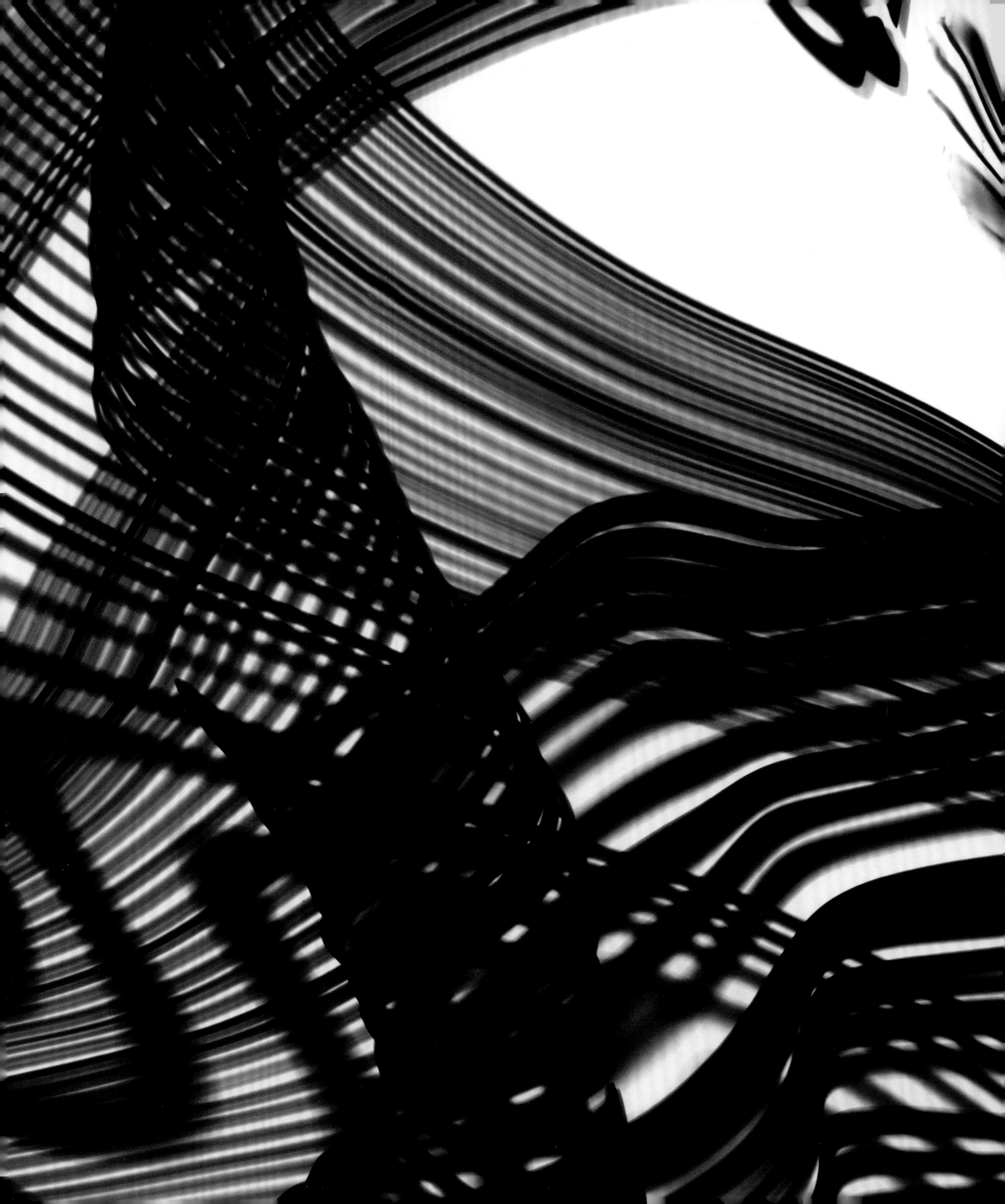

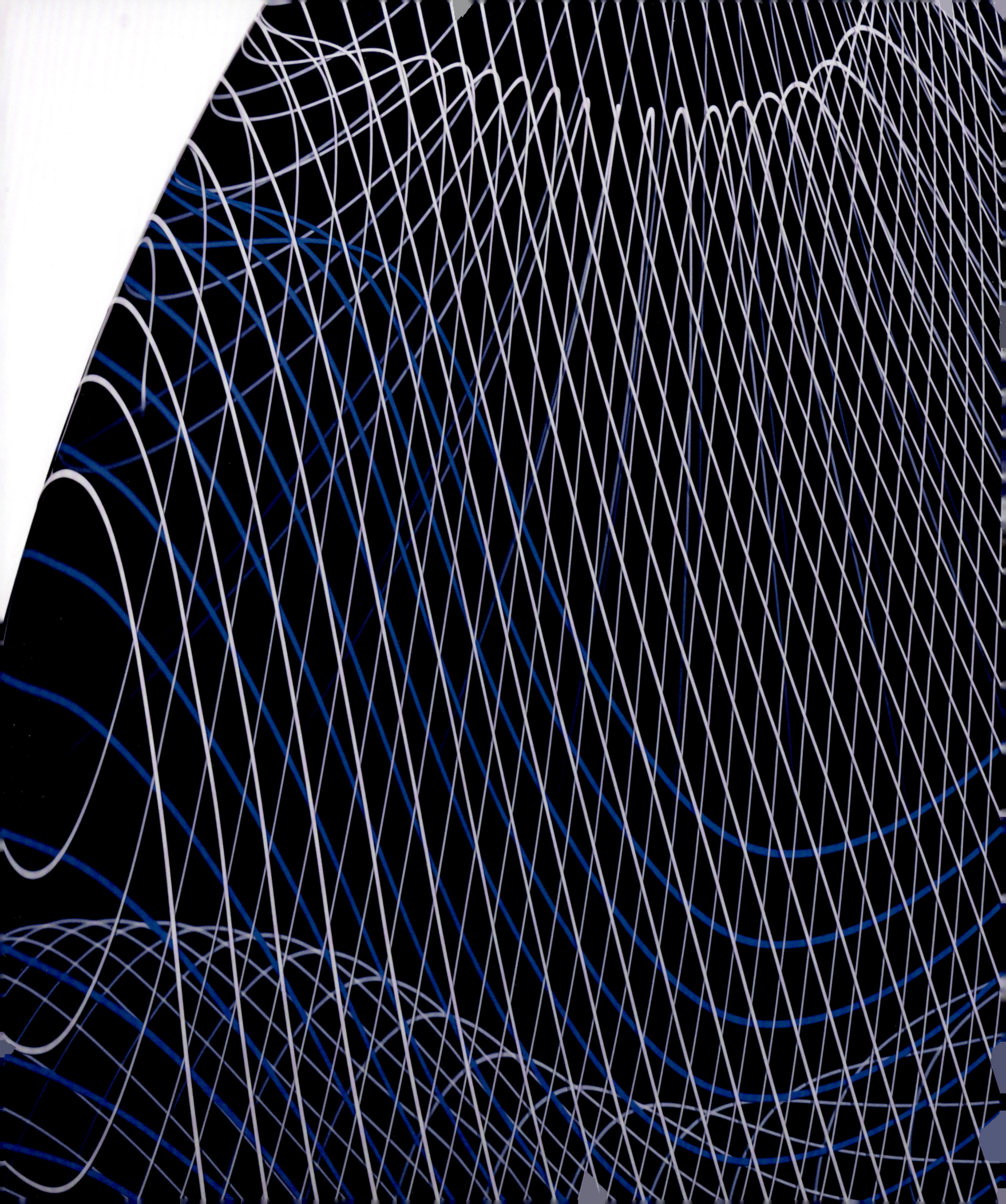

Gayle Clemans

INTERPLAY:
IDENTITY AND INFLUENCE IN THE ART OF NANCY CALLAN

Talking with Nancy Callan in her Seattle studio, as she points to examples of her glass work and some of the many references they hold, is a philosophical colloquy wrapped up in an enjoyable chat, complete with laughter and a little bit of science-fair demo thrown in for good measure.

She nests different objects inside each other to show how she invents new color palettes by layering glass. At one point, she spins a glass sculpture from her *Droplet* series, setting it in motion to further animate the white line that undulates across an inky black surface. This makes her wife—the artist Julia Ricketts—and me nervous. Callan smiles and pulls the sculpture back from the edge before moving on to the next topic.

Over the course of two visits, we discuss, among other things, her observation of pattern in nature, her abiding love of fashion design, the role of humor in her work, the significance of gender roles and fluidity, and her fascination with the endless possibilities she finds in glass.

Another idea that has captivated Callan is string theory, which proposes that tiny filaments vibrate—but vibrate differently—within all particles. Similarly, Callan's work can seem manifestly different from series to series, but it all thrums with connecting elements: witty and conceptual complexity, technical expertise and innovation, and

a dynamic interplay of three-dimensional form with color, line, or pattern.

Like many artists, Callan denies an easy ability to talk about her work, but it's undeniably there, stemming from her wide and deep curiosity about the world. The metaphor of conversation is apt, and one Callan uses to describe the way she enters into dialogue with nature, her own groundbreaking techniques, or the work of other artists.

Callan's conversations with glass artists and the centuries-old tradition of Venetian glass are vital foundations for her mastery of skill and love of the process. Now widely recognized as a preeminent glass artist—and one of the rare female glassblowers at the top of the field—Callan creates work that veers from Venetian conventions into the realm of contemporary art even as she carries the legacies of technique forward. As Callan herself has noted, "I'm a link to the history of Venetian glass."[1]

At the same time, Callan is a key contributor to, and product of, the glass community in the Pacific Northwest of the United States, which launched in the 1970s with artists who quickly gained a reputation as self-taught renegades. They soon sought training, however, from esteemed Italian glassblowers, such as Lino Tagliapietra (fig. 1), who was invited to teach glassblowing at Pilchuck Glass School in 1979. Eventually, Tagliapietra established a team in

Fig. 1 Artist assisting Lino
Tagliapietra in Mukilteo,
Washington, 2012

Fig. 2 *Pop Top*, 2014 (Chk. 21)

Page 14: *String Theory* (detail),
2016 (Chk. 25)

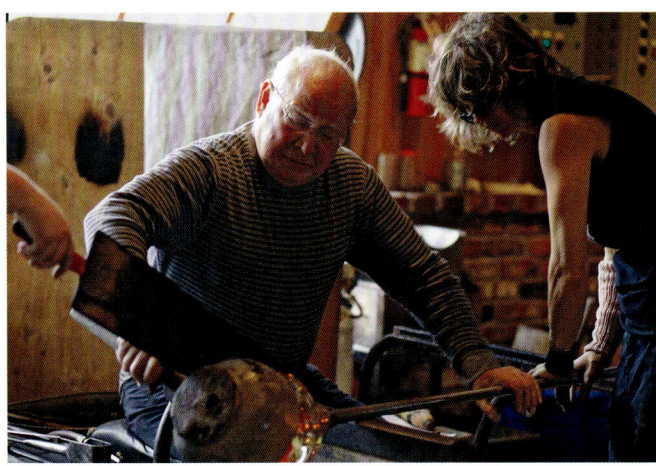

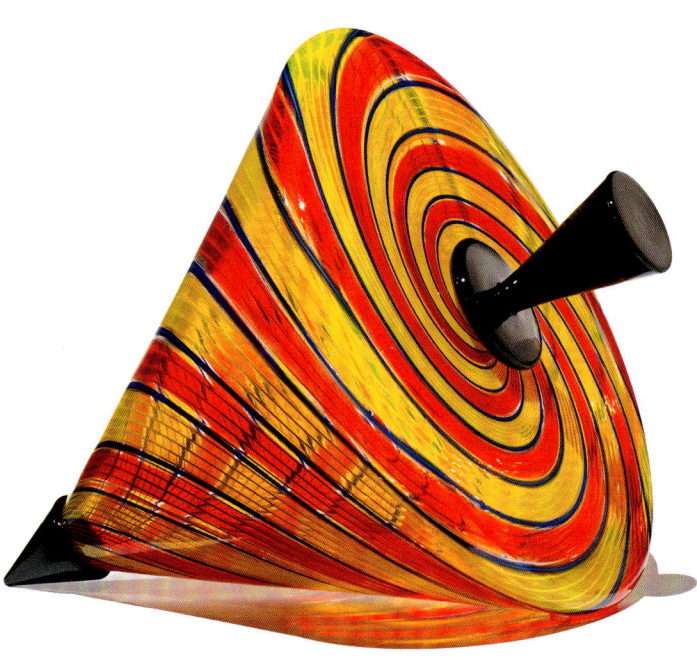

Seattle and, in 1996, procured a job for Callan, who relocated from the East Coast to learn all she could from the scene. Callan went on to work for and with prominent artists working in glass, including Dale Chihuly (American, born 1941), Ginny Ruffner (American, born 1952), Josiah McElheny (American, born 1966), and Flora C. Mace (American, born 1949) and Joey Kirkpatrick (American, born 1952), while traveling all over the world with Tagliapietra's team for 19 years. Callan still calls Seattle home.

This context is vital in understanding Callan's unique "both/and" position in the Studio Glass world. She is both a highly skilled craftsperson and an intuitive, concept-driven artist. As Jerome Harrington states in his study titled *Glass in the Expanded Field*, artists' relationships to Studio Glass can be placed on a spectrum from those who "prioritised craft skill" to those who "prioritised concept."[2] Callan, and other artists emerging in the 1990s and early 2000s, didn't feel the need to choose one pole or the other. Instead, Callan falls into a both/and category described by Harrington as "[a]rtistic concept expressed through skilled making, . . . where craft and concept have a mutually dependent relation."[3]

In this way, Callan is the inheritor of many traditions, including the postmodern one, which rejects absolutes and binaries. Callan's work is both playfully referential and reverently technical. Her fusion of traditional and groundbreaking techniques, along with a set of personal iconographies and intriguing references, aligns with the late postmodernism of the 1990s and 2000s, as irony gave way to sincerity while keeping the postmodern proclivities for humor, reference, and self-reflexivity (wherein the art refers to the process or conventions of the art form). With *Pop Top* (fig. 2), for example, Callan refers to the forms of Japanese toys, the vibrant colors of Pop Art, and the process of spinning a mass of molten glass on the end of a pipe.

These clever meta-allusions to the joys and challenges of working in glass swirl through many—if not all—of Callan's creations and frequently suggest entire series to

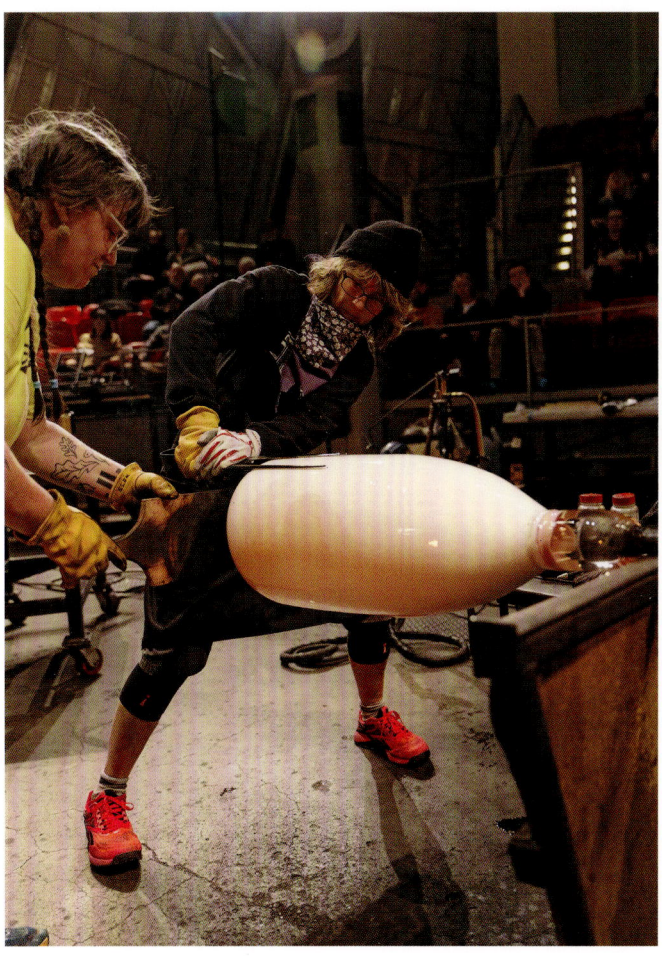

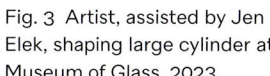
Fig. 3 Artist, assisted by Jen Elek, shaping large cylinder at Museum of Glass, 2023

Fig. 4 Walter Lieberman, *How Nancy Callan makes her flat panels*, 2019

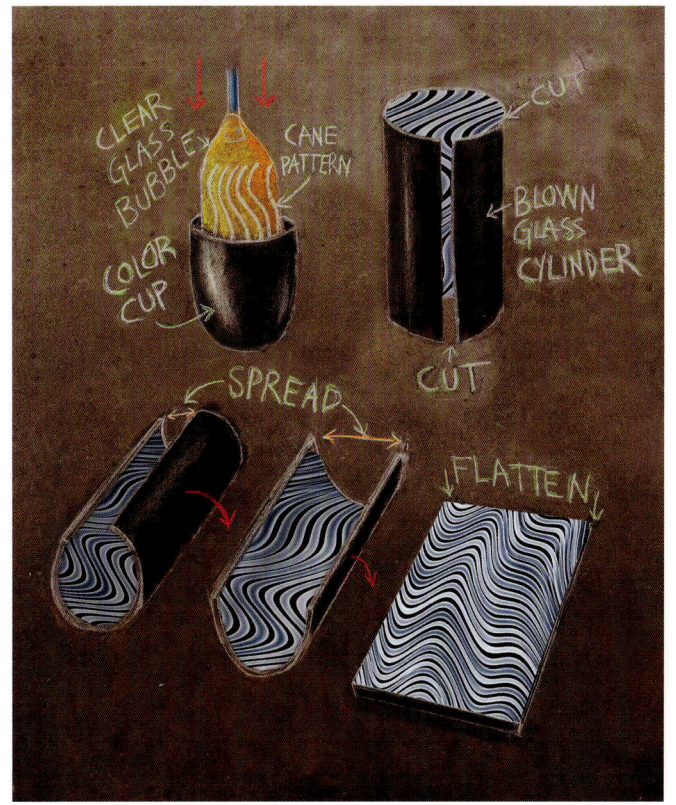

which Callan returns over time. For example, the definitive points within the *Bee Butts*, *Stingers*, *Winkles*—even the *Snowmen*—are humorous nods to the challenges of concluding a form and achieving such precise peaks.[4]

In 2016, Callan's references began to include her own collections of patterns, following the archival impulse so prevalent in contemporary art. A new body of two-dimensional panels was born as she conceptualized those patterns like sketchbooks on the wall, filled with her observations of pattern in nature, textiles, and the work of other artists. Initially created in black and white glass, like the sketches in her notebooks, these panels have recently taken on primary colors and hues of pink, silver, and gray.

The blown and slumped glass panels are technical marvels, born of an old window-pane-making process that Callan has taken in new directions. A very simplified explanation involves creating and laying out the cane or pick-up *murrine*, which she then rolls up and blows into a cylinder; the cylinder is then cut open and laid flat to reveal the panel (figs. 3, 4). All of these translations between two and three dimensions—from observed pattern in the world, to sketches, to blown glass, to flat panel—generate visual and conceptual layers.

Borrowing from the world of fashion, Callan thinks of these panels as large-scale swatches,[5] a term that suggests ideation. In fact, many of the panels collect Callan's keen observations of fashion and textiles. She has been known to stop people on the street to admire a print that they're wearing.[6] In the world of high fashion, Tokyo-based designer Rei Kawakubo (Japanese, born 1942), the founder of Comme des Garçons, has been a font of inspiration, which makes perfect sense given that designer's "in-betweenness."[7] Callan says, "I've always admired her fearless designs, play with contrasts, flow with gender, and cutting edge, sculptural forms. Meditating on her work, I asked myself, 'How can I do that in glass?'"[8]

Some of the answers to that question can be seen in Callan's large-scale installation of panels titled *Comme* les Filles (Chk. 37, pp. 26–27; 80–87). Individual panels were inspired by various patterns, including designs by Kawakubo. With a panel in Comme les Filles (see p. 83), Callan studied a Comme des Garçons layered and dotted skirt, interpreting and translating it through murrine, the slices of layered cane that are, themselves, another play between 2D and 3D, fusion and pattern.[9] The resulting panel ripples and sighs with contrasts between dark and light, hard and soft, surface and depth.

That panel, along with the others, captures Kawakubo's fusion of opposites as well as the concepts of mu (emptiness) and ma (space).[10] Consider the glossy or dense negative spaces of each panel, across and within which flow circles, spirals, swathes, and meshes of color and line. Taken as a whole, when the panels spread across the wall with space in between, they become their own pattern, suggesting an infinite, variegated space of possibilities.

Some of Callan's conversations revolve around artists working in different media who have experimented with the fundamentals of color, texture, and line, and the intertwined relationship of form and surface. The subtle grids and lines of painter Agnes Martin (Canadian-American, 1912–2004), for example, whisper through many of Callan's minimalist yet expressive objects.

Many of Callan's series play with primary and secondary colors and geometric forms; consider, for example, the spheres, cones, or modifications/combinations thereof in her Orbs, Droplets, Winkles, and Snowmen. Callan's engagement with the essential vocabulary of form and color—along with her interest in motion—echoes early 20th-century work by the painter, sculptor, and choreographer Oskar Schlemmer (German, 1888–1943) (fig. 5). Much like Schlemmer, and the Bauhaus design school at which he taught, Callan uses the dynamic power of fundamental forms and colors to rethink artistic conventions and connect with viewers in an elemental, bodily way.

Schlemmer once said that "the stage as a locus for temporal action offers movement of form and colour, first in its main configuration as mobile, coloured or colourless, linear, planar or sculptural single forms, as well as a changeable movable space . . ."[11] This kind of locus can also be found in the glass studio, with the choreography of the team working in unison amidst swirling color and changing form. Callan loves the process of orchestrating the plan and moving alongside others in the creative dance of the hot shop.

These qualities of movement and form, along with the influence of the Bauhaus, can be seen in the Snowman series, particularly The Robber (fig. 6), which Callan says is just about the favorite thing she's ever made. Not only is it a technical marvel, it's a kinetic piece—the knob on the bottom allows it to roll around in circles, which Callan calls "playful but a little dangerous!"[12] She cites the way the Bauhaus artists used "costumes, play, and silliness alongside sophisticated formal investigation"[13] as a strong tie to this work.

Other actual or imagined dialogues include Louise Bourgeois (French-American, 1911–2010), Anni Albers (German, 1899–1994), Richard Marquis (American, born 1945), Jun Kaneko (Japanese-American, born 1942), and Callan's friends and occasional collaborators Mel Douglas (Australian, born 1978) and Katherine Gray. And then there's Andy Warhol (American, 1928–1987).

Warhol, whom Callan refers to as a hero, offered many things to her early in her creative journey: a sense of playfulness with color, line, and subject matter. As Callan puts it, "He used familiar subjects but made you look at them in a new way."[14] He was also an example of someone living boldly in defiance of conventional gender norms and sexual orientations. Callan says, "When I first learned about Andy Warhol as a young adult, it gave me permission to be who I was."[15]

These ideas of freedom, acceptance, gender, and sexual orientation still resonate with Callan as a member of the LGBTQ+ community and as a woman working in the world of glass, which has been traditionally aligned with male heteronormativity. Callan states, "As a gay woman in

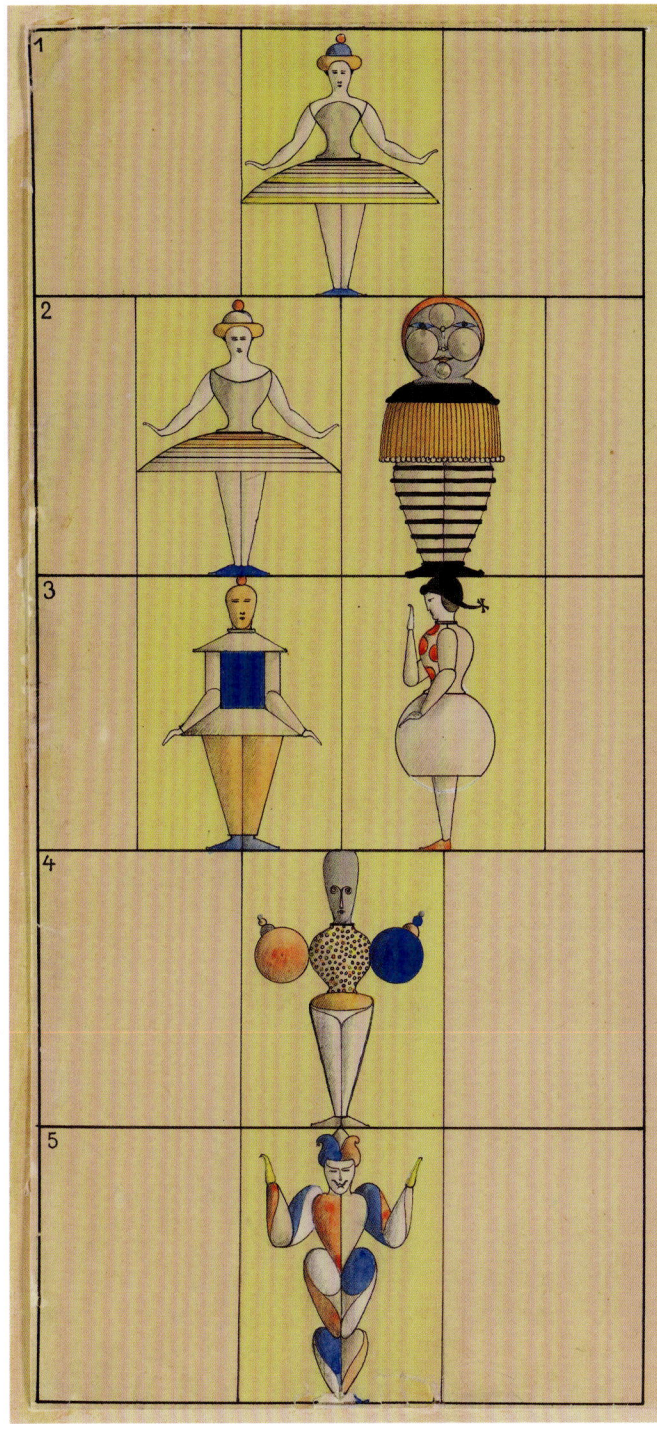

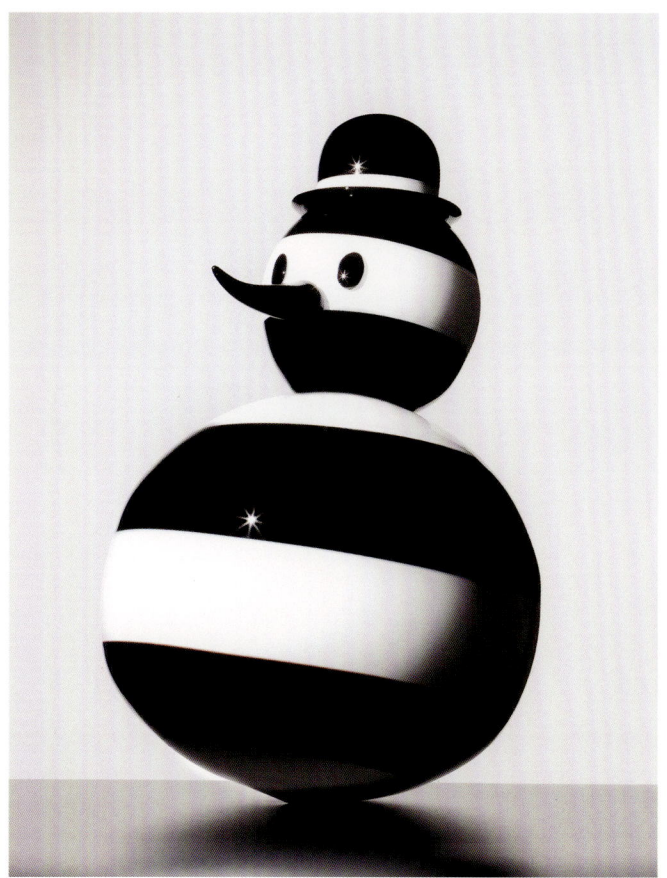

Fig. 5 Oskar Schlemmer, *Costume Designs for Das Triadische Ballet* [The Triadic Ballet] (detail), 1926

Fig. 6 *The Robber*, 2016

a male-dominated field, I would joke that the only women I saw in the hot shops were pin-up girls, on calendars and on the hot shields. Being gay made it easier in some ways. You're not quite in the boys' club, but you're closer. And it was always a way of getting out of the come-ons."[16]

Callan's exploration of these topics appears in early work like her *Pinup Girls* series (Chk. 2, p. 38), with their cheeky silhouettes of nude women in poses that suggest sexual allurement or availability. Furthermore, the bottle forms themselves have full shapes and bodily language: rounded shoulders, thin necks, and bulbous stoppers. A later group, *Beefcake Boys* (Chk. 4, p. 39), flips the script by depicting musclemen frozen in their "ideal man" poses.

A more recent work, *Road Trip with Keith* (fig. 7 and Chk. 34, pp. 58–59), is a thank you, of sorts, to Keith Haring (American, 1958–1990), another queer artist who has been a key figure for Callan. "His work is fun and joyful and an expression of freedom. He was part of my journey."[17] The colorful, linear qualities of Callan's multi-paneled work connect with Haring's graphic style. And Callan's white lines not only suggest paths or streams, they also recall Haring's early chalk drawings on advertisement substrates in subway stations.[18]

If you personally identify with some of these positionalities, or if you recognize some of these cultural or humorous

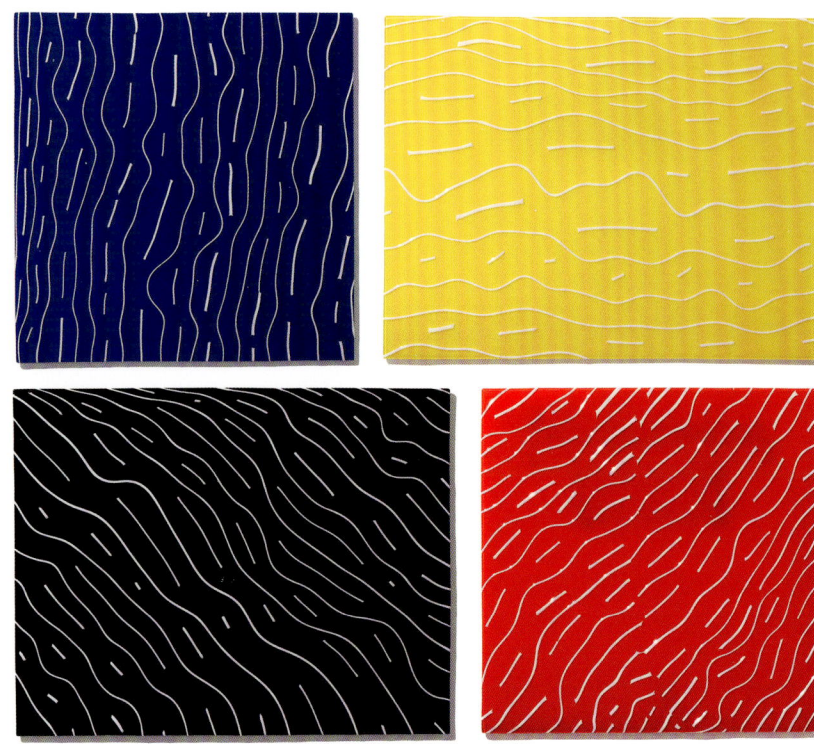

references, you'll be on common ground with the artist. But this is not the only way to be in conversation with Callan's work. It is vital to approach the work with an eye toward the beautiful, inextricable relationship between object and surface, what Callan calls "the synergy between the form and the pattern, the form and the lines."[19] Many works are driven by technical challenges that Callan sets for herself. After years of building her skills and striving for perfection, Callan can push those skills into myriad, experimental directions.

Another large-scale installation of panels titled *Shadow Realm* (fig. 8 and Chk. 47, pp. 28; 119–126) captures Callan's very recent experiments with reductive colors and highly textured surfaces. Her excitement about—and absorption in—these technically difficult processes are embedded in the work. Reducing can be an undesirable effect for glass artists given its unpredictability and its impact on color, but here, Callan has embraced the challenges and developed reduced color into a new visual language. Working with *granulare* and *murrine*, in layers of stiffer and softer colors, Callan torches oxygen and propane into cylinders to create these metallic and textured effects. The possibilities are endless. Callan says, "I just love to blow my own mind. The glass blows my mind and also the amount of knowledge behind it. This new work is all about discovery and what is possible. It's magic."[20]

The reflective, topographical panels are downright primordial with their slick or knobby surfaces. The work is so fresh that Callan hasn't had time to sit and sift through the possible references that were on her mind when planning and making them, but she's excited about how open ended and associative they are. We, as viewers, might conjure up allusions to landscapes, geology, cellular structures, or otherworldly terrains. Dark, mysterious, and alluring, our eyes can travel across their textured surfaces or get lost in their inky, sparkling depths.

This kind of engagement is possible and important in all of Callan's art, whether we find access through a humorous reference or marvel at the skilled craftsmanship. And so, allow yourself to become immersed in the way that textures and lines seem to slide across a panel as if extending infinitely outward, or the way that a *Winkle* or *Droplet* contains and stretches the lines within and around its body. Allow the movement to remind you of the process of the object's creation, as the molten glass spins, forms, and reforms in all of its changeable glory. And consider the incredible, liminal moment when movement becomes still, when Callan allows the hot, fast, ephemeral process to solidify and rest.

Callan says, "Something I always think about is how I'm able to freeze a moment in glass. To be able to stop something in time—that's powerful."[21]

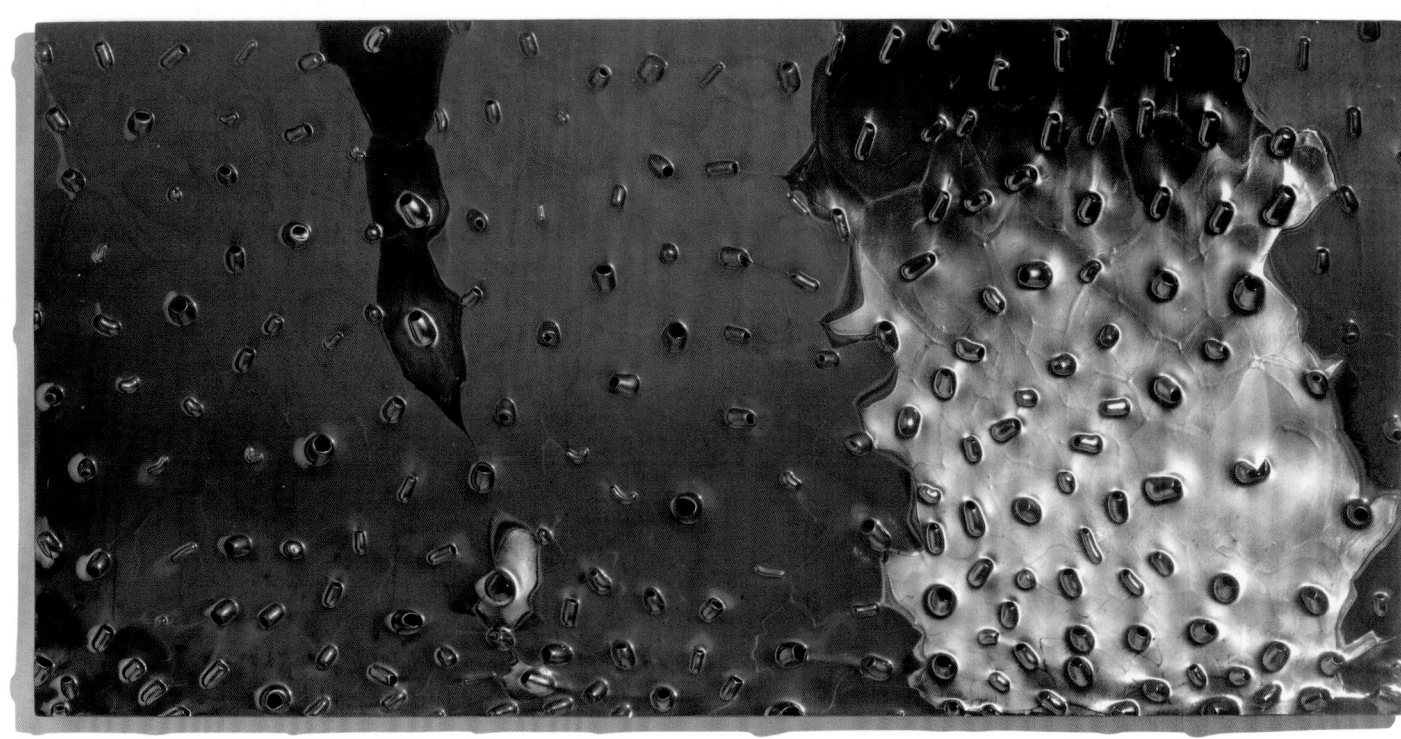

Notes

1 Nancy Callan, "Nancy Callan–21st Century Glassblower," TEDxEast, 2011, http://youtube.com/watch?v=XpWZIr6yDt0, accessed August 9, 2023.

2 Jerome Harrington, *Glass in the Expanded Field* (Amsterdam: Gerrit Rietveld Academie, 2012), 4.

3 Harrington, *Glass in the Expanded Field*, 4.

4 Nancy Callan, interview with the author, August 22, 2023.

5 William Warmus, "Behaving Boldly," *Glass: The UrbanGlass Art Quarterly*, No. 154 (Spring 2019): 53.

6 Callan, interview with the author, June 4, 2023.

7 This phrase comes from the exhibition *Rei Kawakubo/Comme des Garçons: Art of the In-Between*, The Metropolitan Museum of Art, New York, May 4–September 4, 2017.

8 Callan, interview June.

9 For images of the skirt that inspired Callan, see https://assets.vogue.com/photos/58ebbd843d34201718f28102/master/w_1600,c_limit/03-cdg-book.jpg, an image extracted from https://www.vogue.com/article/met-gala-2017-comme-des-garcons-rei-kawakubo-andrew-bolton-costume-institute, p. 2: Borrelli-Persson, Laird. "Runway: How 10 Photographers Captured Rei Kawakubo's Genius for the New Met Catalog," *Vogue*, April 10, 2017.

10 *Rei Kawakubo/Comme des Garçons: Art of the In-Between*, exhibition guide (New York: The Metropolitan Museum of Art, 2017).

11 Oskar Schlemmer, quoted in "Art in the Age of Movement," an interview with Jan Bartoszek, *Bauhaus Kooperation Magazine*. Accessed October 20, 2023, http://bauhauskooperation.com/kooperation/project-archive/magazine/dance-the-bauhaus/art-in-the-age-of-movement/.

12 Callan, written exchange with the author, October 13, 2023.

13 Callan, written exchange.

14 Callan in Warmus, 52.

15 Callan, interview August.

16 Callan, interview August.

17 Callan, interview June.

18 For examples of Keith Haring's *Subway Drawings*, see https://www.haring.com/!/art-work/40.

19 Callan, interview June.

20 Callan, interview June.

21 Callan, interview June.

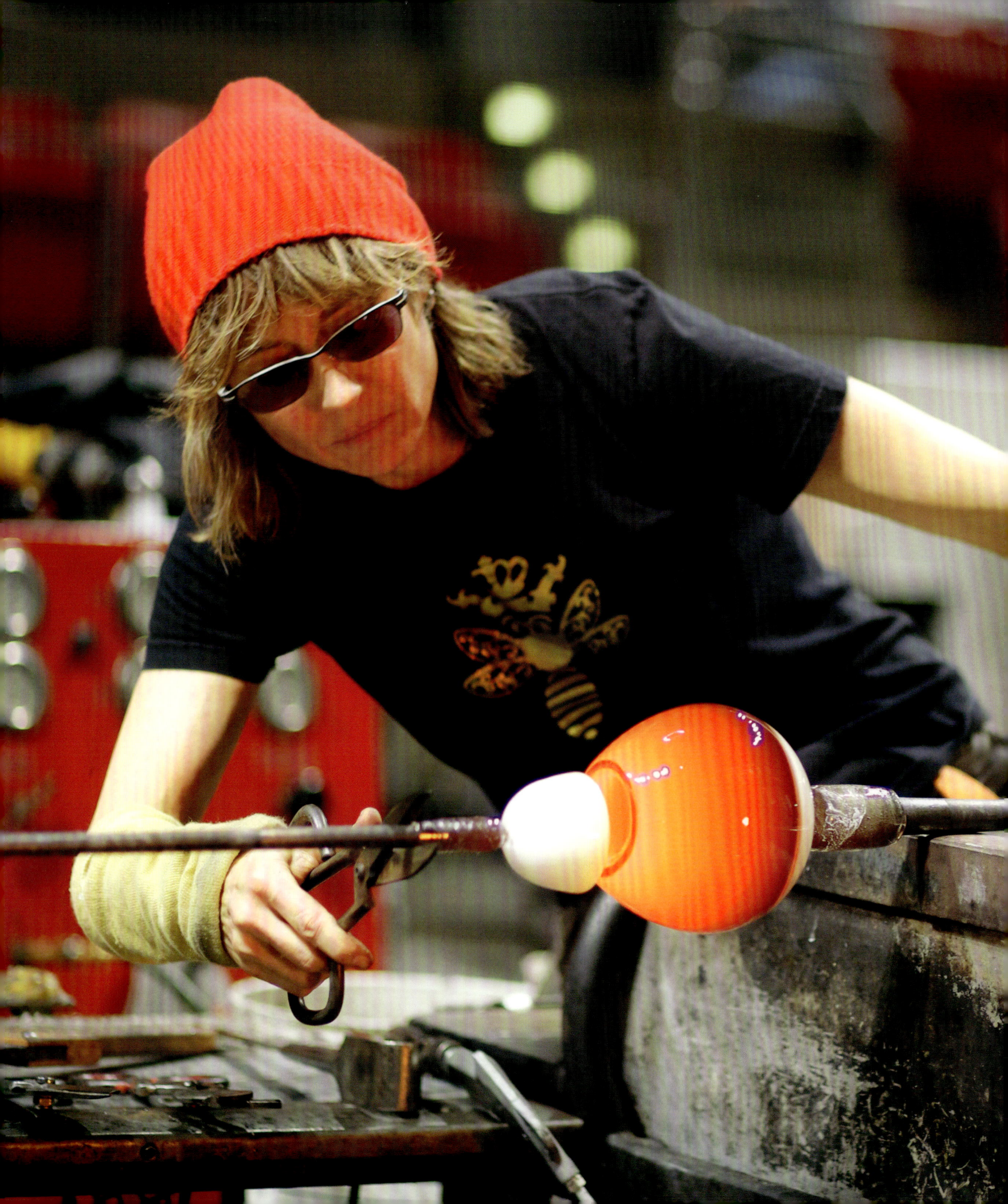

Kim Harty

NANCY CALLAN:
PLAYING TO HER STRENGTHS

Nancy Callan: Forces at Play presents over two decades of glasswork in which Nancy Callan's deep expertise in glassmaking meets her exuberant and playful approach to the material. Driven by a desire for excellence and exploration, Callan works in series so that she can continually revise, rework, and discover different varieties of form, pattern, and color. In *Forces at Play*, we witness an evolution where traditional Venetian glass techniques transform into an expressive language, pioneering new ways of working with glass.

Gen X Aesthetics

The first gallery, *Pop Art and Graphics*, presents a collection of artworks originating in the early 2000s. As a member of Generation X, Callan came of age during a transformative period marked by the explosion of consumerism, ubiquitous advertising, and shifting gender norms. The work in this gallery is a burst of color and abstraction, which is complemented by custom wallpaper, showcasing Callan's personal collection of toys. Superhero figurines, whimsical troll dolls with their pointy hair, and jack-o'-lantern trinkets adorned in witches' caps offer a window into the abstract forms and vibrant hues that define Callan's creative inspirations (fig. 1).

An early glimpse into Callan's aesthetic, the *Medicine Bottle* series marked a significant milestone as some of her first pieces displayed in a gallery. The brightly colored

bottles use pictorial cameo-carved tiles to pose the question, "What do you need?" Answers are provided in the form of simple visual puzzles that pair a word or phrase ("Ask Alice") with an image (a white rabbit) (Chk. 3, p. 34). Presented as singular objects or grouped in small cabinets, the series combines cheerful color with a personal language of symbols, at times commenting on the allure and dangers of various addictions. For example, *Night Cap* (Chk. 5, p. 33) offers "one for the road" from a large (and slightly lopsided) black bottle. Touching on narrative, graphic design, and the exploration of glass technique, these early bottle-form works foreshadow Callan's exploration of color, coded symbolism, gender tropes, and humor.

In subsequent works in *Pop Art and Graphics*, viewers encounter the familiar made strange through Callan's rendering in glass and her shifting of scale. Recalling strategies of Pop artists like Claes Oldenburg (Swedish-American, 1929–2022) and Andy Warhol, Callan's larger-than-life objects evoke themes of play, dreams, and childhood wonder. Balanced elegantly on their sides, her oversized *Tops*, with elaborate cane and *murrine* patterning, entice the viewer to play while they coyly threaten to roll away. Then there is the mischievous *Snowman* series, whose upturned, pointy noses have a slightly cheeky

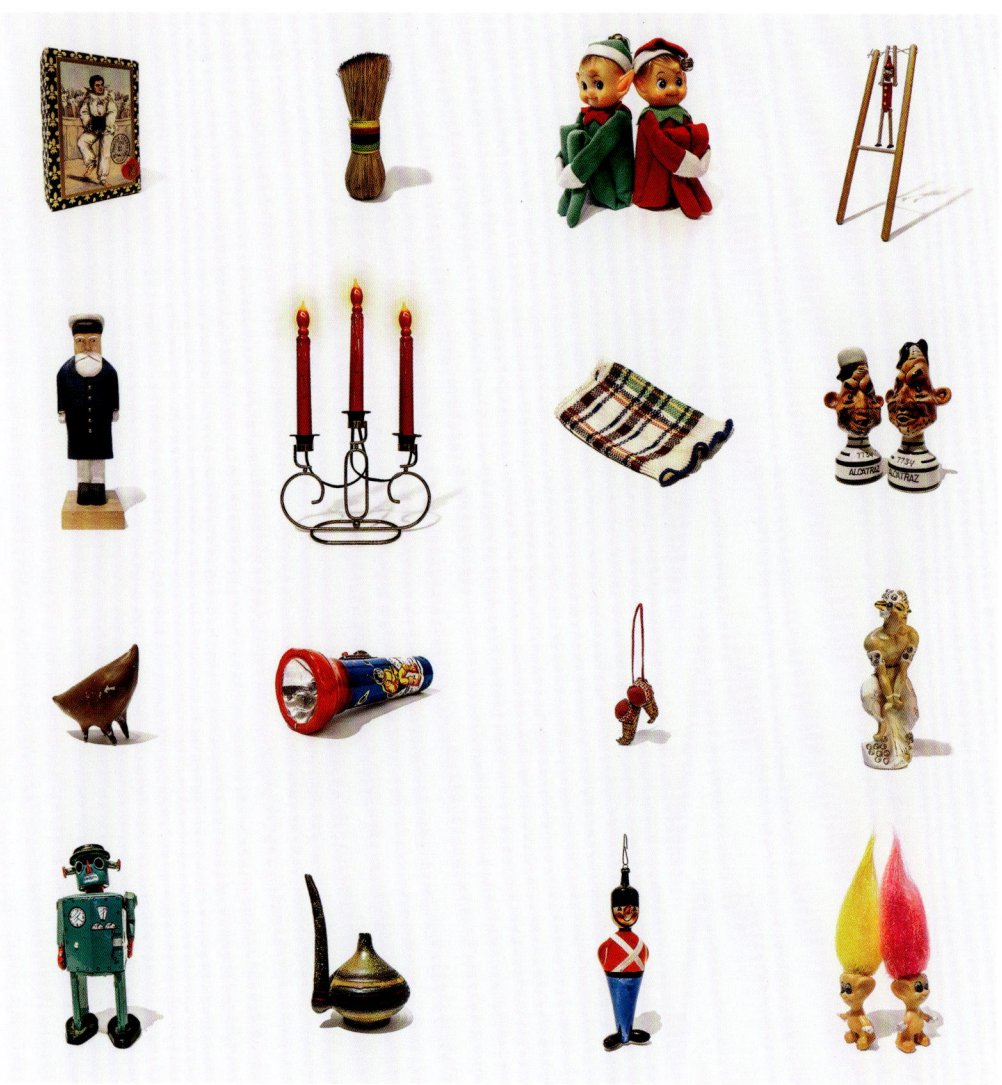

Fig. 1 *Toy Wallpaper* (detail), 2023

tilt, infusing them with a naughty attitude. These full-scale snowmen are iconic and immediately recognizable forms that Callan injects with wit and a touch of irony, simply by making them out of hot glass. Her comical motifs in *Big Spender Snowman* (Chk. 15, p. 40) are accented by gold-leaf buttons and a glass top hat set at a jaunty angle.

Throughout this section, Callan's explorations of objects move from representational forms like *Snowmen* or *Tops* to more abstract forms like *Bee Buoys* and *Bee Butts*. Like the mysterious riddles on her *Medicine Bottles*, Callan makes intuitive connections between a bee's stripes, the pattern of floating buoys, and the buoyancy of glass. The enigmatic combinations of rounded and spiky forms subtly suggest androgyny and queerness, and foreshadow her monumental *Stingers*.

Callan revisits one of her most iconic series, *Stingers*, in *Forces at Play*. These deliberately ambiguous works, perched at slightly dangerous angles, resist the symmetry of blown glass and confront the viewer with a sense of

tension and precarity. For her recent *Stingers*, Callan drew inspiration from female superheroes and considered how costumes can be transformative to a character. She notes that it was a challenge to find female superheroes who aren't sidekicks. Her muses Catwoman, rendered here in black, purple, and sparkly green aventurine glass (fig. 2 and Chk. 33, p. 53), and Mystique, who is capable of shifting between female and male forms (Chk. 42, p. 57), were originally supervillains, though both characters have developed recent anti-hero storylines that challenge traditional notions of heroism. These eponymous objects command attention due to their confrontational size and unique sculptural form. Here Callan exploits the medium's capacity for delivering pure and flat color application to achieve a graphic effect. The assembly of colored cups through *incalmo* gives the sculptures precise lines and hues, evoking vector graphics, which can be scaled infinitely without any loss of detail or resolution. Such mastery of technique is so convincing that viewers may not comprehend

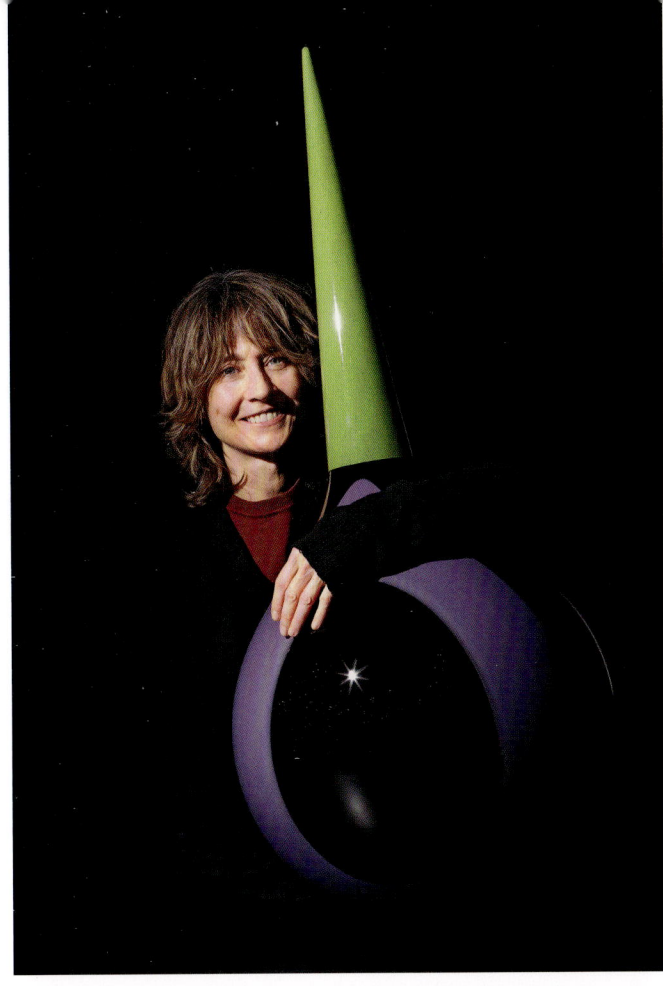

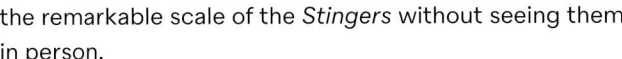
Fig. 2 Artist with *Catwoman Stinger*, 2022 (Chk. 33)

Fig. 3 *Aqua Silk Crinkle Winkle*, 2006

the remarkable scale of the *Stingers* without seeing them in person.

Callan's enduring fascination with pop culture extends into her most recent work in this section, *Road Trip with Keith*, from 2022 (Chk. 34, pp. 58–59). Made of four brightly colored panels with wiggling white lines, the piece nods to the Pop-Art aesthetic, with subtle references to Haring's bold lines, Henri Matisse's (French, 1869–1954) flat colors, and the Memphis Milano attitude. This centerpiece of the *Pop Art and Graphics* section showcases Callan's artistic evolution, incorporating the myriad influences and references she has absorbed over time.

Playing with Pattern

The mechanics of laying out colorful rows of glass cane provokes an inherent desire to play with patterns. For Callan, the exploration of plaid as a visual reference and technical challenge was a springboard for much of the three-dimensional work in the next section in *Forces at Play*, titled *Pattern and Textiles*. In a 2006 piece, *Aqua Silk Crinkle Winkle* (fig. 3), she stretches a translucent plaid pattern to extreme heights, as the coned shape reaches upward, terminating with a slight tilt. *Sonia Winkle* (Chk. 24, p. 69), from 2015, inspired by knitwear designer Sonia Rykiel (French, 1930–2016), illuminates Callan's interest in how textiles relate to the body. In this towering 36-inch-tall piece, crisscrossing patterns stretch toward the top of the cone as if the glass form is pressing against elastic fabric. Here, Callan works with *duro*, a type of colored glass with a very stiff formulation that holds a sharp line no matter how far it is stretched; this type of glass becomes critical to Callan's development of thread-like patterns. Hints of translucent color and a soft, sanded surface make palpable the reference to knitwear.

In the *Paloma* series, Callan's interest in fabric and the body evolves into figurative contrapposto forms, and she begins to use more irregular and unconventional approaches to cane. *Nikkita Paloma*, (Chk. 29, p. 76), a

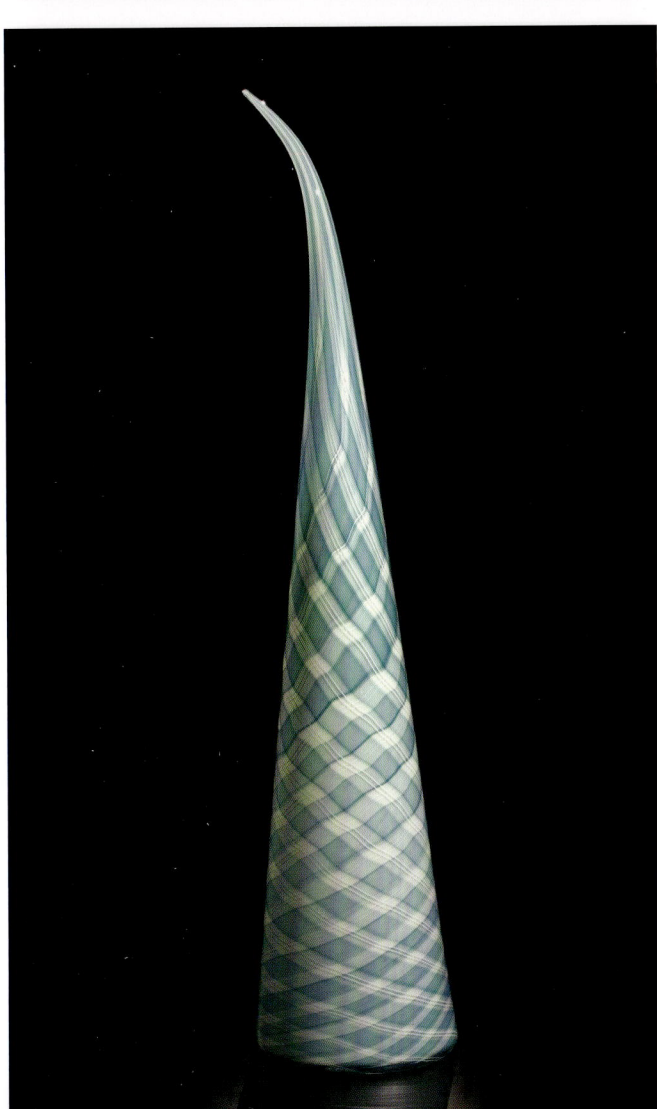

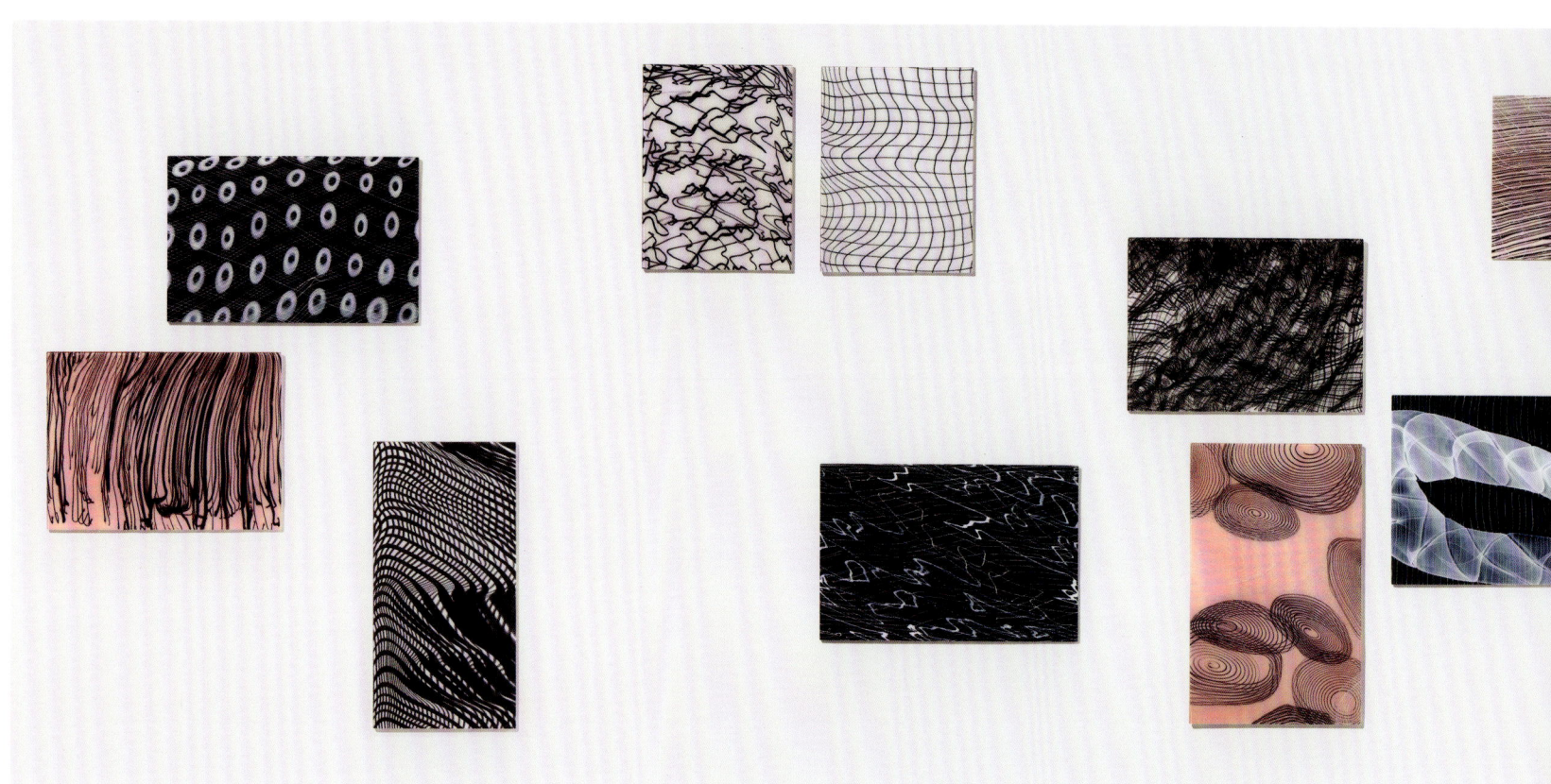

Fig. 4 *Comme les Filles*, 2023
(Chk. 37)

memorial work made after the death of the musician Prince (American, 1958–2016), is created from large pieces of multistrand and transparent flat canes, some of which are then distorted into a swirl pattern. Random blue canes placed unexpectedly within the composition further disrupt the regularity, yet the effect is cohesive and harmonious. These pieces show an increasing freedom and creativity with cane, foreshadowing a shift to a more expressive and free-form approach to surface.

The most ambitious piece in this section, *Comme les Filles* (fig. 4 and Chk. 37, pp. 80–87), represents Callan's full pattern- and image-making aspirations in an homage to Rei Kawakubo, the founder, designer, and creative director of clothing line Comme des Garçons. In *Comme les Filles*, Callan employs a limited palette of black, white, and soft pink, using the contrasts of stiff *duro* glass alongside softer blacks and whites in an approach akin to drawing. The thread-like imagery evokes close-ups of weaves, embroidery, or printed motifs. Callan deliberately chose to work with the color pink, which she acknowledges is a difficult color with a lot of baggage, a color she has never really liked—a choice that echoes the creative strategies

of the iconoclastic Kawakubo. By incorporating subtle hues of pink, she effectively references the body and adds an unexpected dimension to the high-contrast composition. The 19-panel piece is installed on a 30-foot wall in an arrangement that resists a strict or obvious grid pattern, incorporating negative space and creating relationships in subsets of the pieces. *Comme les Filles* propels Callan's work to an assertive stage of image development as she innovates new methods of working with cane to add to her growing library of processes and techniques.

Forces of Nature
In the final section of the exhibition, *Nature and Wonders*, Callan takes a deep dive into the connections among water, light, and glass. In her *Droplet* series, she creates buoyant and shimmering sculptures, each one resembling a blown-up droplet of water. Using veiled cane, a technique in which stiff white glass encases clear glass, Callan creates a tube-like graphic that is reimagined in different pieces throughout this section. *Azure Droplet* (fig. 5), from 2016, the first of the series, is bulbous and bright blue, with orderly tubes wrapping the surface, receding to the

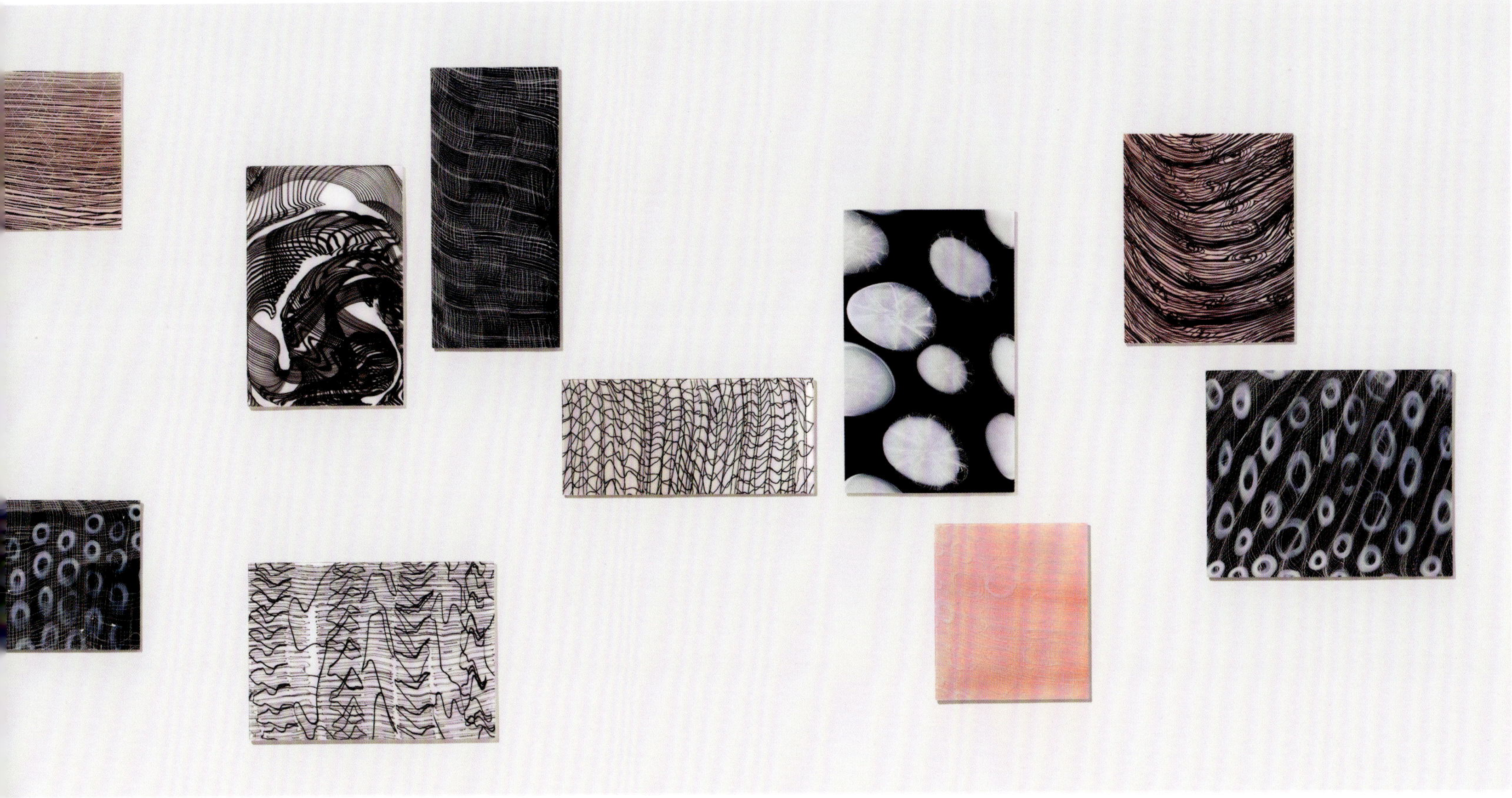

Fig. 5 *Azure Droplet*, 2016

pinnacle. Sandblasting and hand-sanding give the exterior a luminescent quality, as light dances along the edges of the white canes, evoking the ground glass found in early cameras and scientific instruments. Through ongoing experimentation, Callan continues to evolve the *Droplets*, producing works that seem to glow, as canes of varied density float and gleam across richly colored backgrounds. In *Luminescence Droplet* (Chk. 32, pp. 104–105), Callan masterfully plays with color and contrast, layering electric blue canes behind dancing white canes on a deep plum background.

These innovations in layering activate many of Callan's pieces, allowing her to explore other natural phenomena, and *Witching Hour* (Chk. 30, p. 101) stands out as particularly electric. With bright pinks glowing through blues and purples, the piece is reminiscent of bioluminescence in the deep sea or the radiant linings of clouds during a sunset. In another recent series, *Spires*, elongated teardrop forms are enhanced with line work that mimics the swirling or churning of water. In *Cypress Spire* (Chk. 39, p. 109), the color transitions from blue on the bottom to pale lime green at the peak; black lines

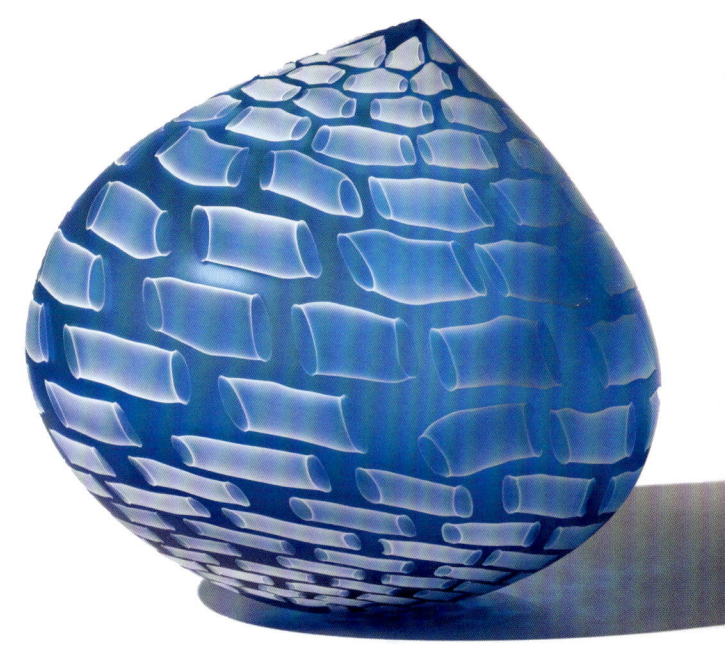

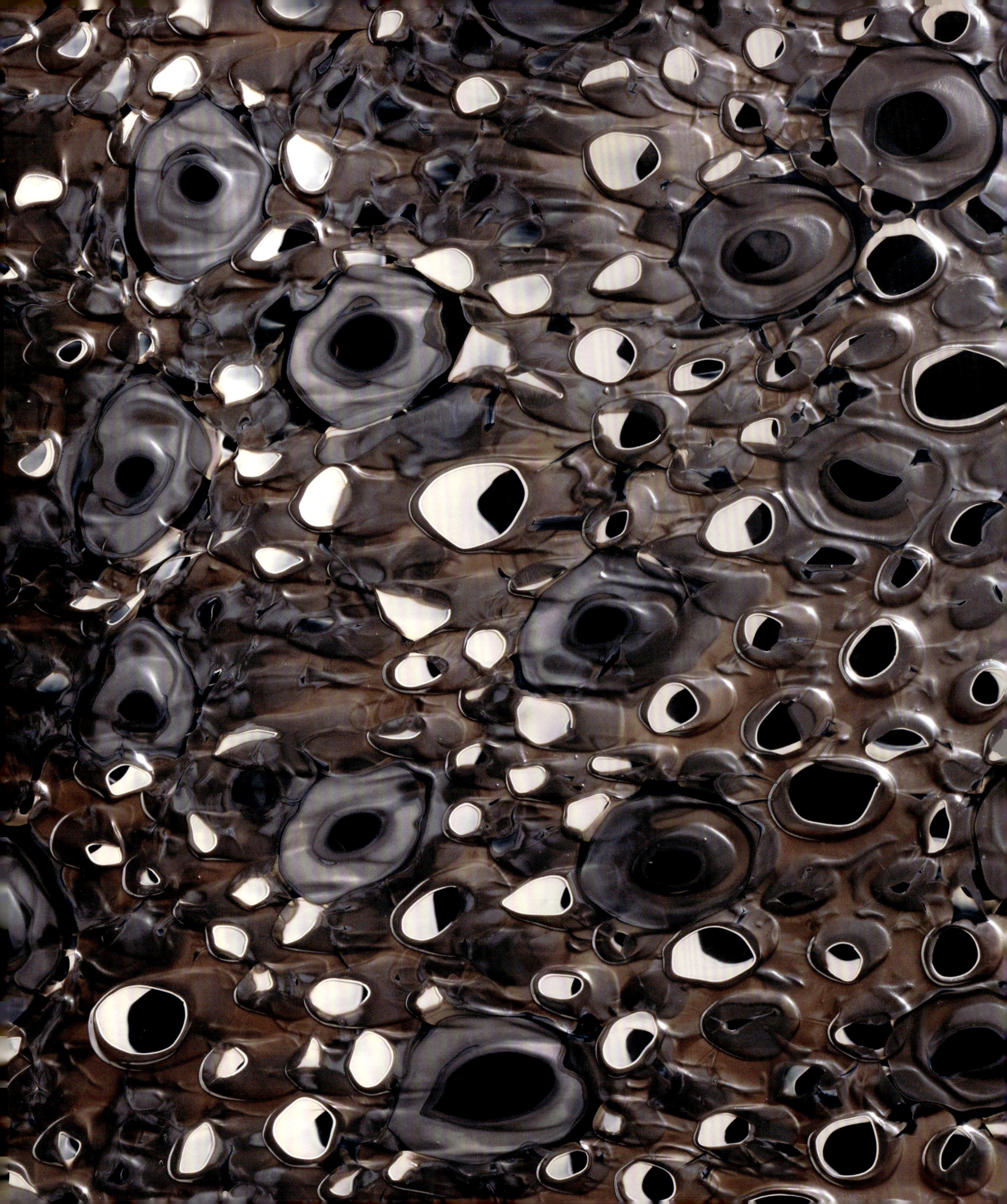

crisscrossing the piece recall tidal patterns or topographic maps. The matte glass surface amplifies the brightness of the colors, imbuing them with an illuminated quality.

In *Nature and Wonders*, Callan also explores the potential for glass to evoke both macro- and microcosmic realms. *Ghost Oasis* (Chk. 31, pp. 92–93) is a four-panel installation that draws inspiration from the deep ocean. The imagery walks the line between figure and pattern with forms that might be schools of mysterious swimming creatures or calligraphic marks. Likewise, *Amber Shimmer Orb* (Chk. 27, p. 98) and *Laguna Shimmer Orb* (Chk. 28, p. 99) conjure images of bacteria and the vibrant colors found in scientific imagery through use of veiled cane and roller-wrapped glass threads. In contrast, the stark *Cosmic Waves* (Chk. 38, p. 111) panel contemplates the vastness of space and the invisible forces exerted by celestial bodies. Sculptural pieces like *Stellar Net* (Chk. 35, p. 115), *Traverse* (Chk. 36, p. 113), and *String Theory* (Chk. 25, p. 110) evoke the emptiness of spaces big and small and the solitary forces that may dwell within them. These glossy, black forms, subtly nodding at their pinnacles, are covered with swirling lines that seem to trace the paths of cosmic winds, the pull of gravitational forces, or the reverberations of planet-shaking vibrations. In this work, Callan executes these unconventional designs flawlessly, contending with the uneven properties of the varying glass viscosities to create sleek, precise, patterned forms.

The exhibition concludes with Callan's *Shadow Realm* (fig. 6 and Chk. 47, pp. 21, 119–126), a new panel installation created at the Museum of Glass Hot Shop. Here, Callan delves deeper into the study of nature by considering the alchemy of glass's material properties. During the glassblowing process, she creates a reducing (low-oxygen) atmosphere that pulls the reflective particles to the surface of the glass, evoking the sheen of an oil spill or a metallic surface. Here, Callan's approach feels closer to abstract painting, as the eye bounces around the surface, texture, and gesture of the composition. In *Shadow Realm*, Callan transmutes the very nature of glass into something strange and nearly unrecognizable.

Lines Converge

Although it spans more than two decades, *Forces at Play* feels more like the start of a new chapter than a retrospective. Much of the work represents a creative eruption following Callan's retirement from Lino Tagliapietra's team in 2016. Her approach, while honoring the meticulous craft and ambitious spirit of her most important teacher, significantly diverges from that of the *Maestro* and the traditional Venetian aesthetic, breathing fresh life into familiar techniques, offering innovative, experimental, and even radical applications. Callan's pieces speak to Studio Glass, but also offer insights into the expanded practices of drawing, painting, and abstraction.

Forces at Play commences with works that exude ambition and culminates in pieces that are profoundly transformative. Callan invites the viewer on a journey where seemingly disparate influences—such as kitsch culture and avant-garde fashion—coalesce through her discerning lens. We see how lines echo through the tapestry of nature and textiles in analogous ways. We ponder the parallels between the universe's expansion and the unfurling of a glass bubble. Her playful sense of material and effortless execution allow the viewer to bask in wonderment of the patterns, forms, and surfaces on display. With profound technical knowledge to guide her exploration, Callan pushes technique and tradition beyond its known boundaries.

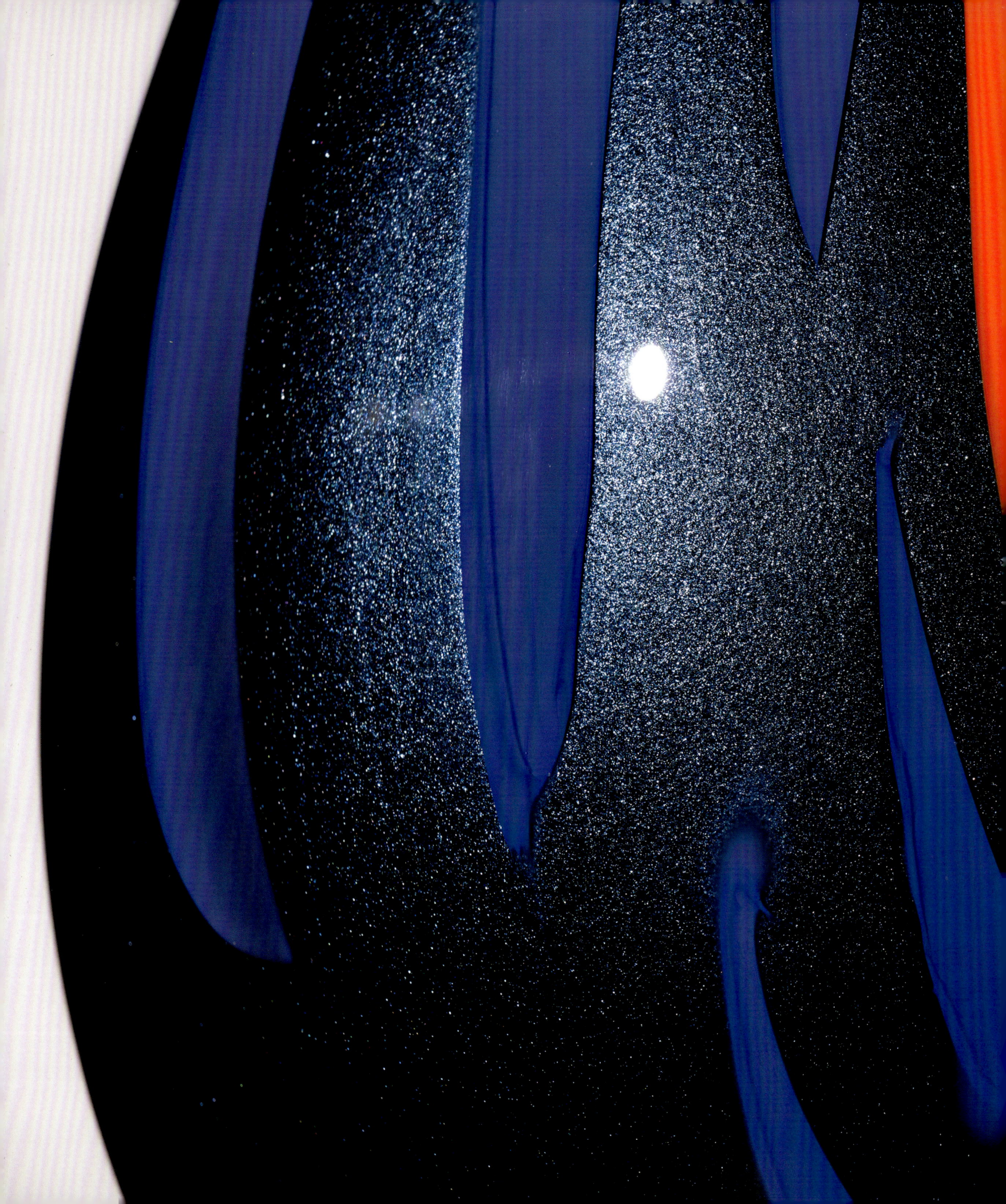

P O P A R T
A N D
G R A P H I C S

My early work in glass draws on the
language of graphic design—that feeling
you get when you look at a certain
font, and the impact of symbols and
images. In my twenties, I designed logos
for sports teams and album covers for
local bands around Boston. This really
influenced my work as a young artist.

—Nancy Callan

CHK.5 *Night Cap, 2003*

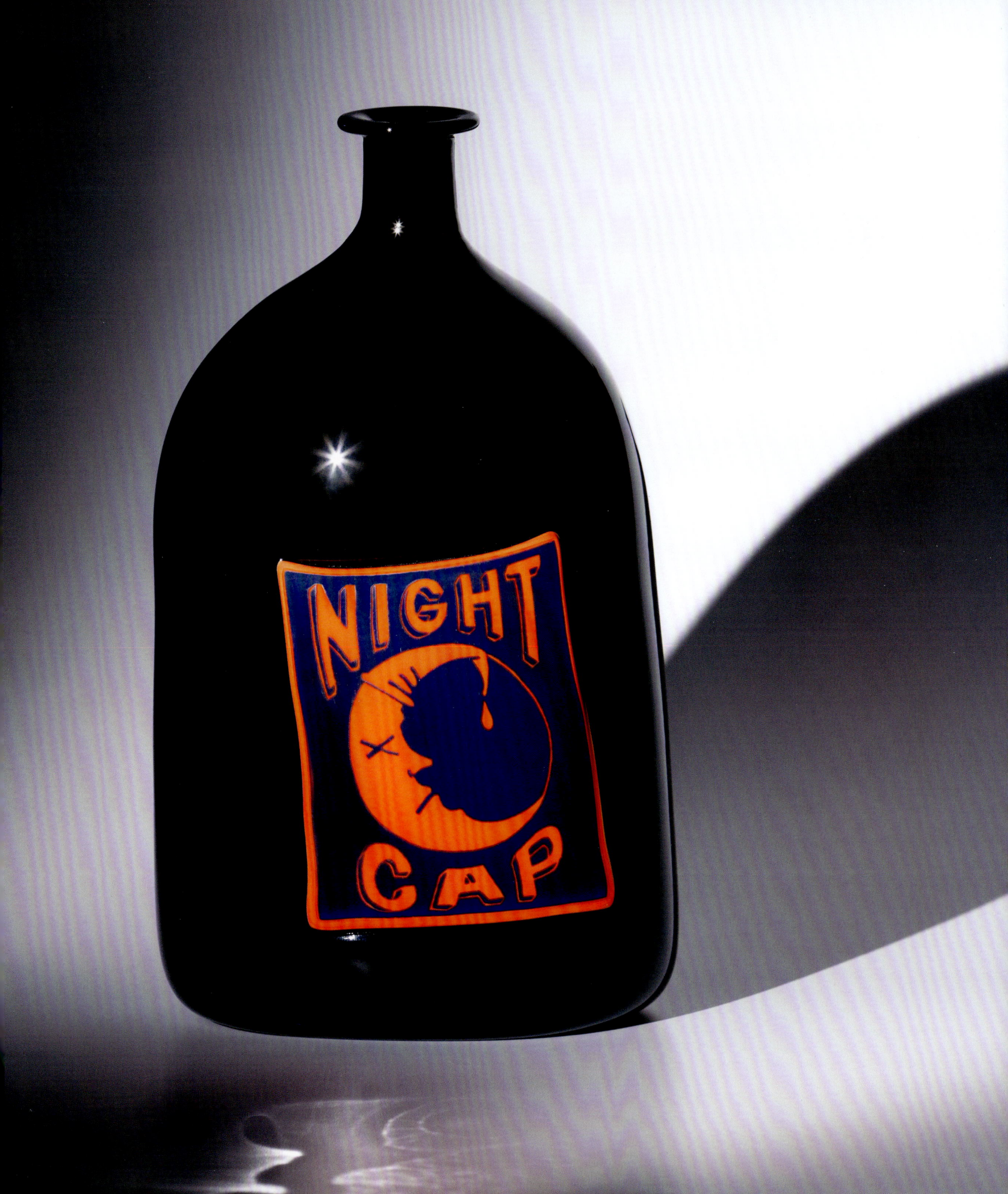

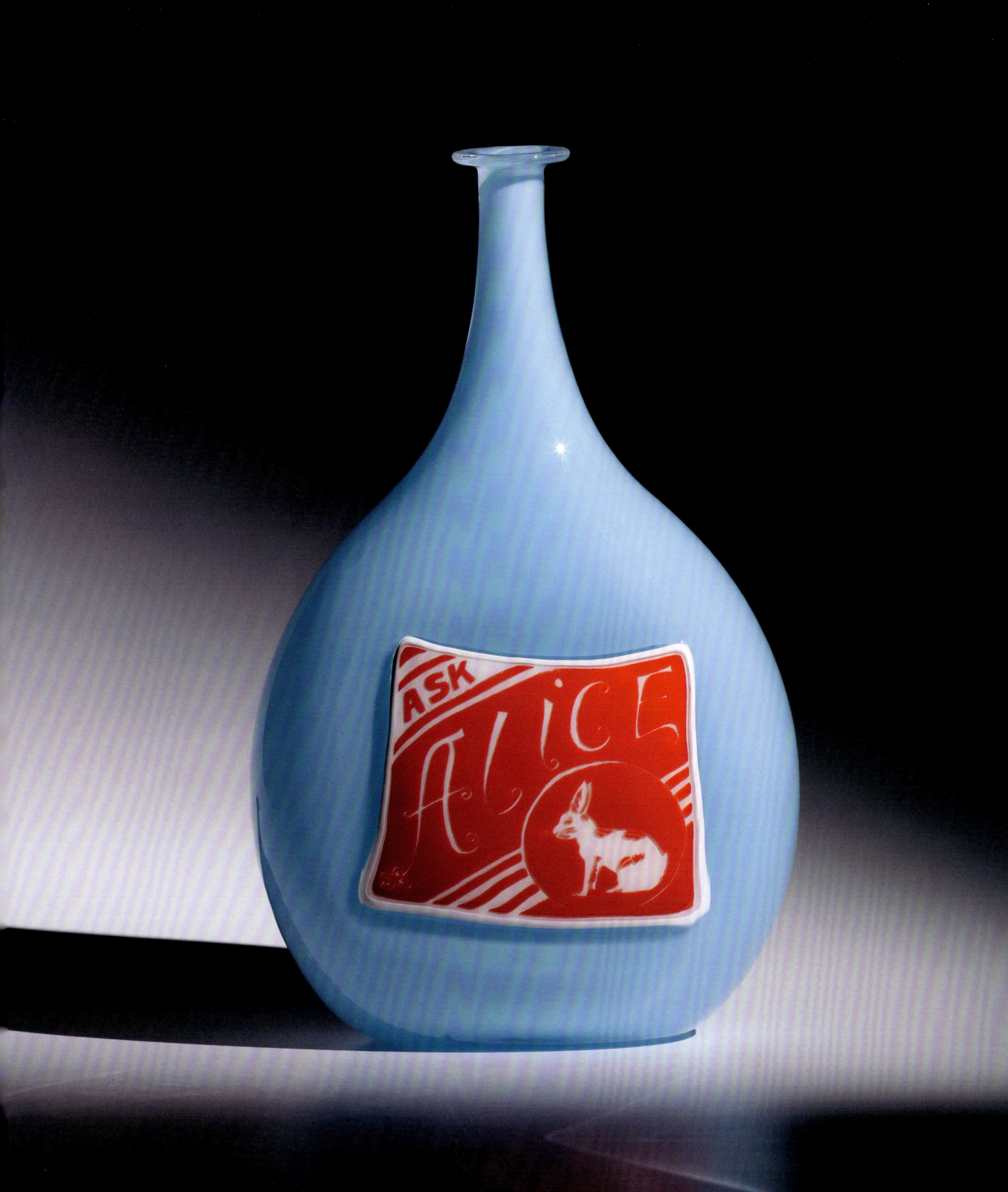

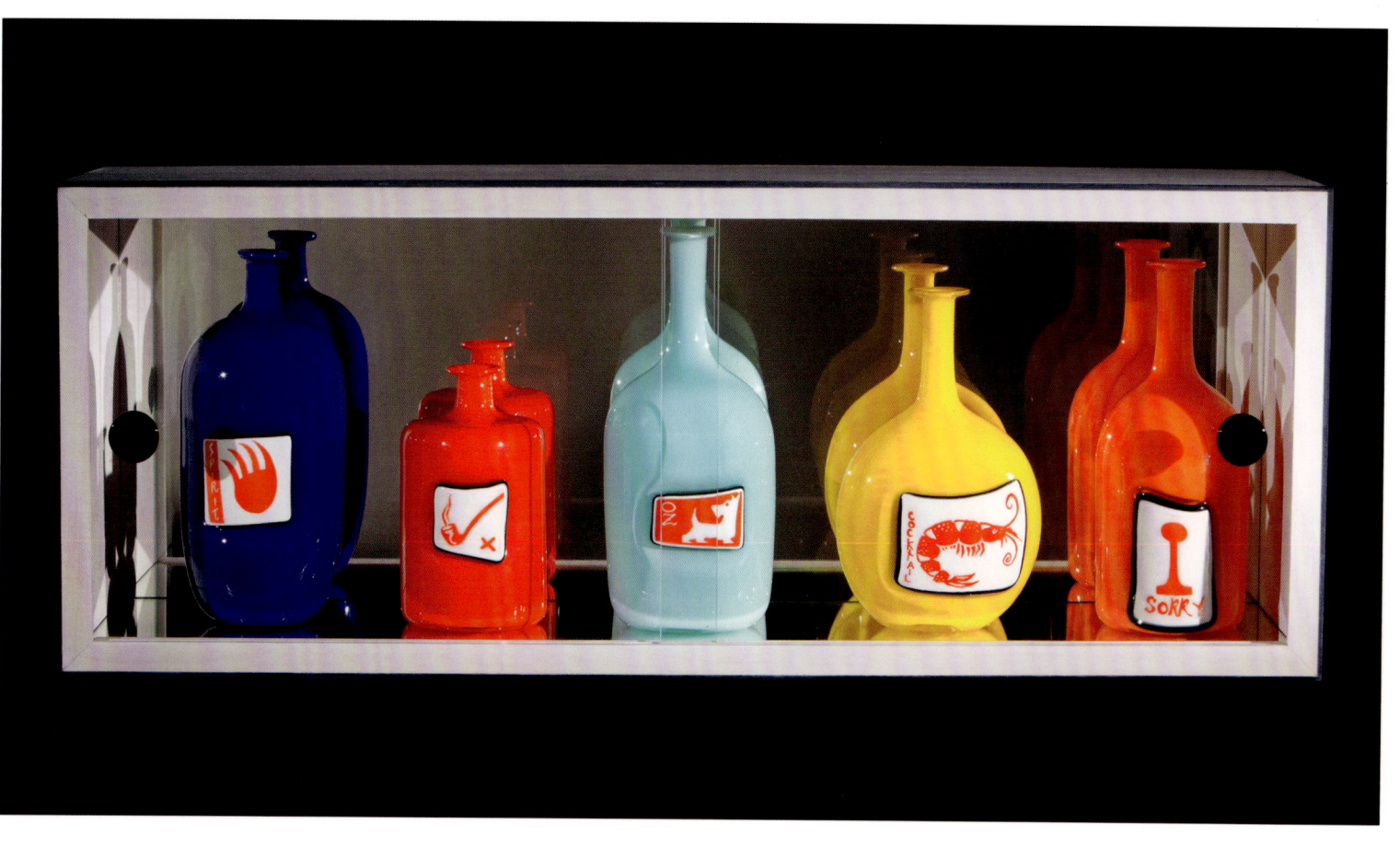

CHK. 3 *Ask Alice,* 2003

CHK. 12 *Medicine Cabinet,* 2009

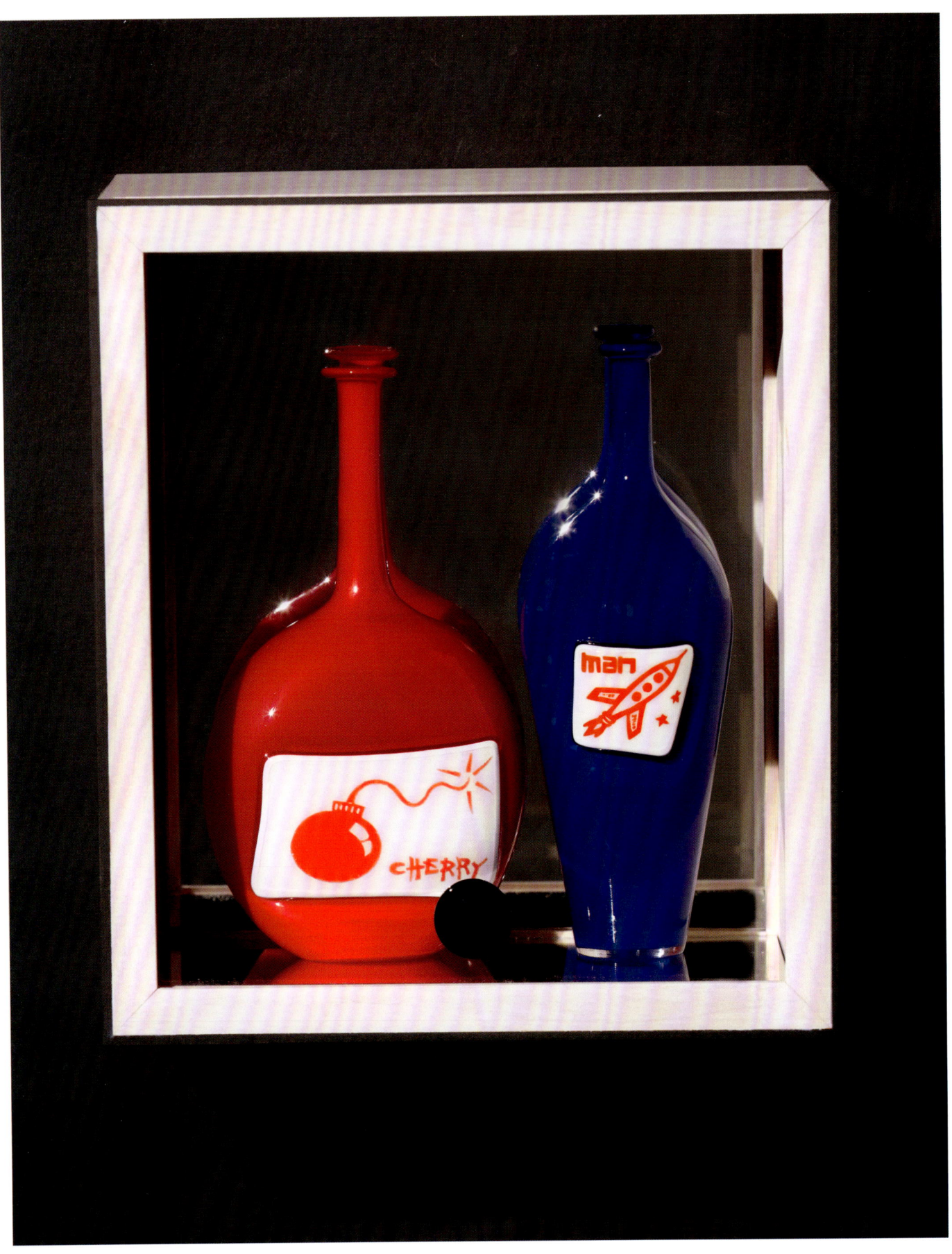

CHK. 11   *Chemistry Set, 2009*

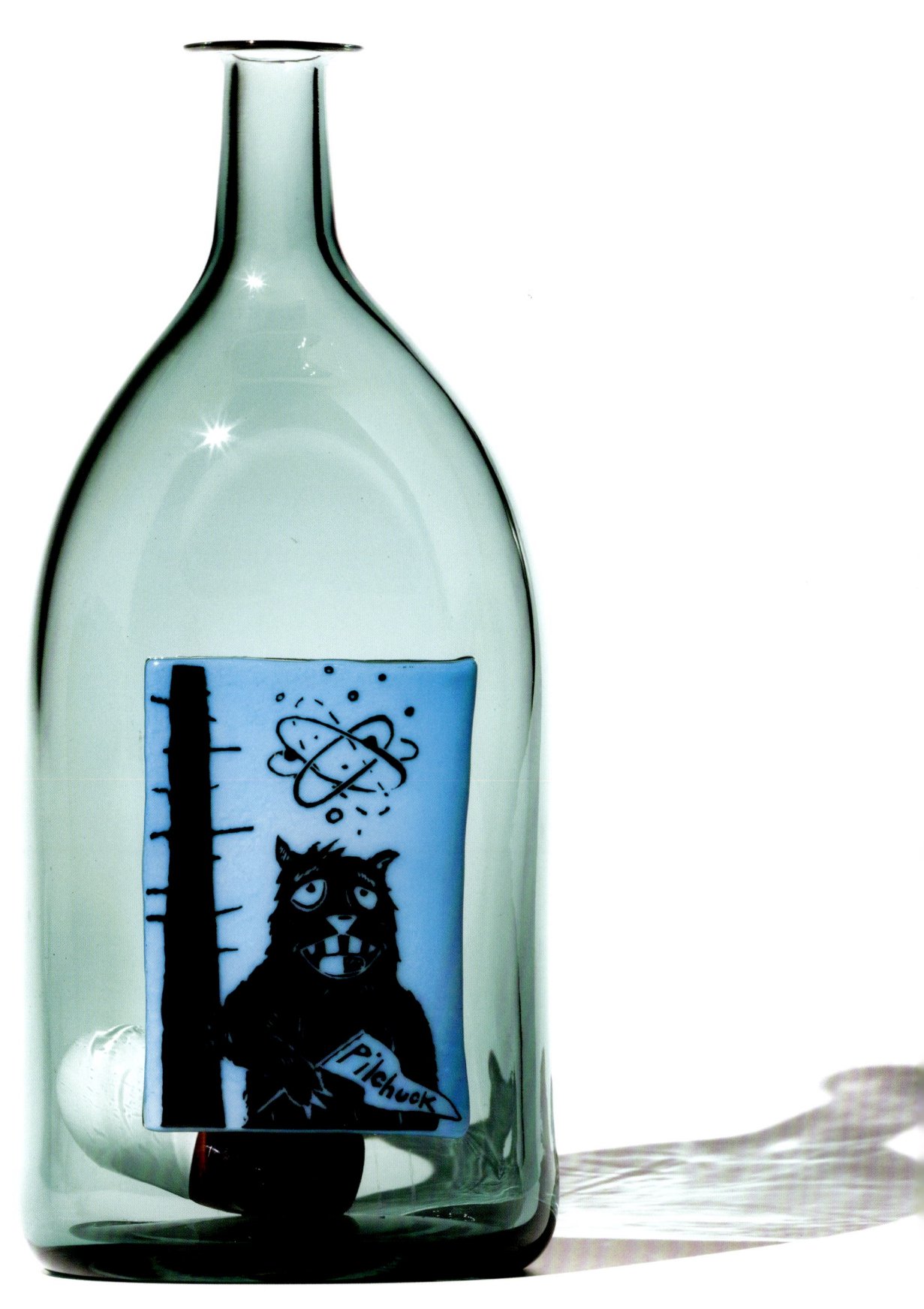

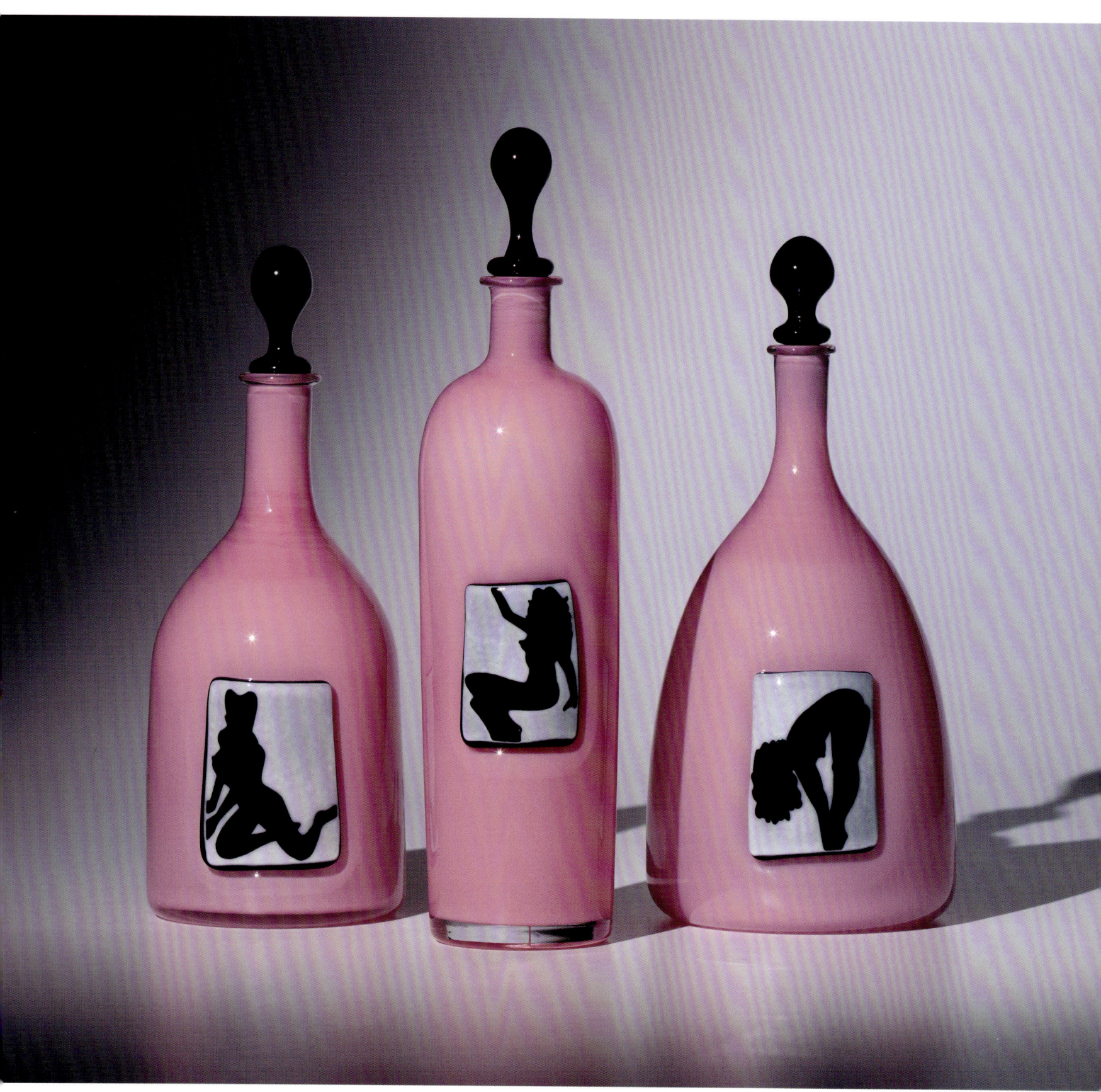

CHK. 2 *Pinup Girls,* 2002

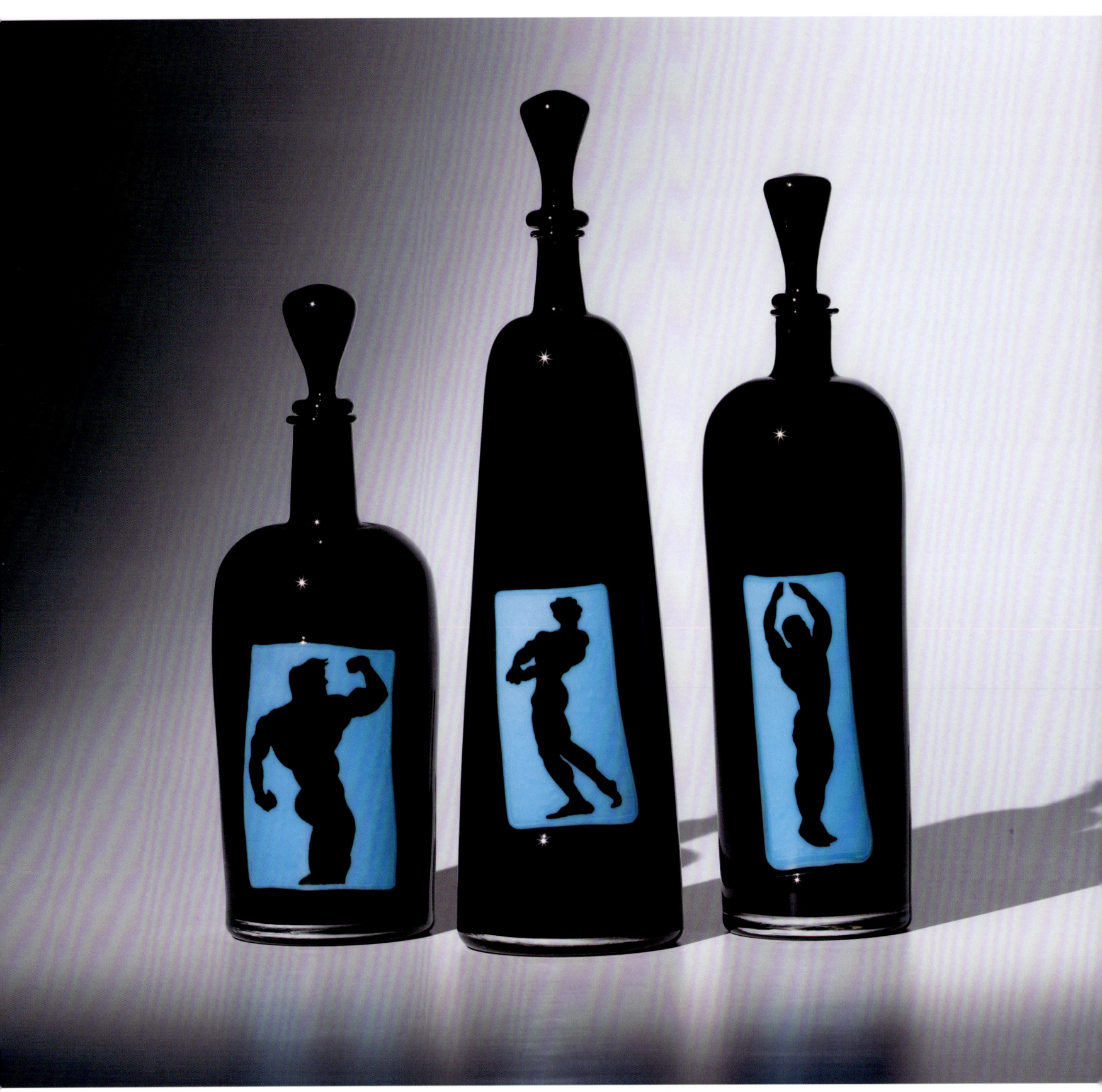

Beefcake Boys, 2003

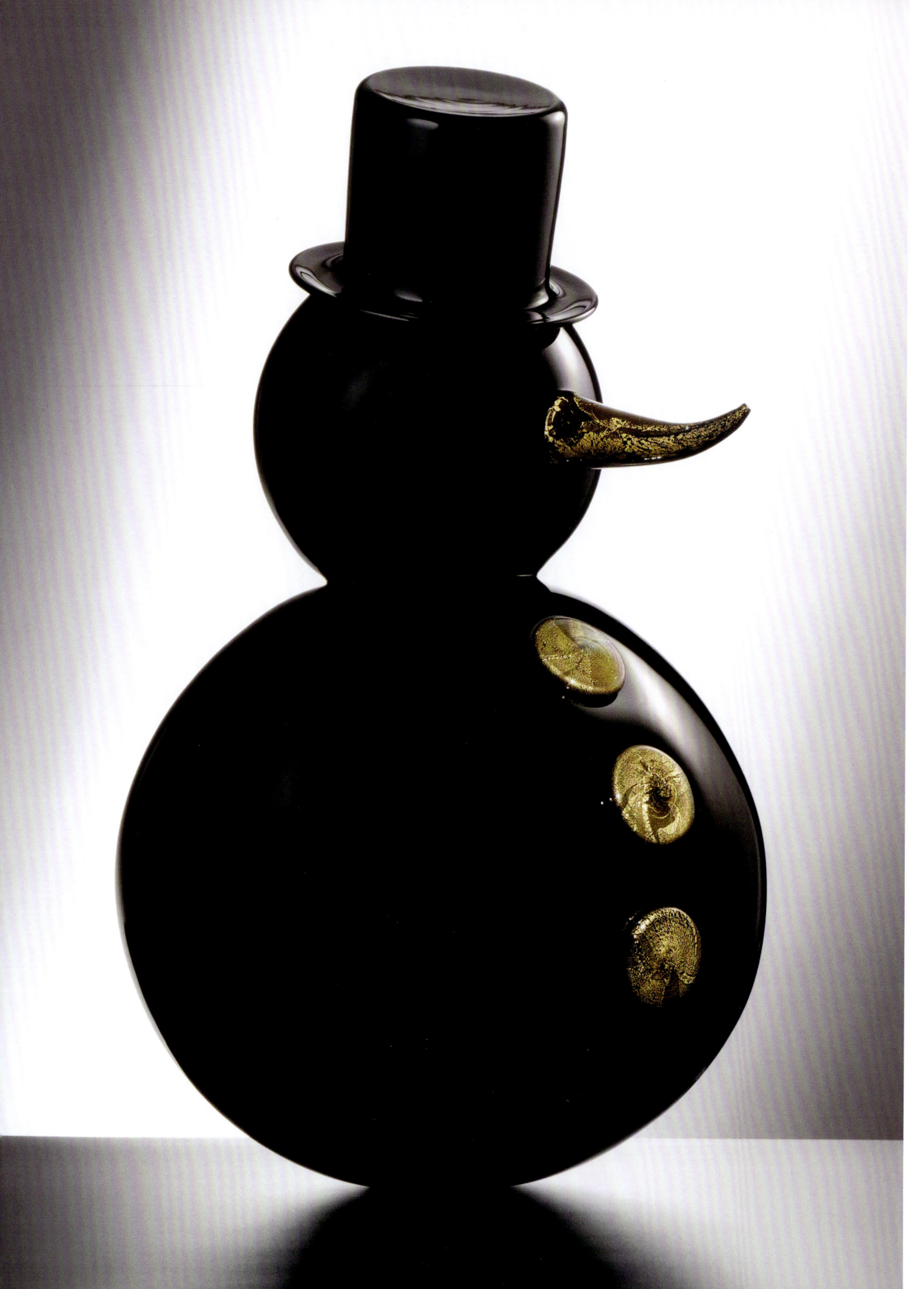

While creating each piece, I try to balance the fluidity of hot glass with the sense of wonder and fun I felt the first time I gathered from the furnace. I believe play is essential not only for the artist but for everyone. When we daydream or play games, we return to our childlike state of mind, where we are free to explore and imagine. This simple joy is a counterweight to our busy lives, and is central to my artistic process.

—Nancy Callan

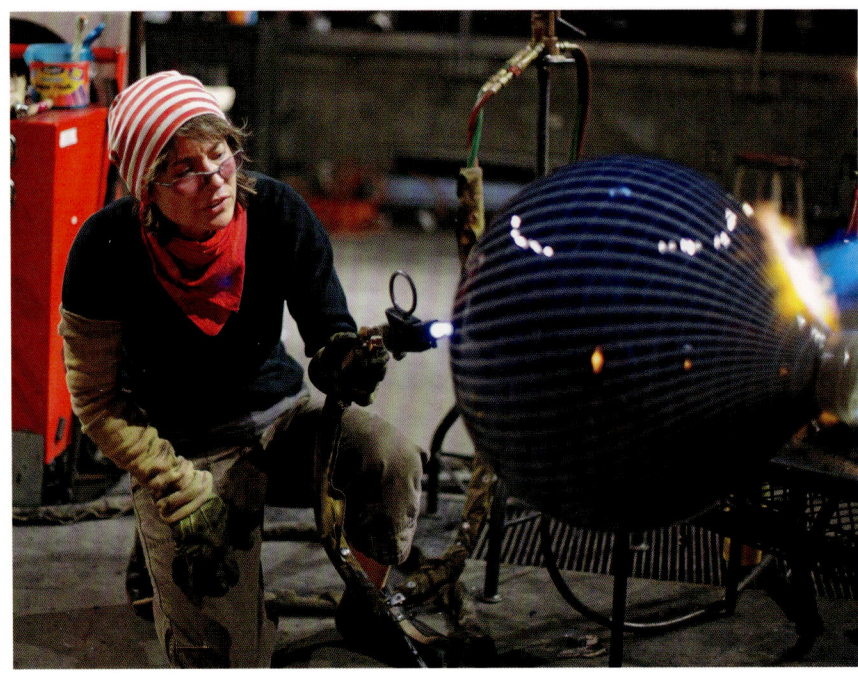
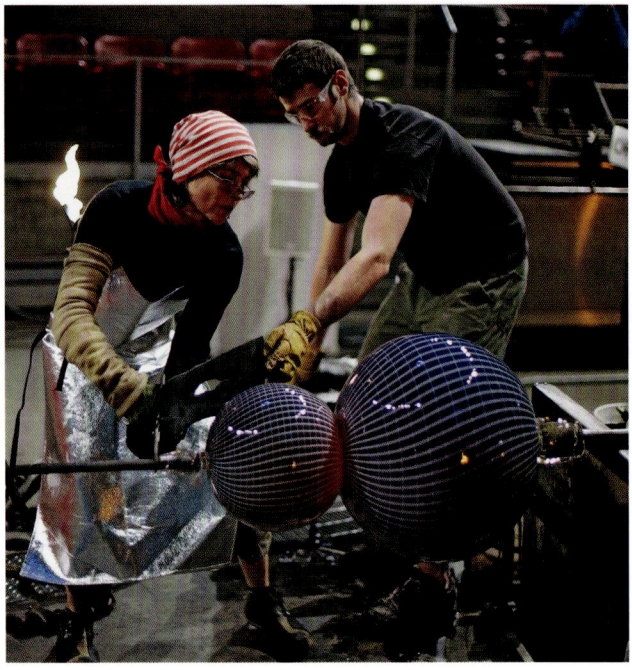
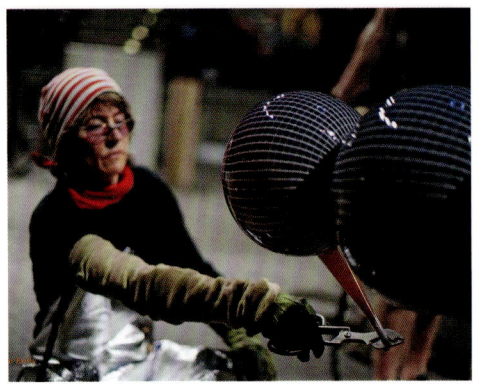
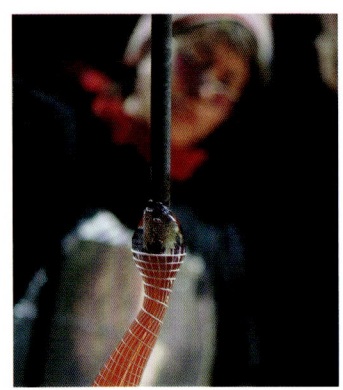
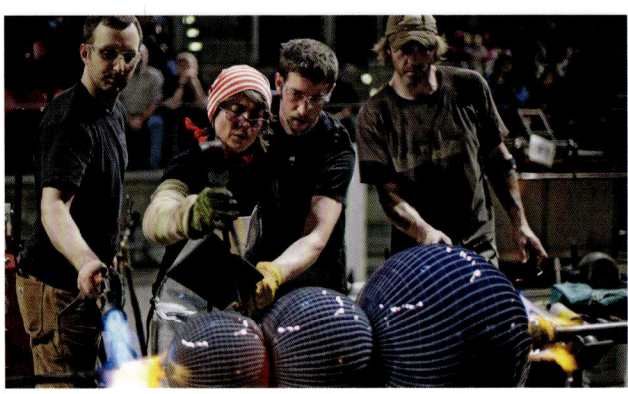
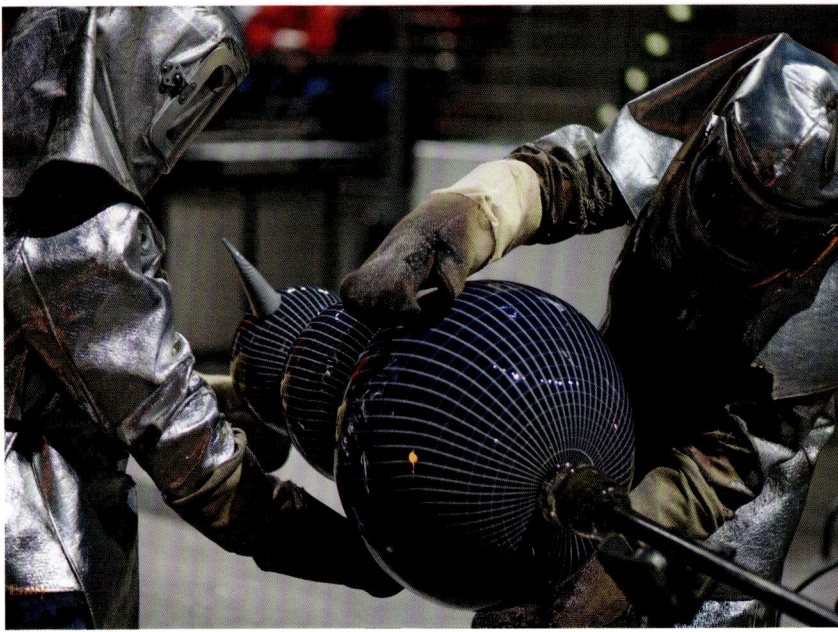
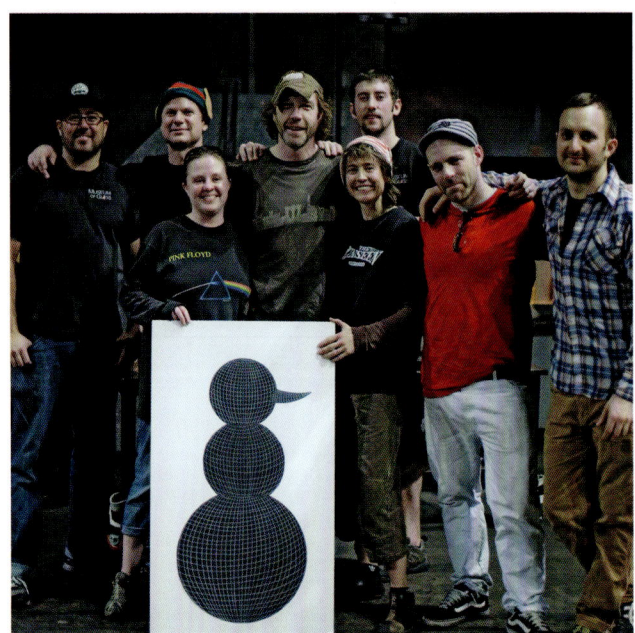

Artist and Museum of Glass Hot Shop team making *Blueprint for a Snowman I*,
2012 (Chk. 16), at Museum of Glass Snowman Blow, in 2011

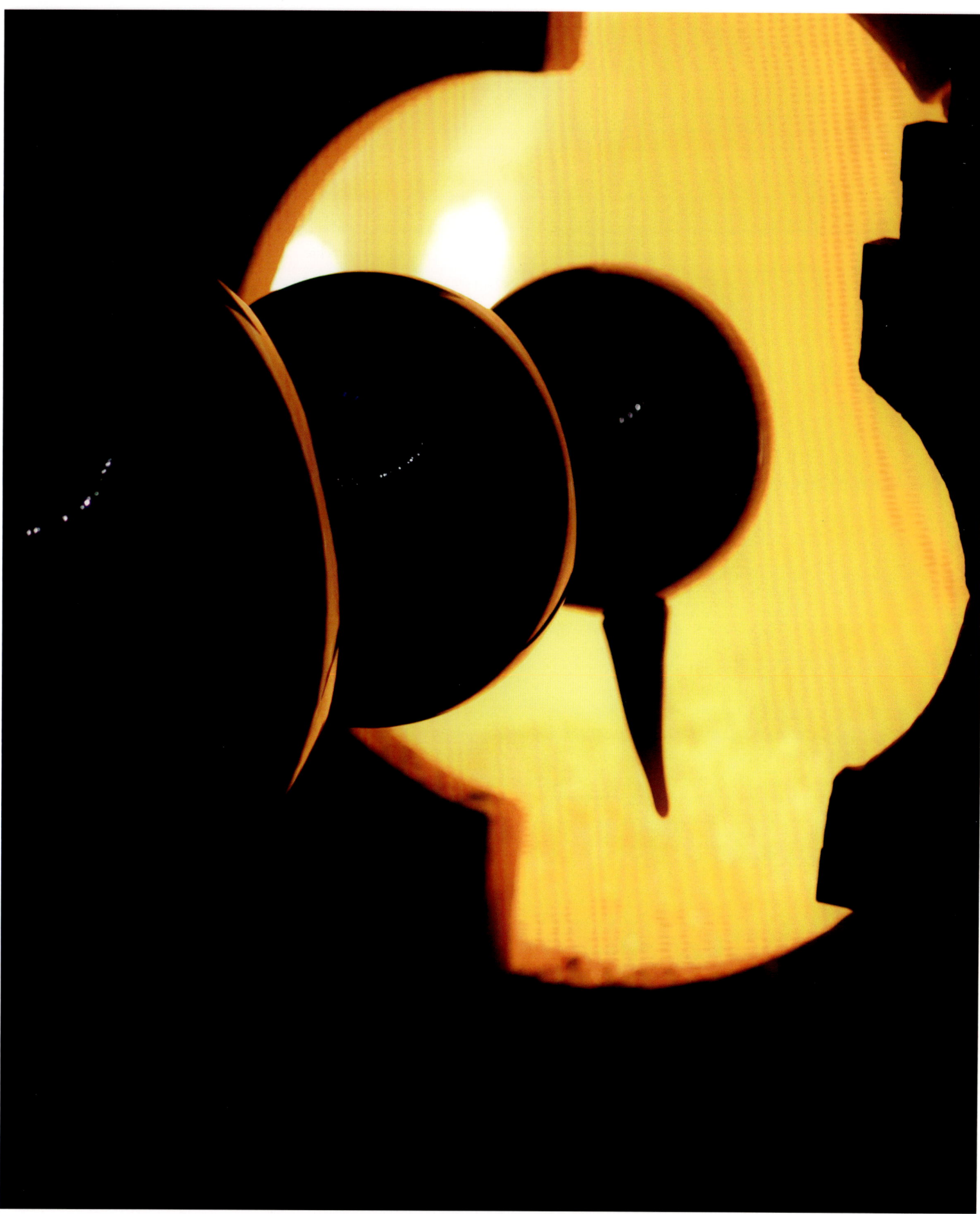

CHK. 16 *Blueprint for a Snowman I,* 2012

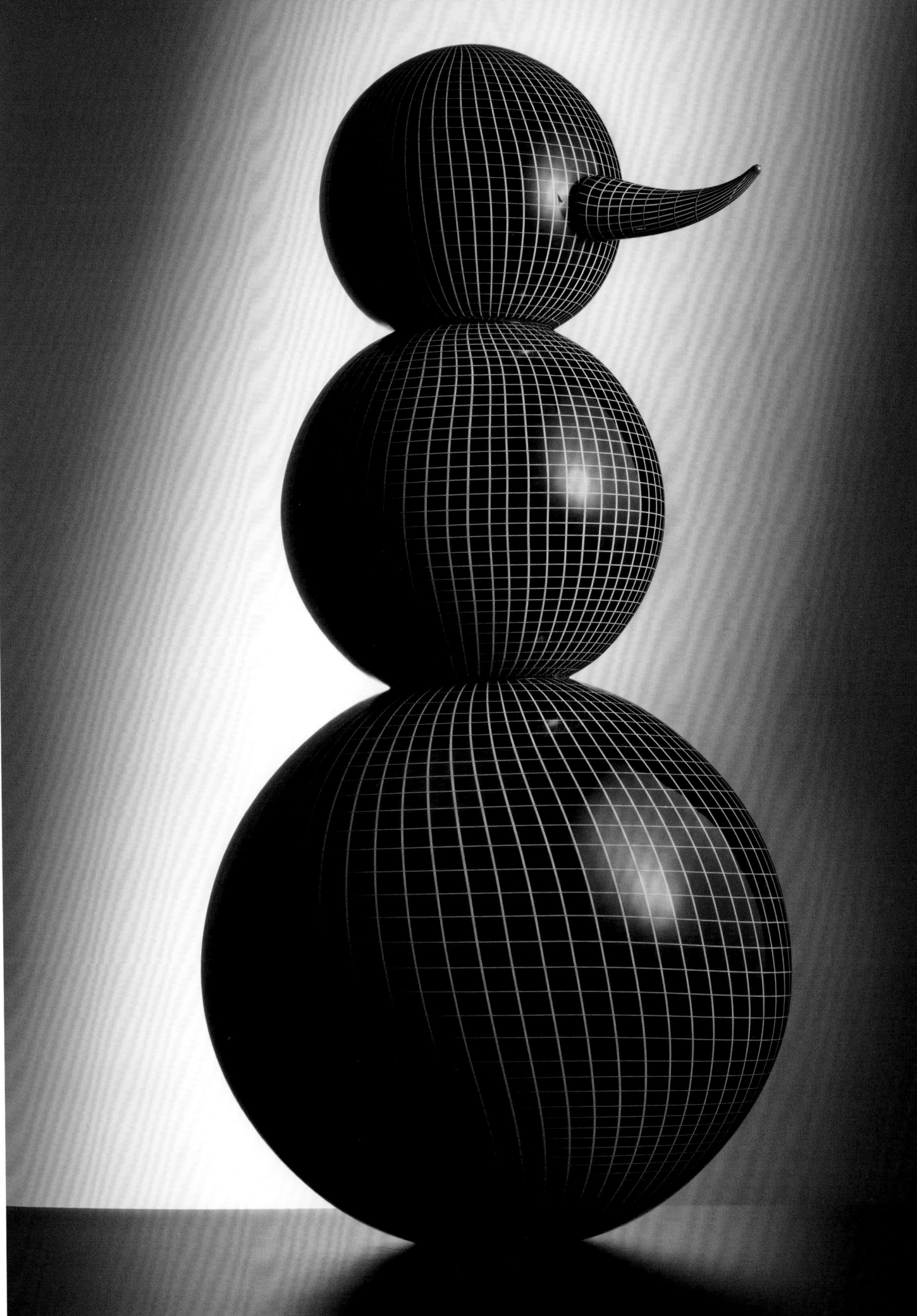

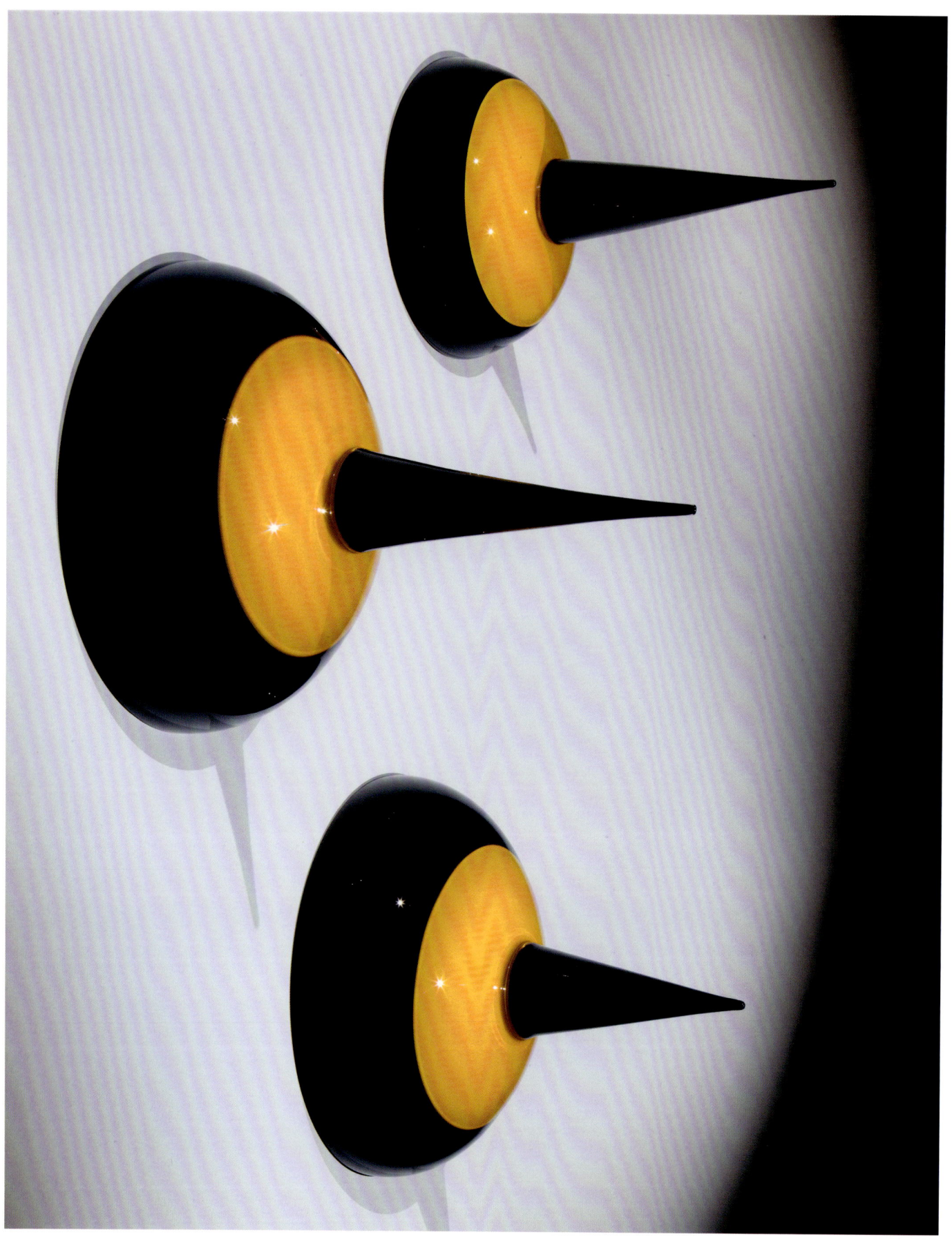

CHK. 8 *Bee Butts, 2007–2008*   **CHK. 10** *Bumble Bee Buoy, 2009*

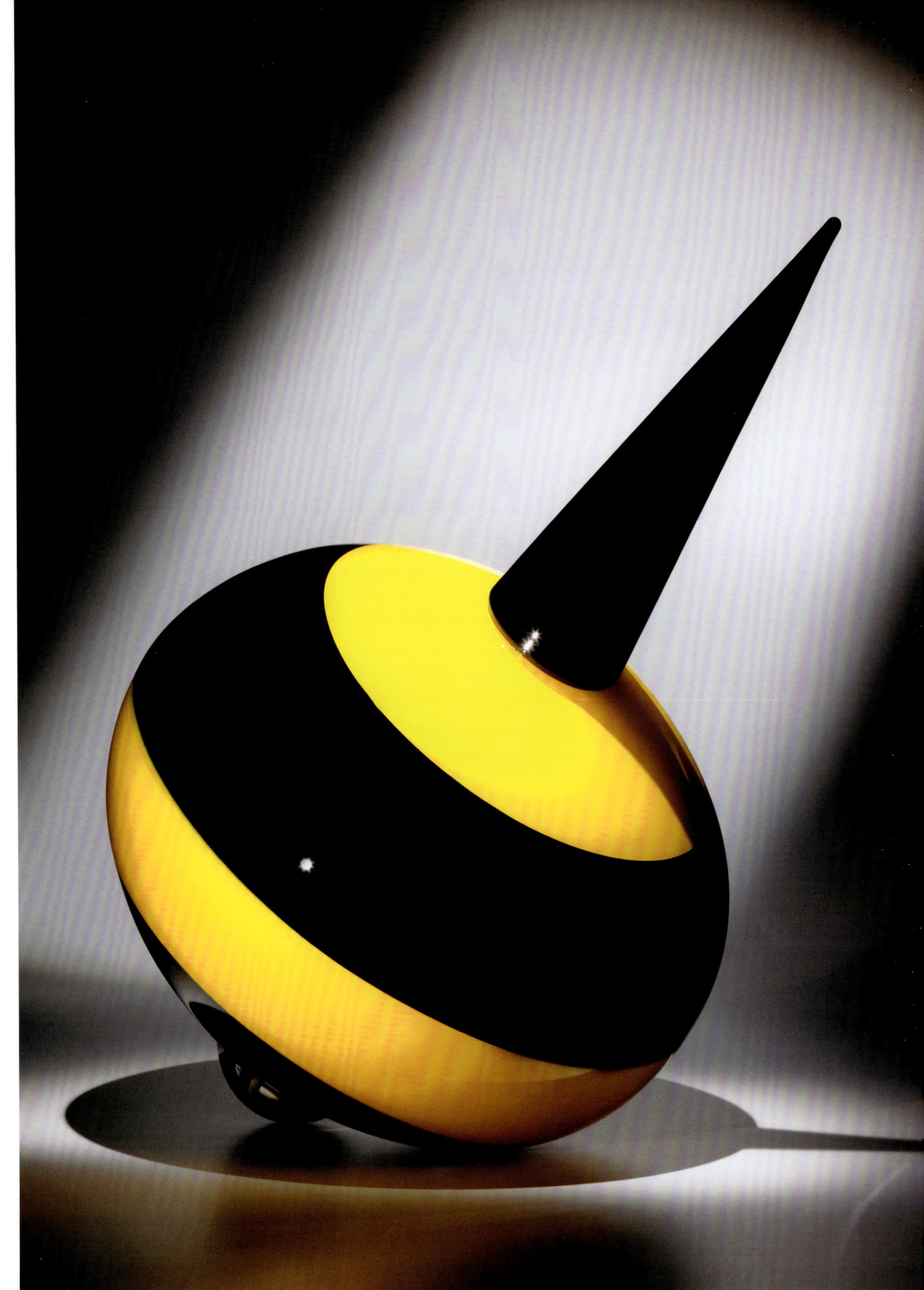

CHK. 13 *Mod Candy Cloud*, 2009

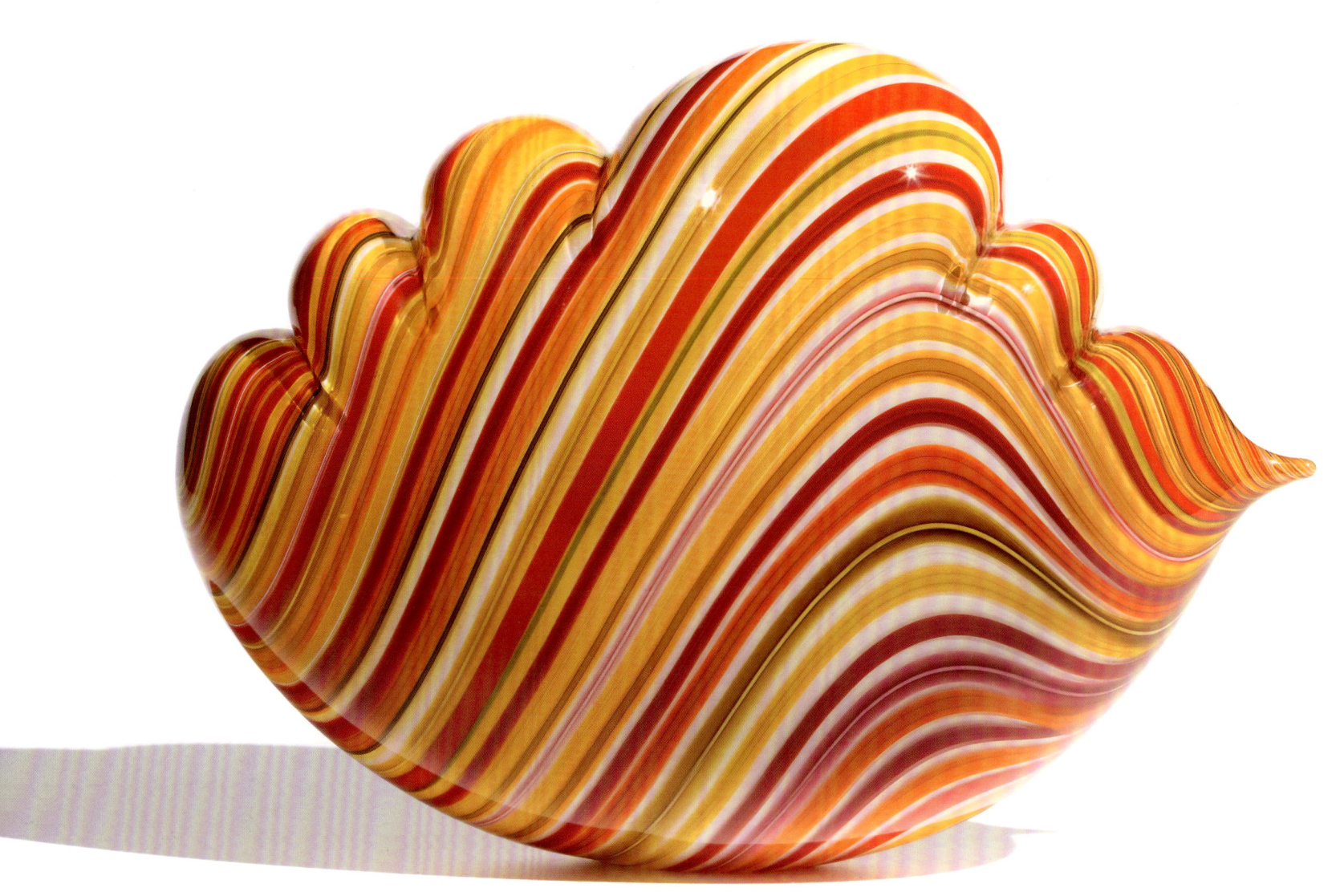

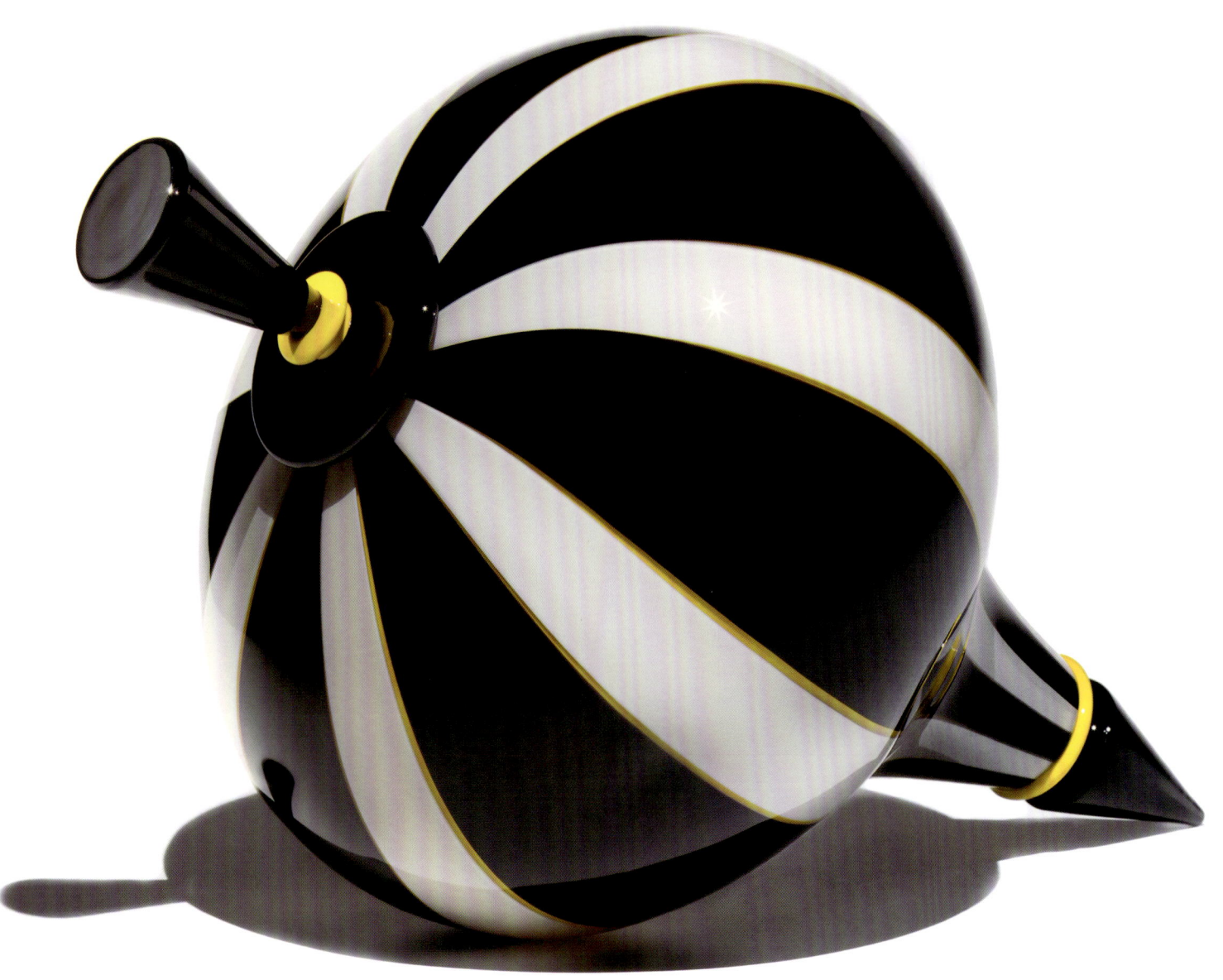

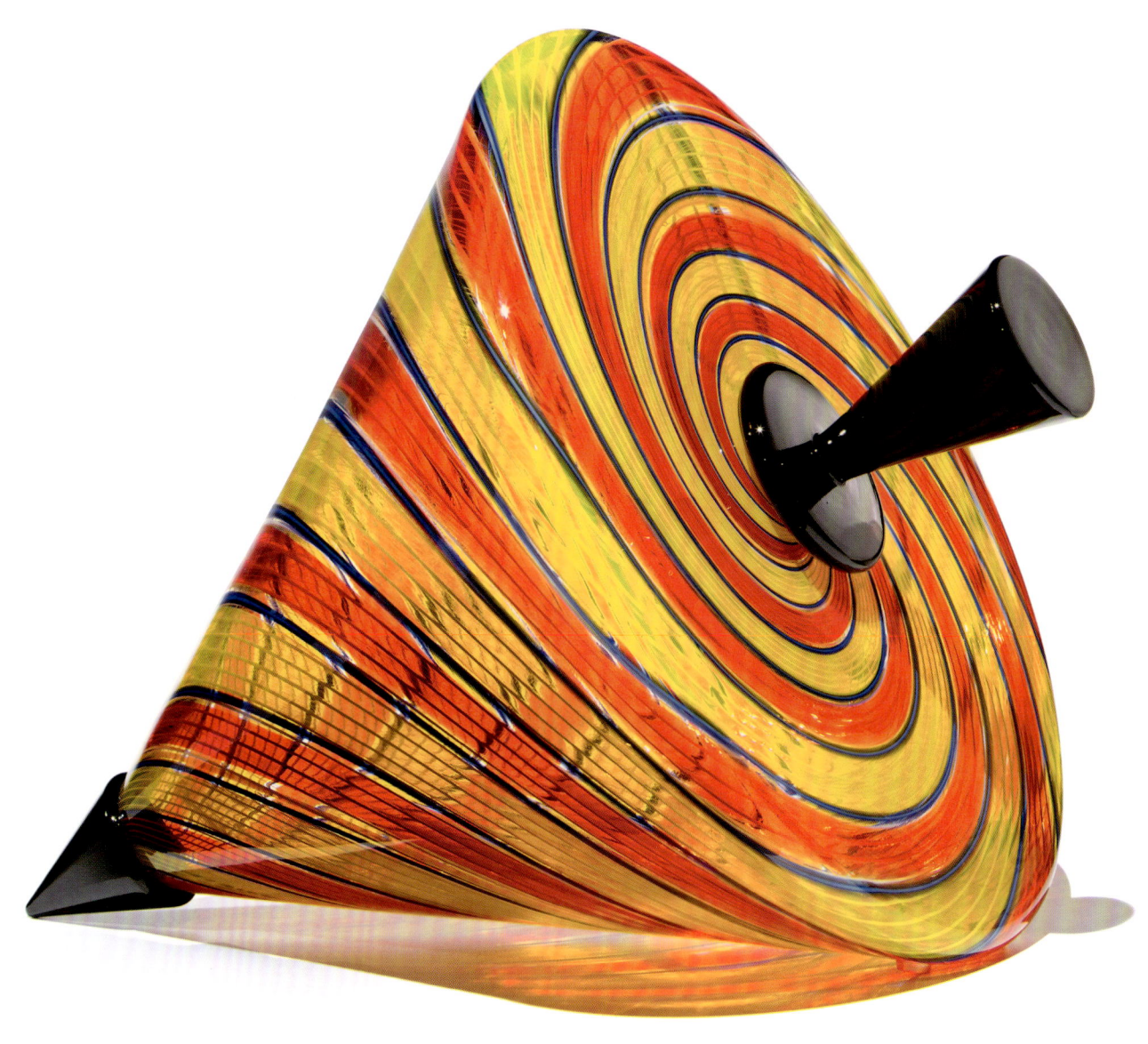

CHK. 22 *Tuxedo Top, 2014*   CHK. 21 *Pop Top, 2014*   51

I've always loved bright, punchy colors and bold graphics—that Pop-Art aesthetic. It's sophisticated, but it also reminds me of being a kid, reading comic books and watching Saturday morning cartoons. I was fascinated by the tight costumes and flowing capes of the superheroes, flying through the air . . . The *Stingers* express that larger-than-life feeling in scale and presence.

—Nancy Callan

CHK. 33 *Catwoman Stinger*, 2022

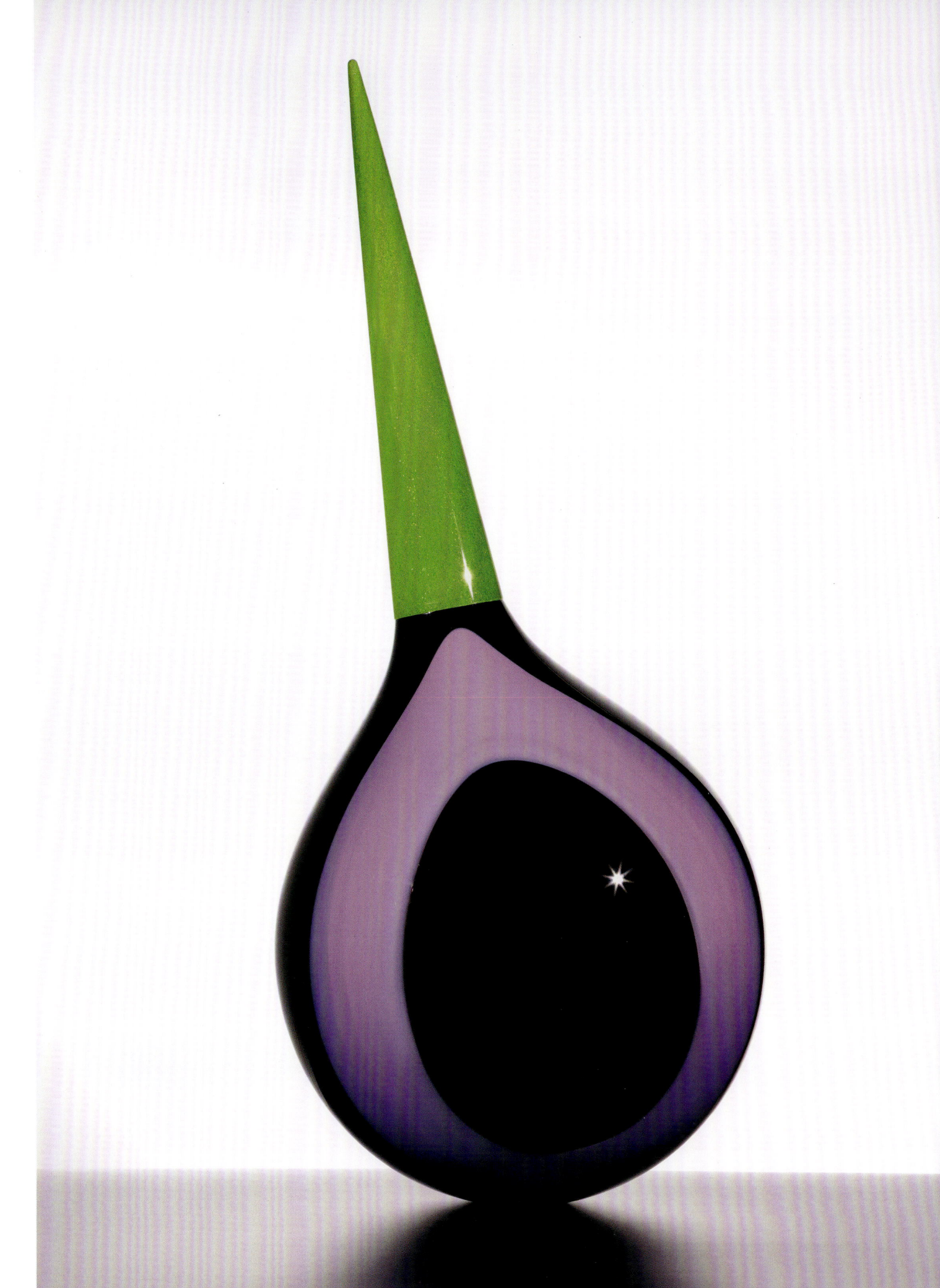

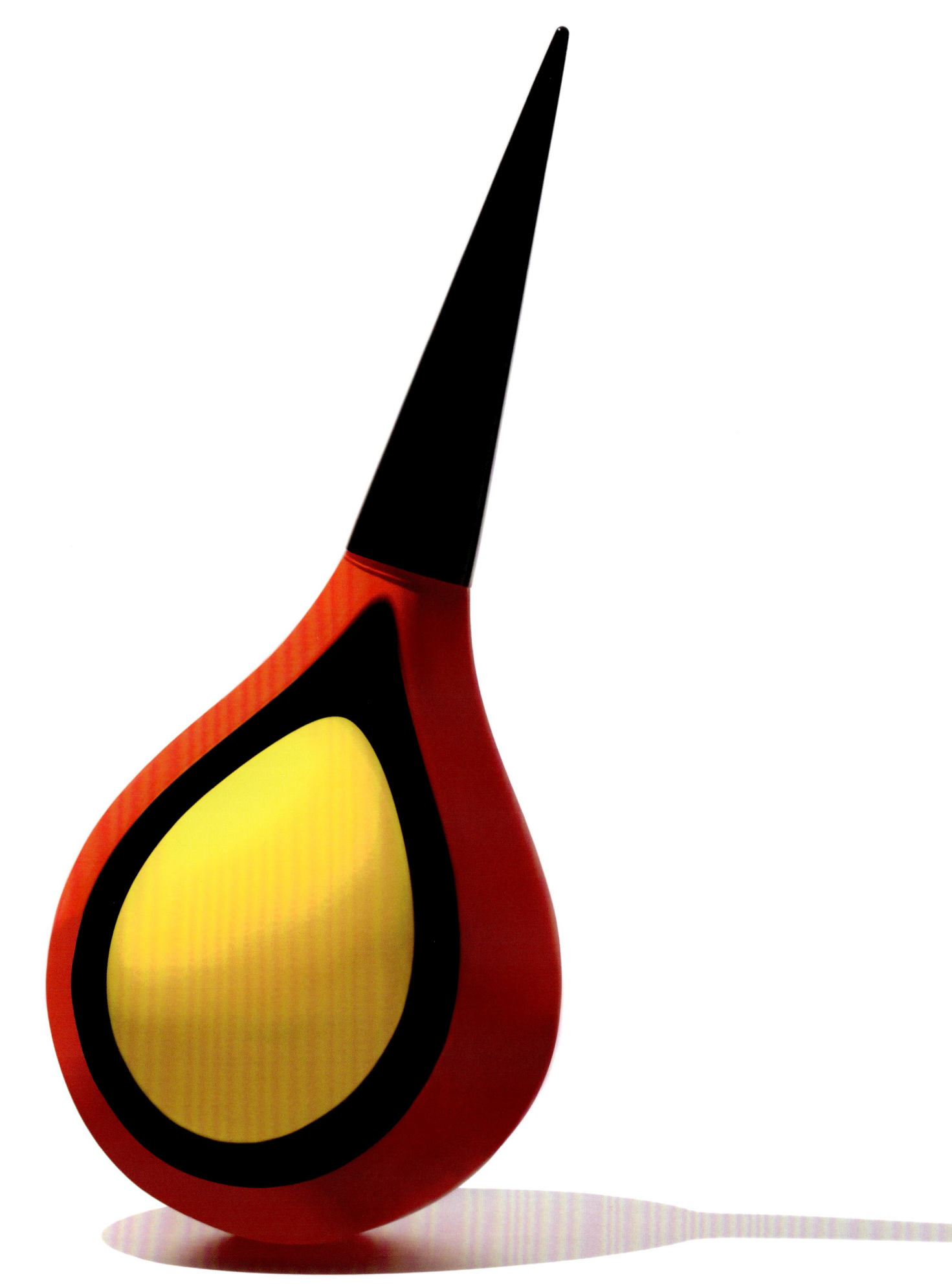

A *Stinger* takes shape from molten glass in the Museum's Hot Shop, 2013

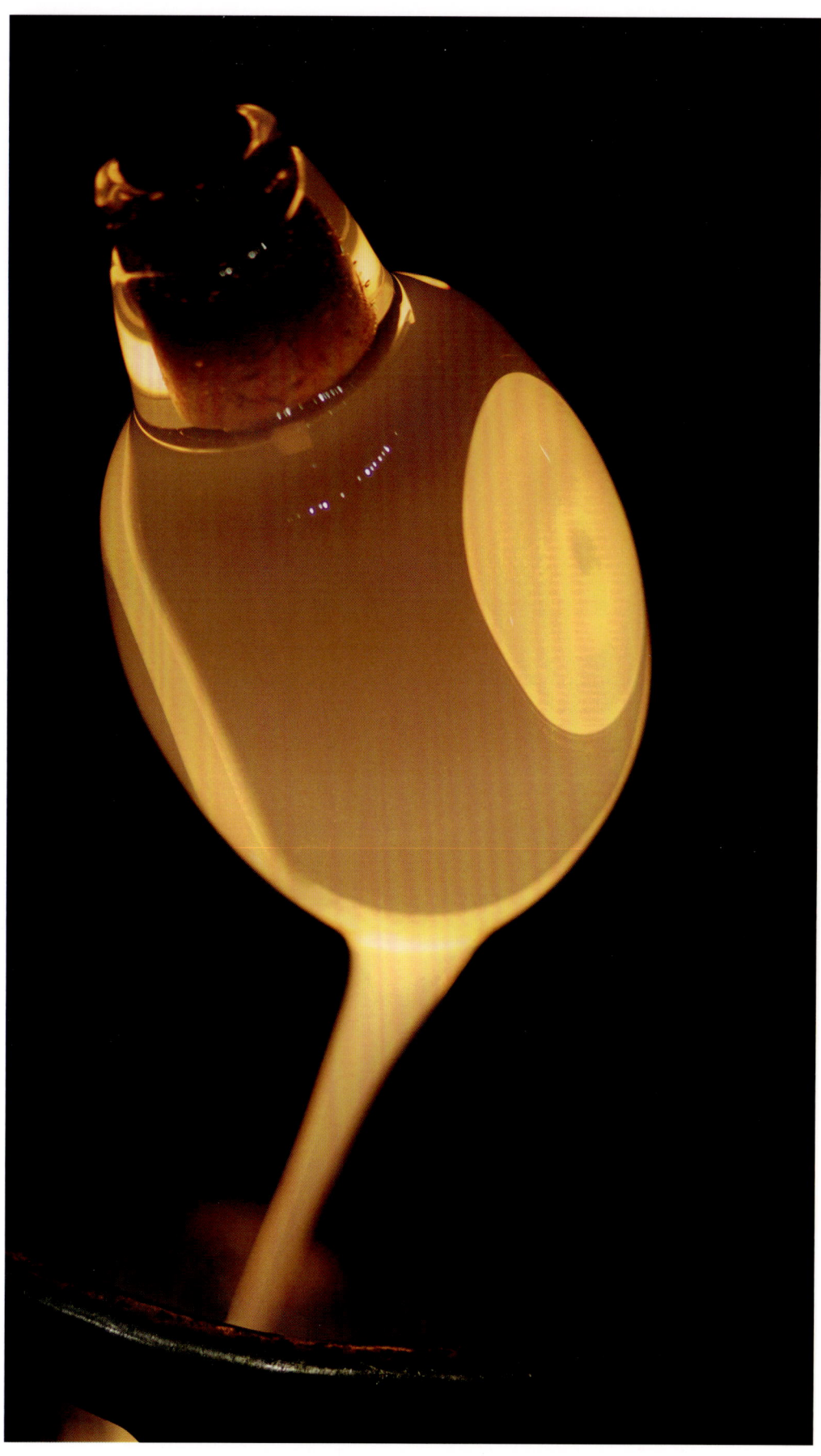

CHK. 41 *Kitty Pryde Stinger, 2023*

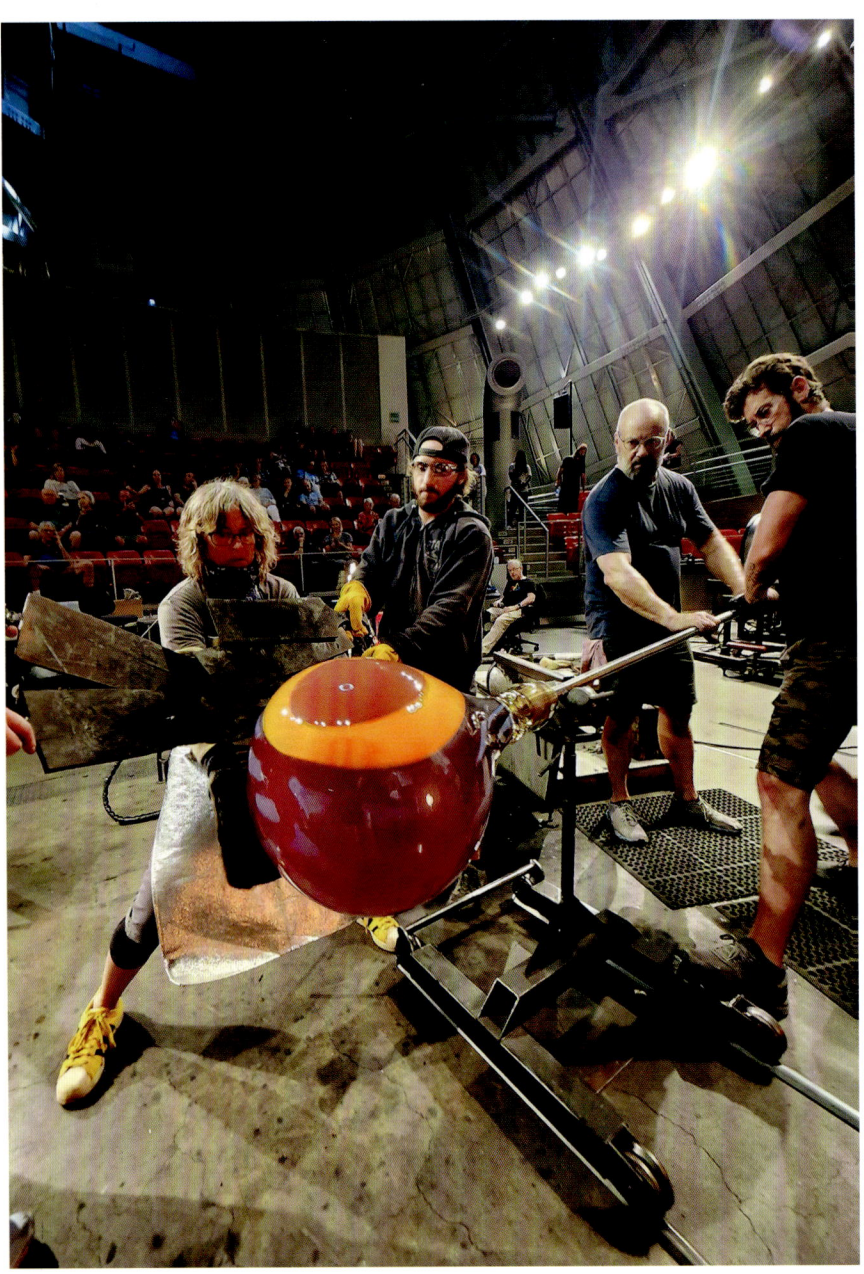

Artist making *Mystique Stinger*
(Chk. 42) at the Museum of
Glass Hot Shop, assisted by
Tanner Weiss, David Walters,
and Benjamin Cobb, 2023

CHK. 42   *Mystique Stinger,* 2023

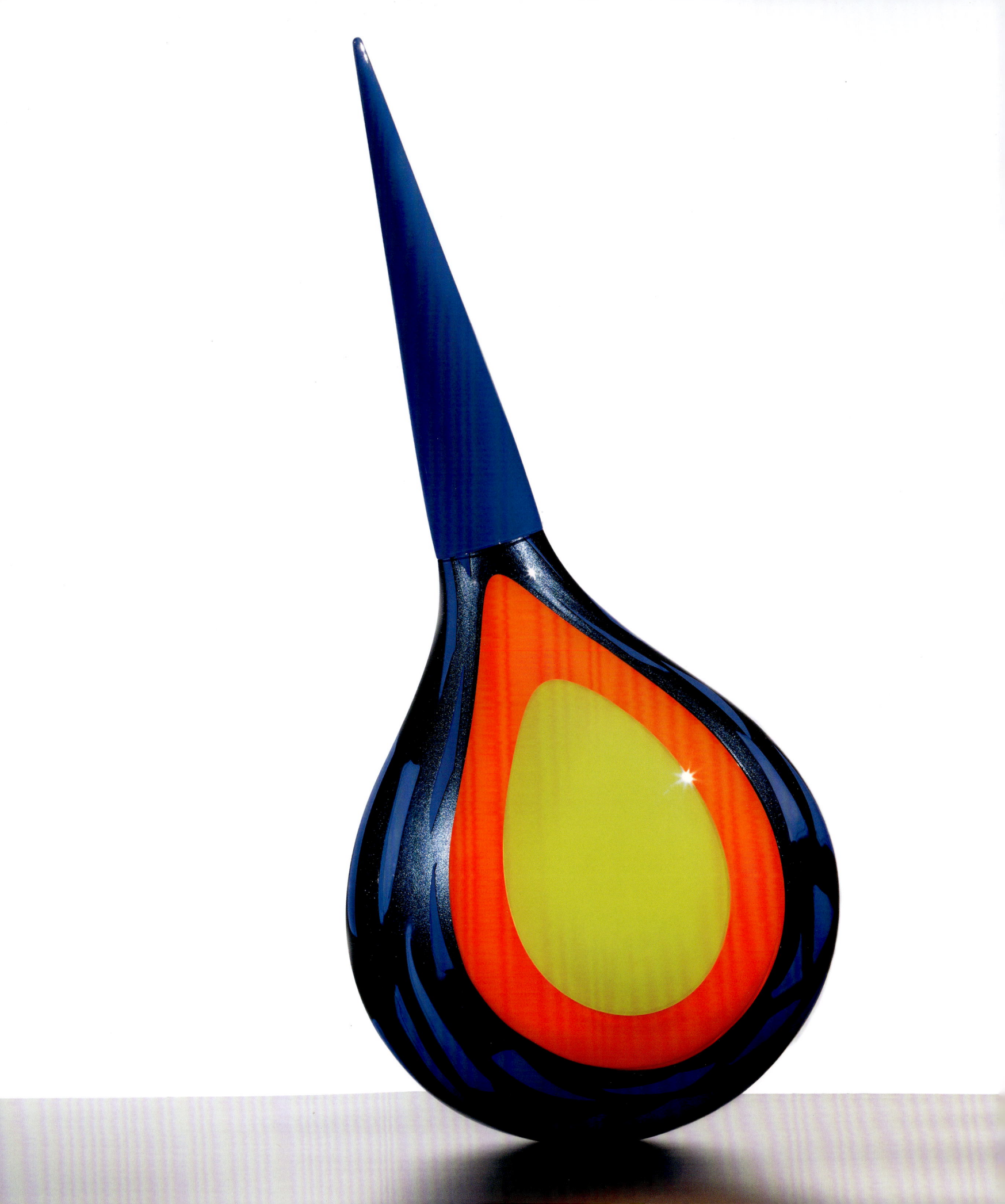

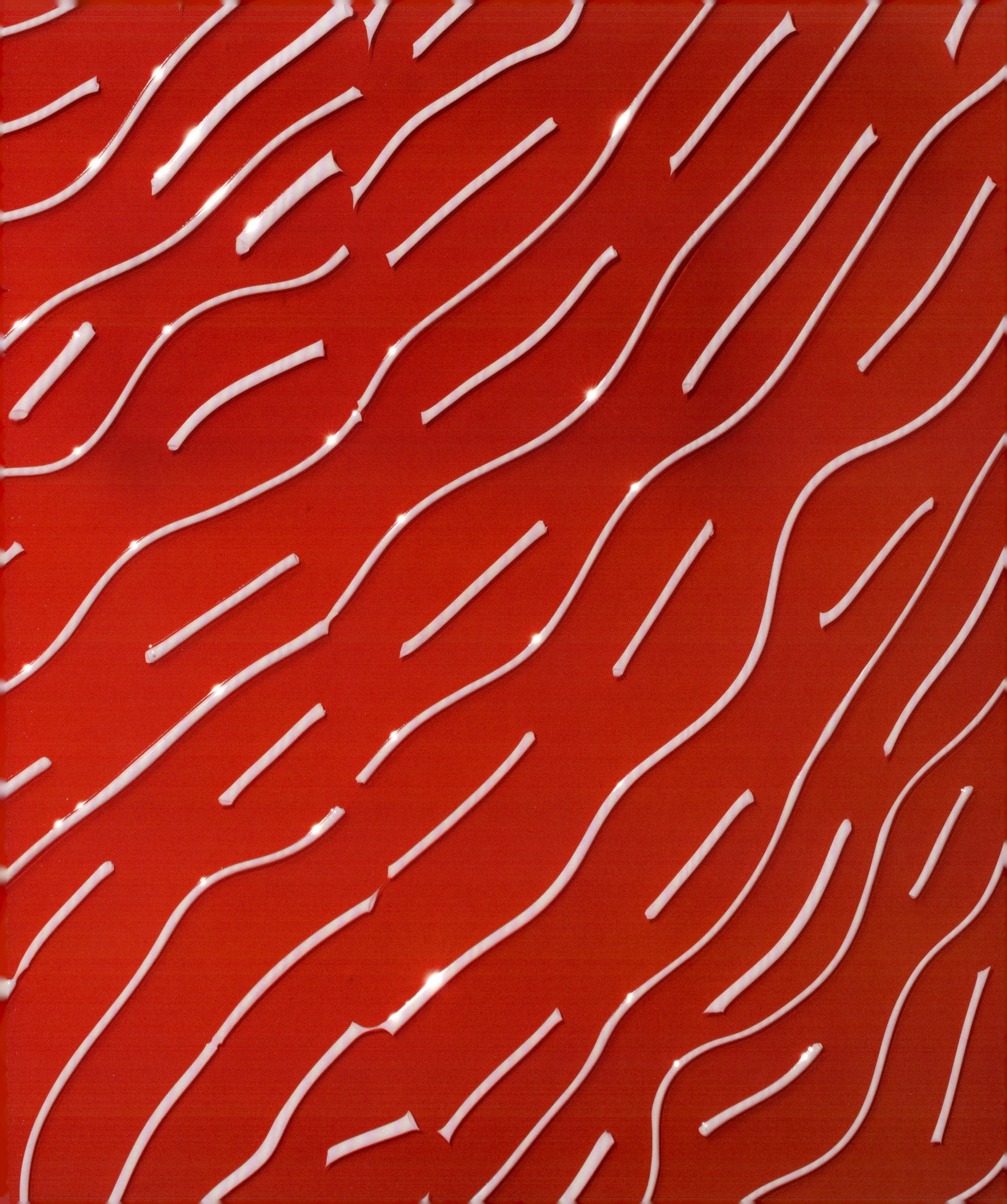

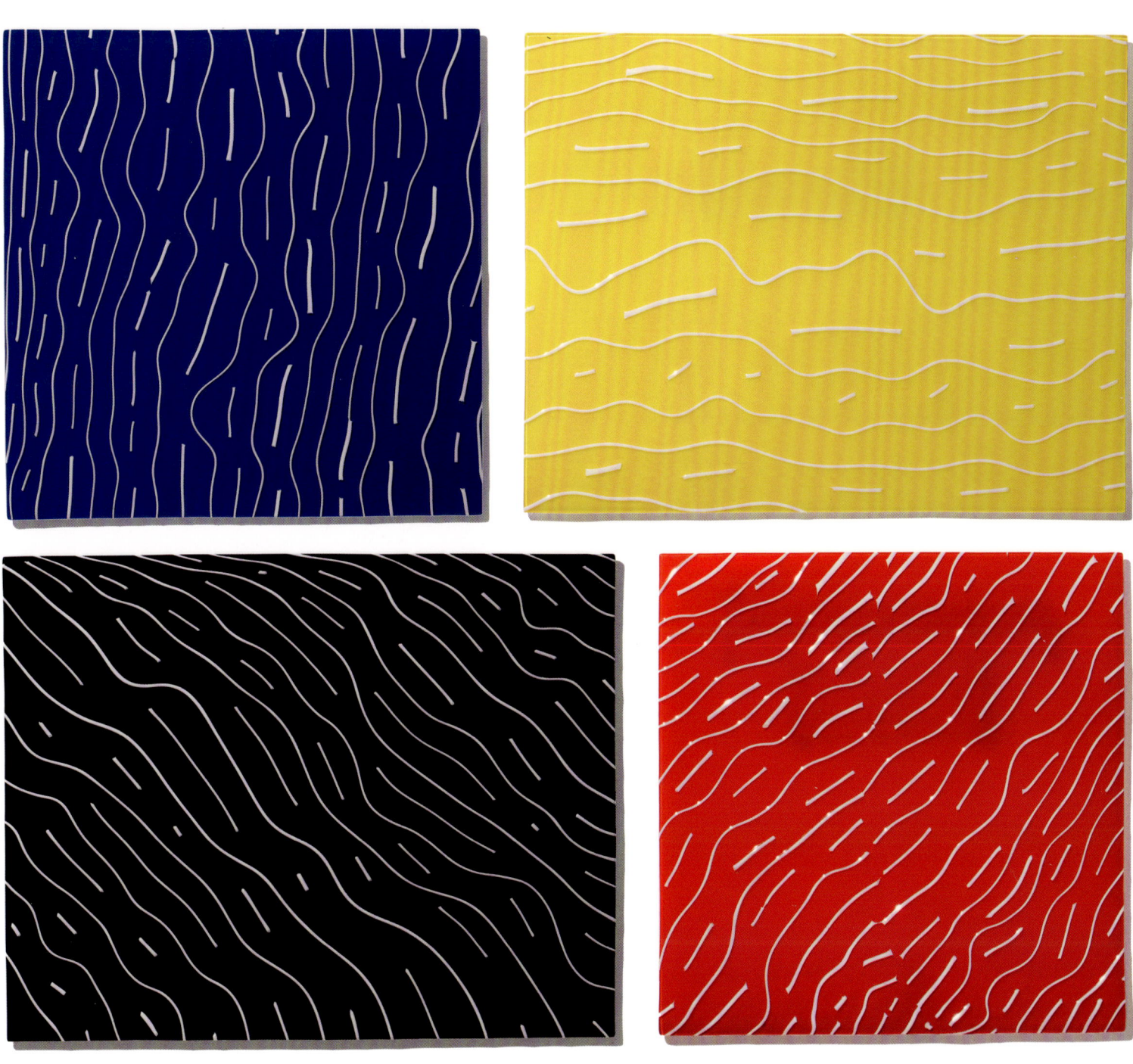

CHK. 34 *Road Trip with Keith,* 2022

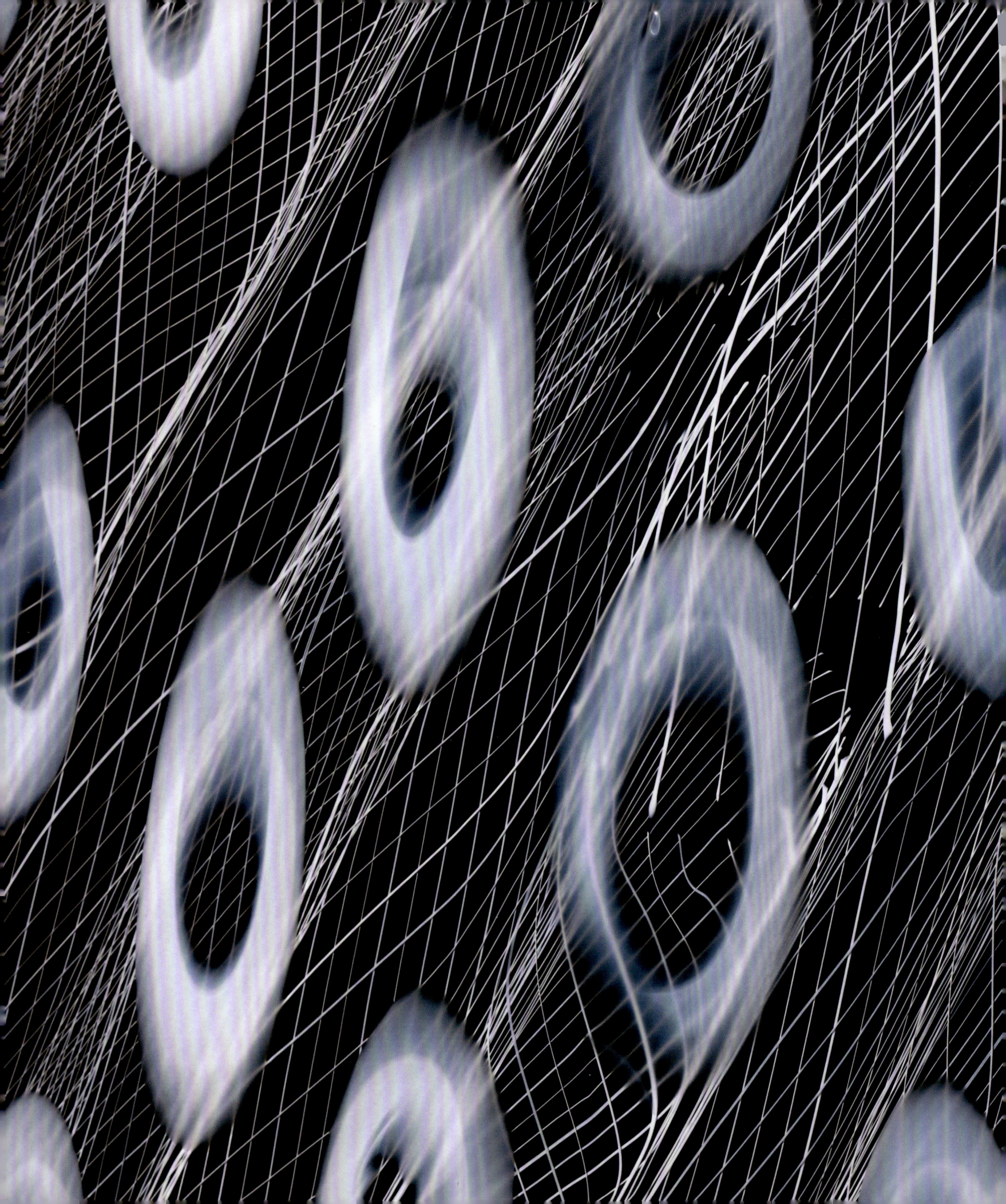

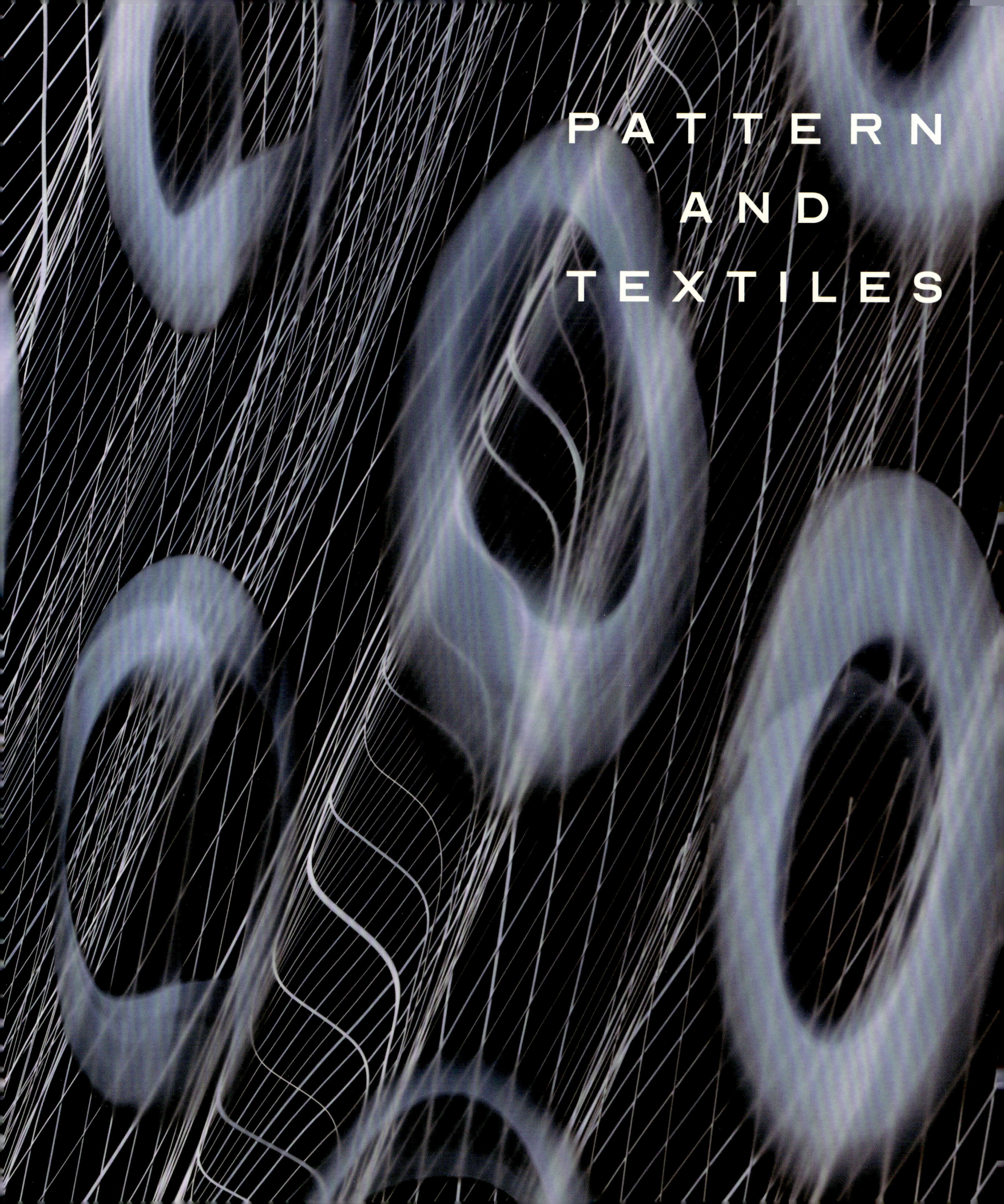

PATTERN
AND
TEXTILES

Pages 60–61: *Comme les Filles* (detail), 2023 (Chk. 37)

CHK. 9   *Speedy Blue Winkle,* 2008

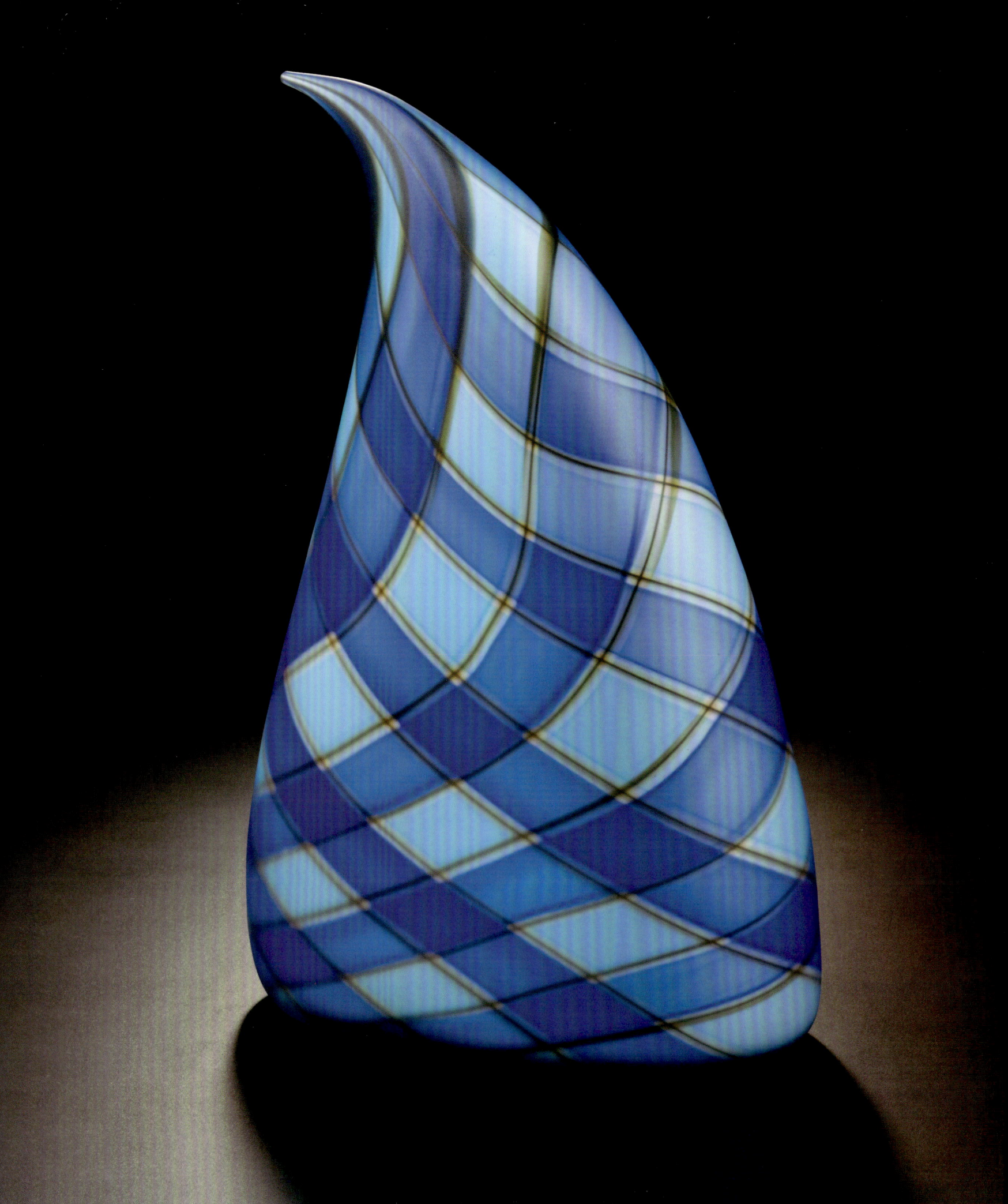

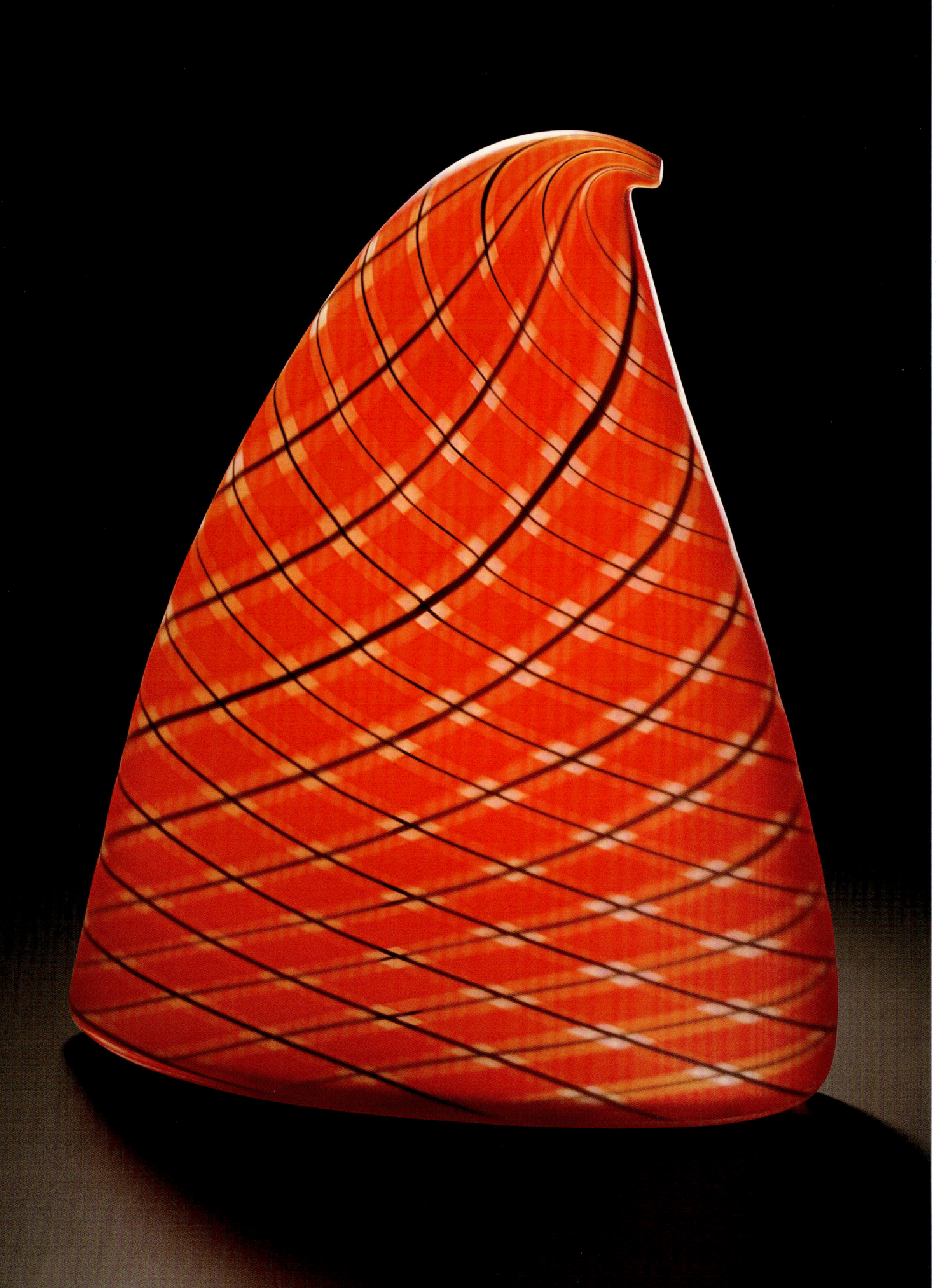

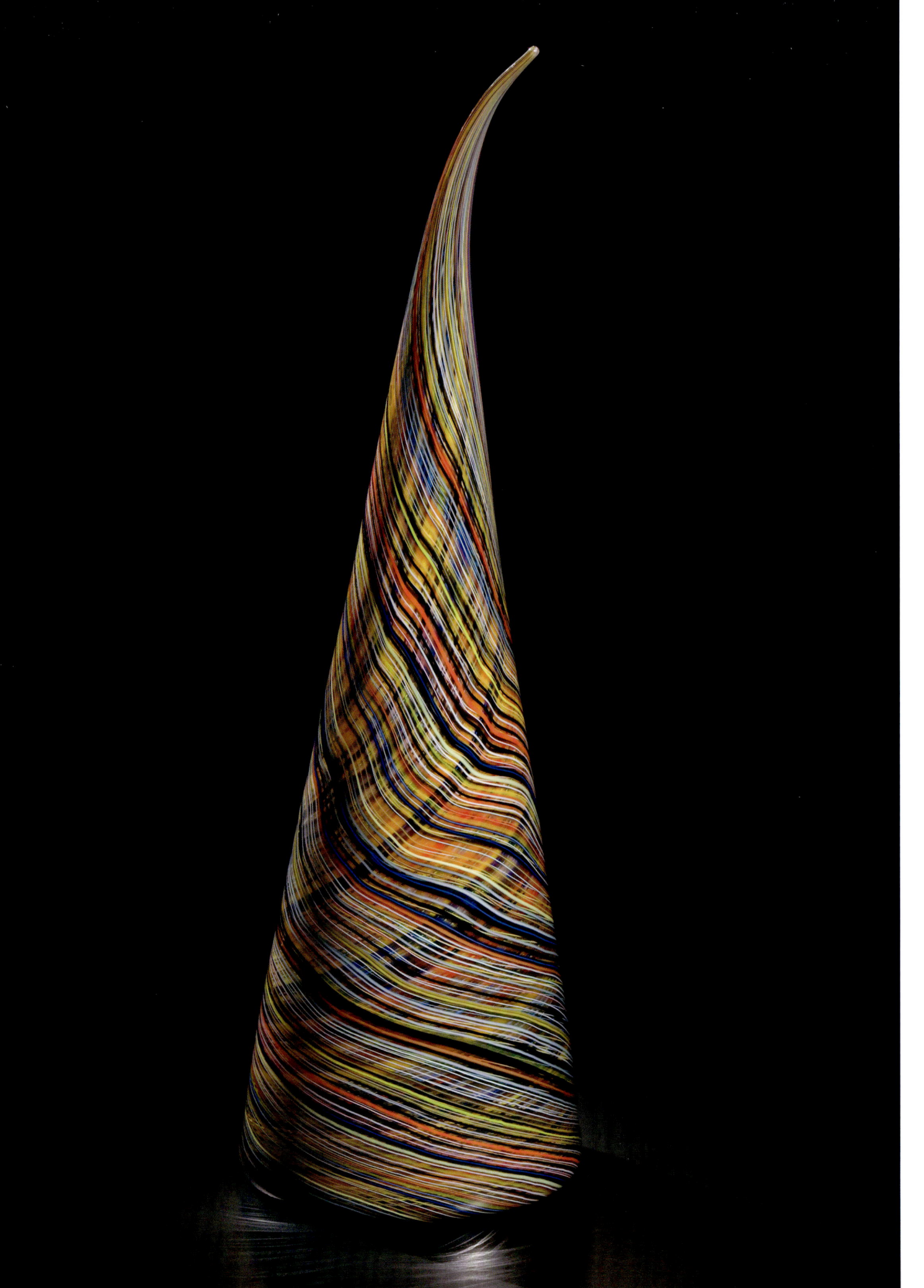

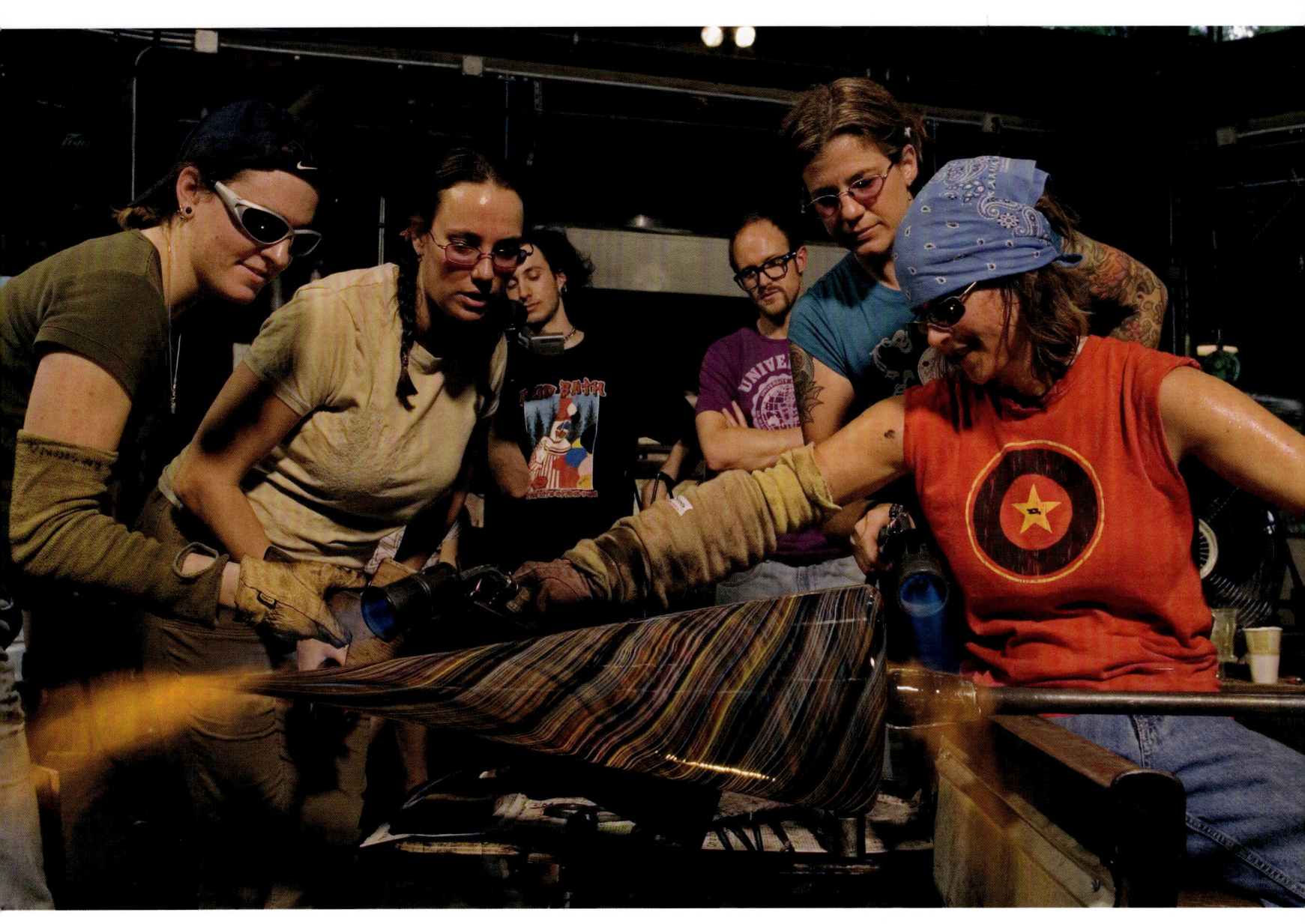

Artist making *Missoni Winkle*
(Chk. 6) at Pilchuck Glass
School, assisted by Anne
Rushing, Kait Rhoads,
and Kelly O'Dell, 2007

There is a real connection for me
between textiles and glass. When I see
a pattern drape over a form or bend
and fold with motion, I wonder how I
can make that happen in glass. I love to
see the deconstruction of a garment,
the distress or wear…those moments
capture my imagination.

—Nancy Callan

CHK. 24   *Sonia Winkle,* 2015

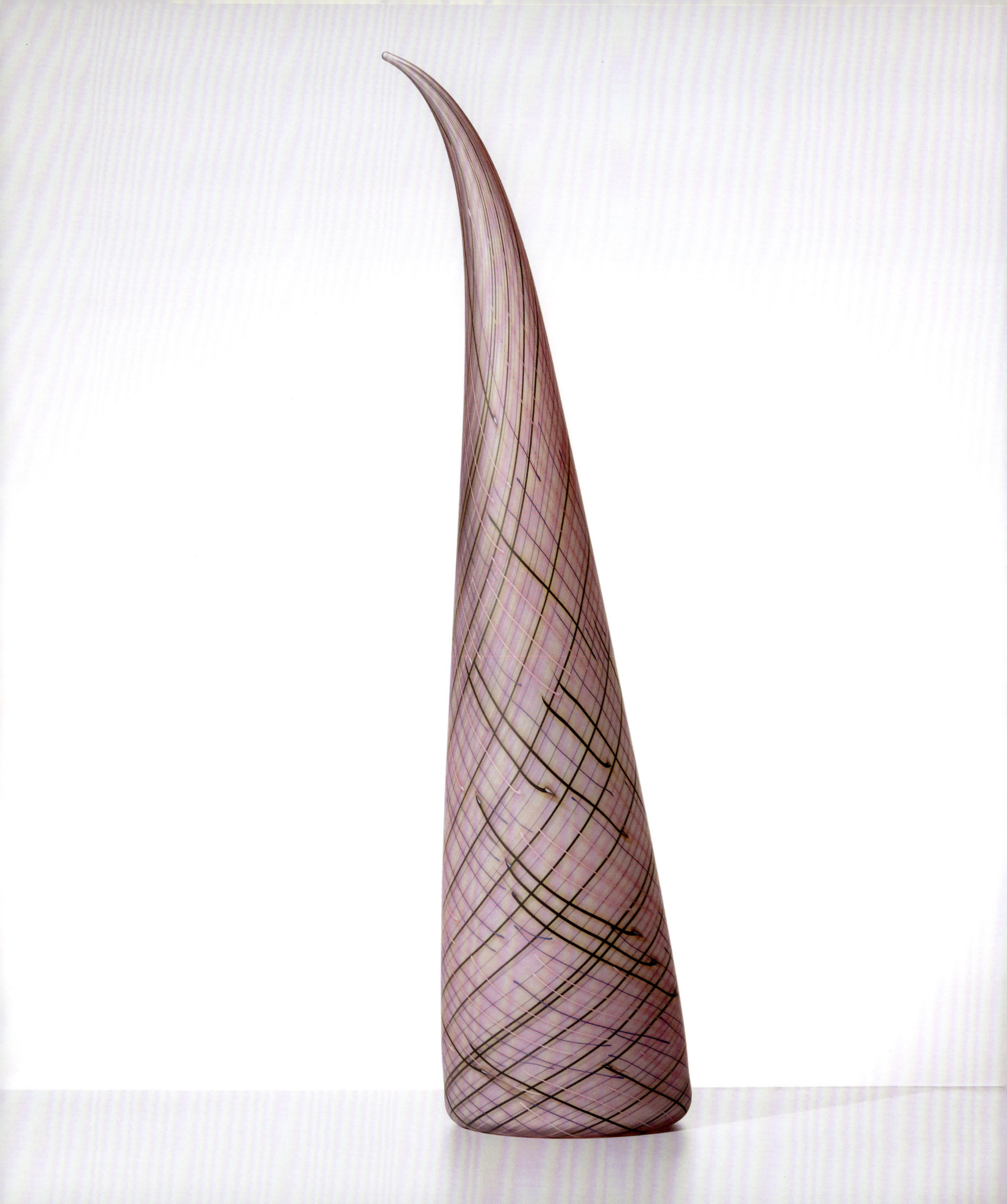

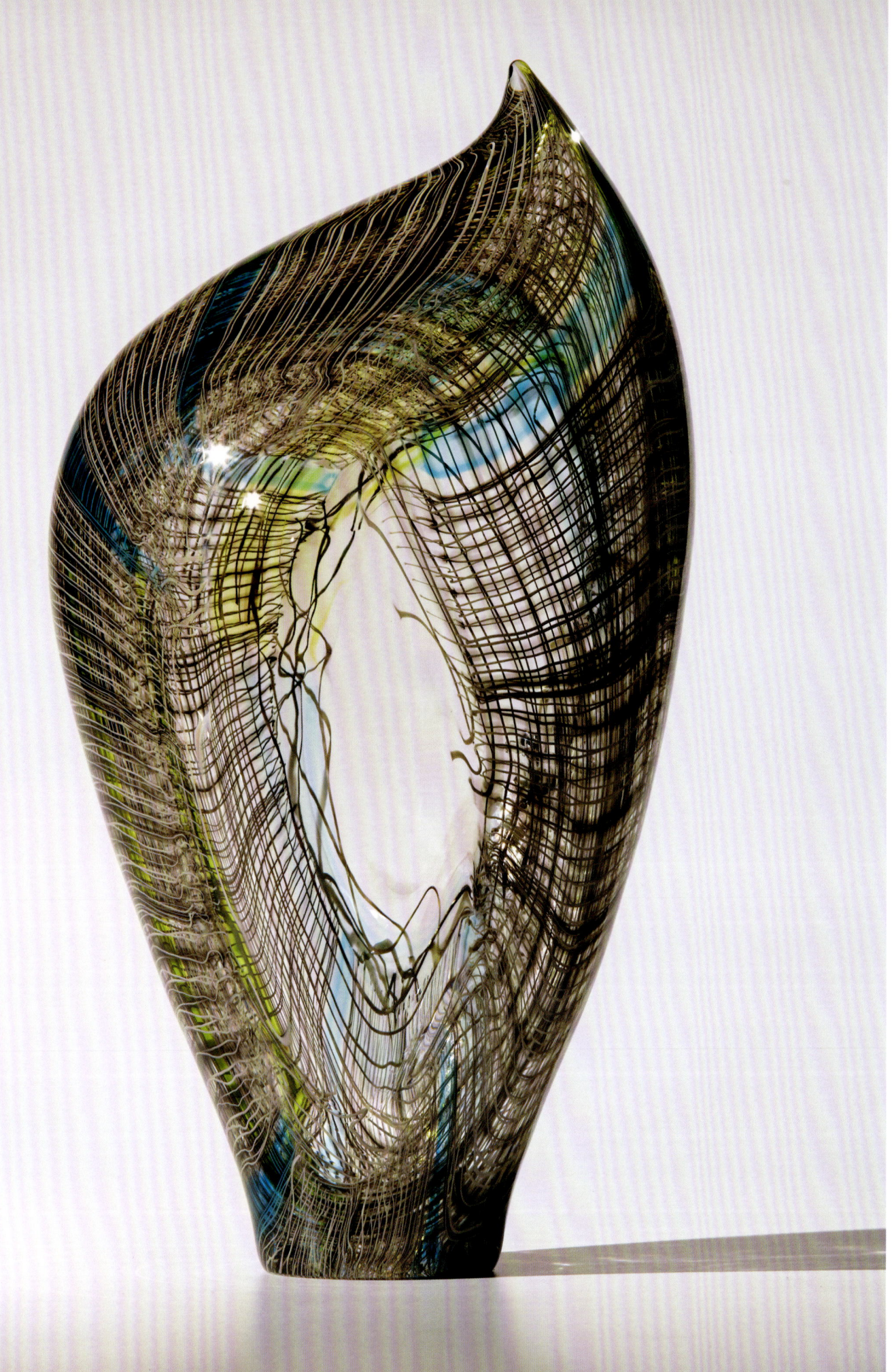

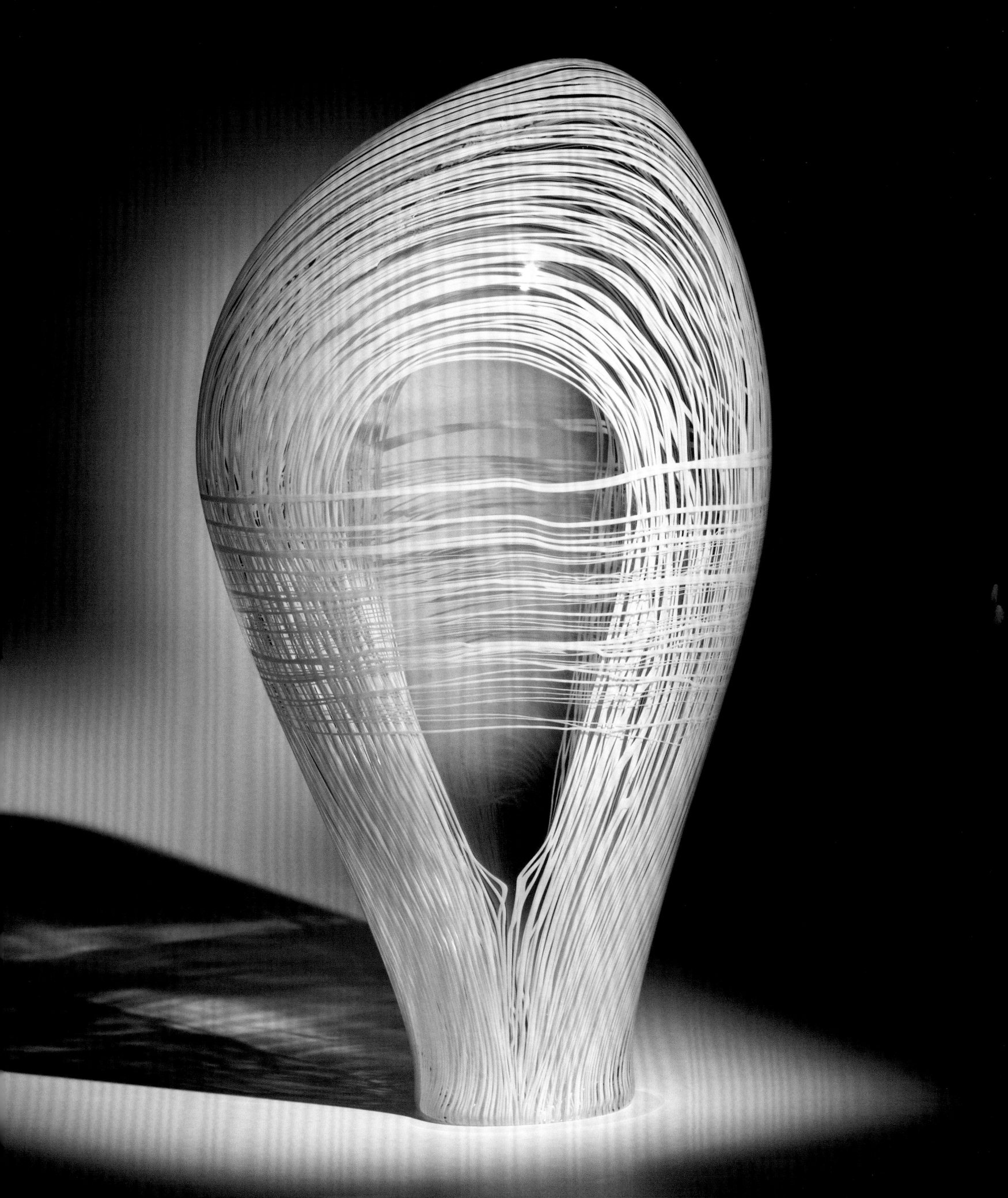

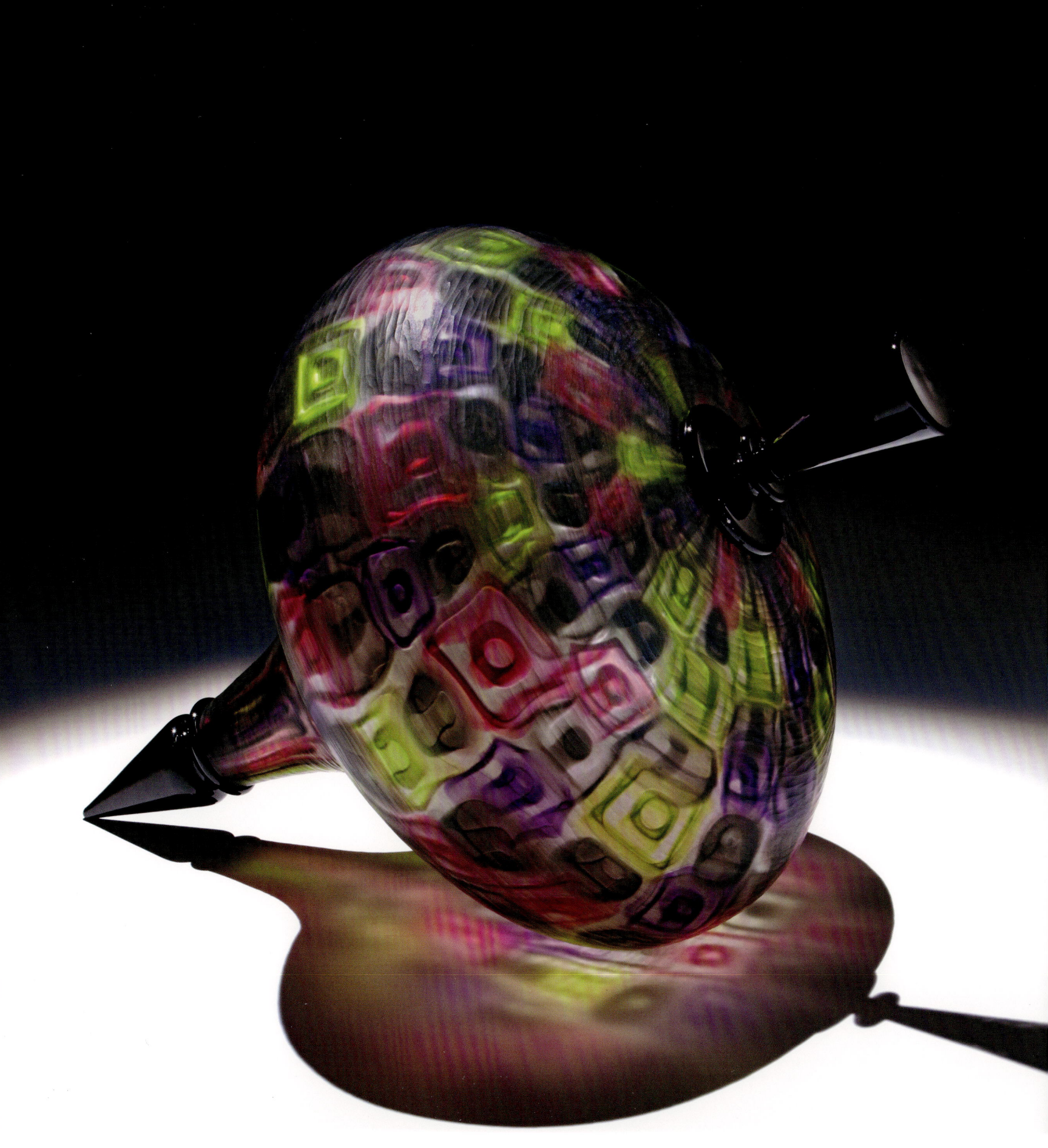

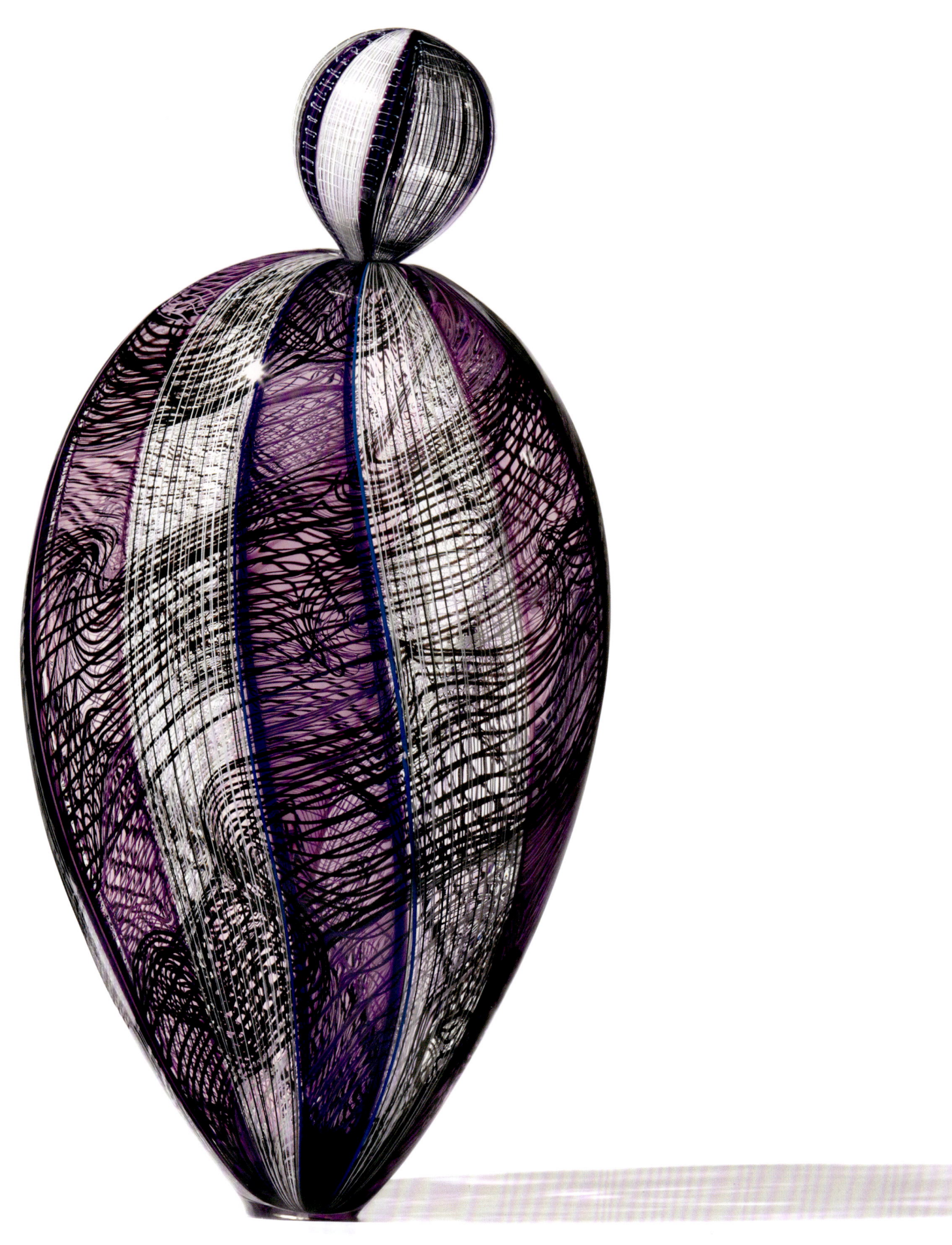

CHK. 26 *Natalia Paloma, 2017*   **CHK. 37 (GATEFOLD)** *Comme les Filles, 2023*

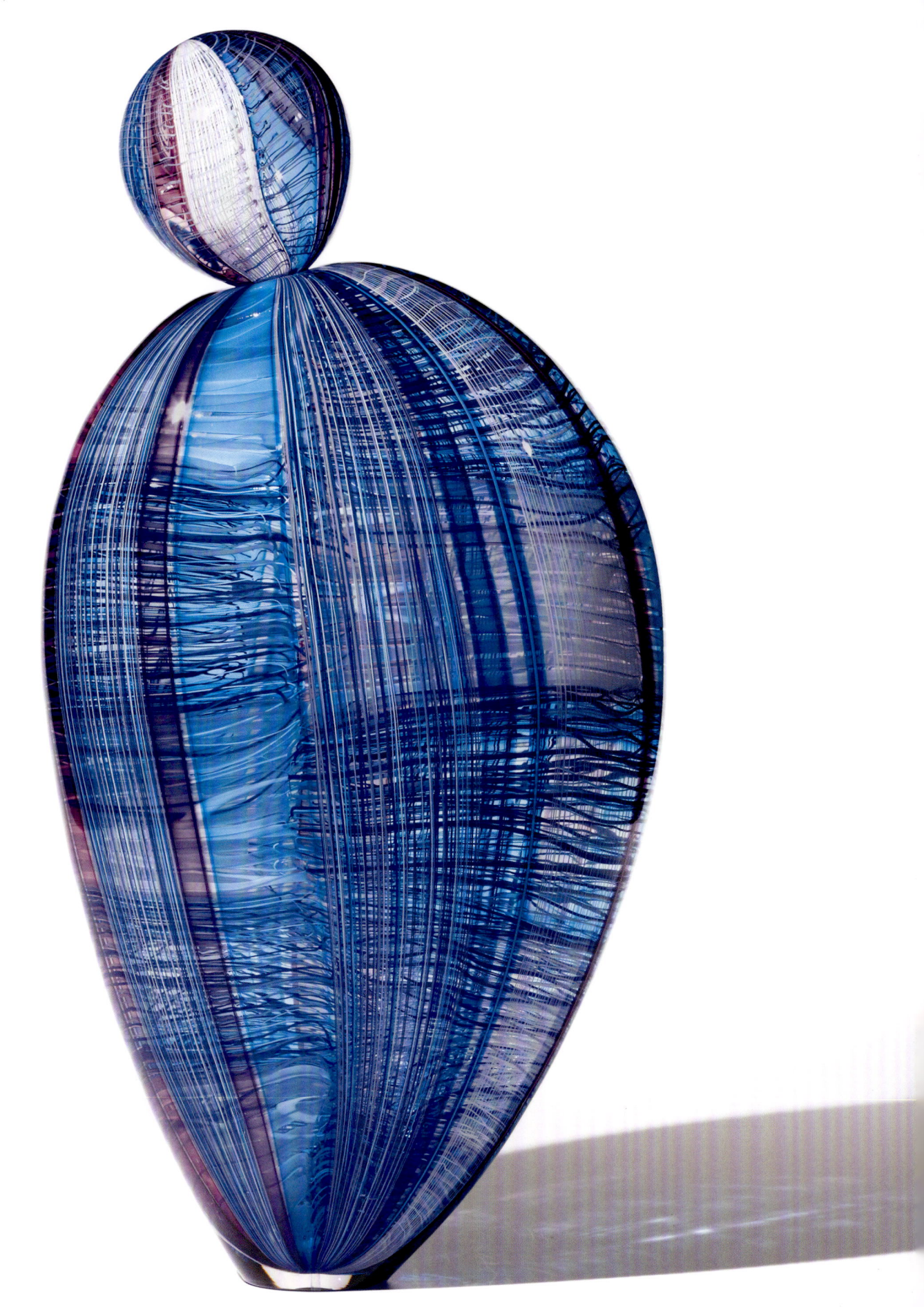

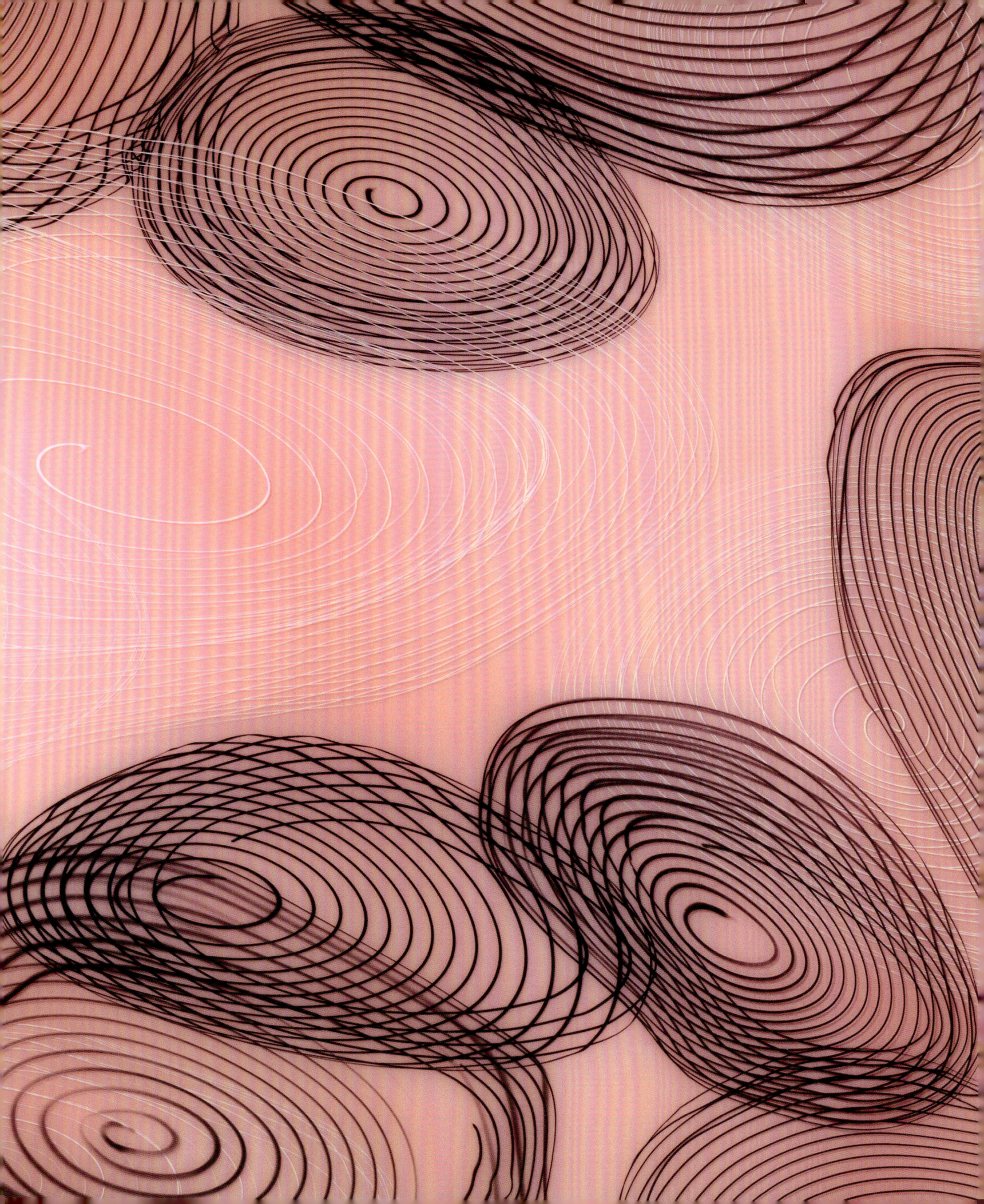

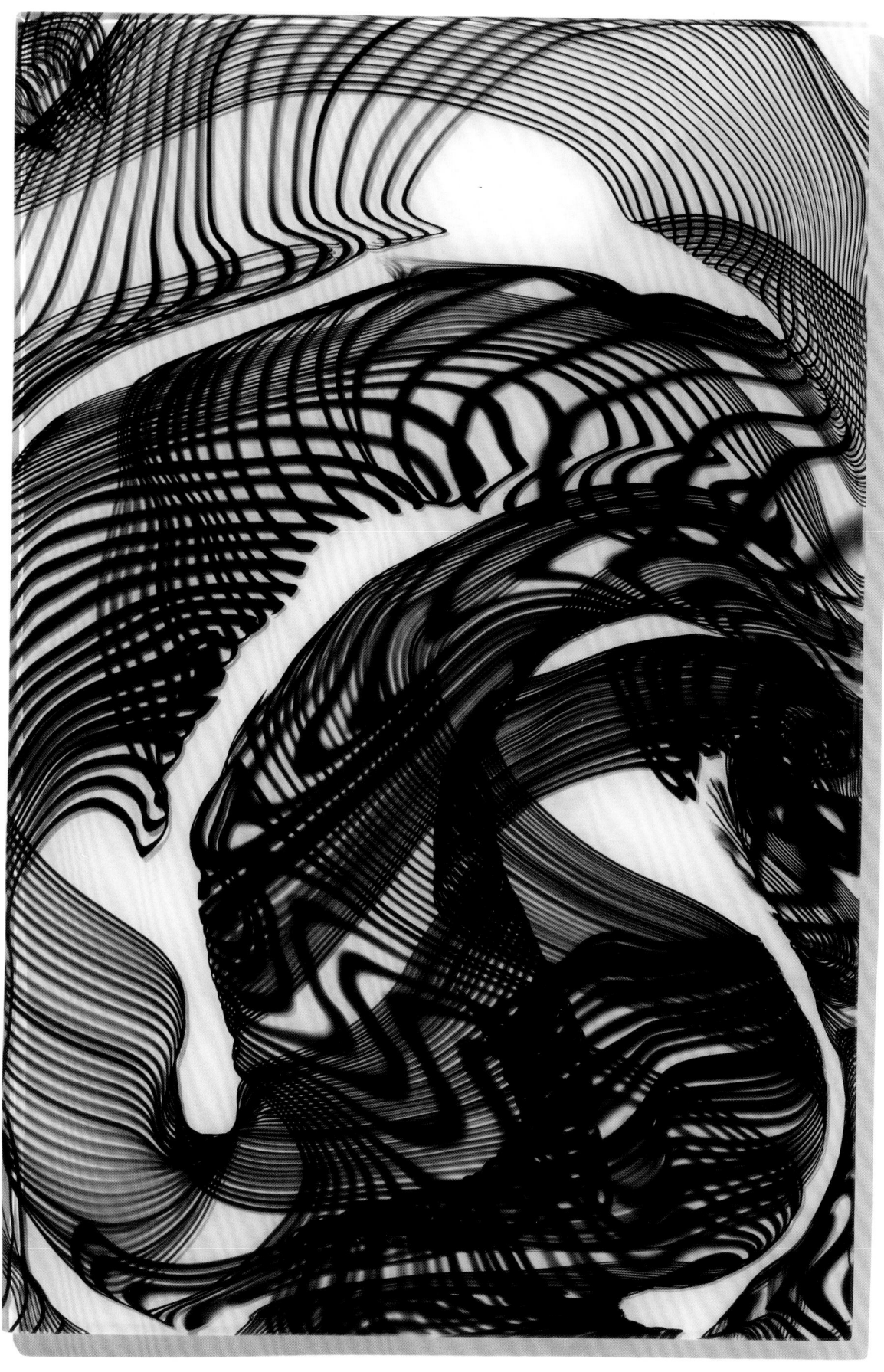

CHK. 37 *Comme les Filles* (detail), 2023

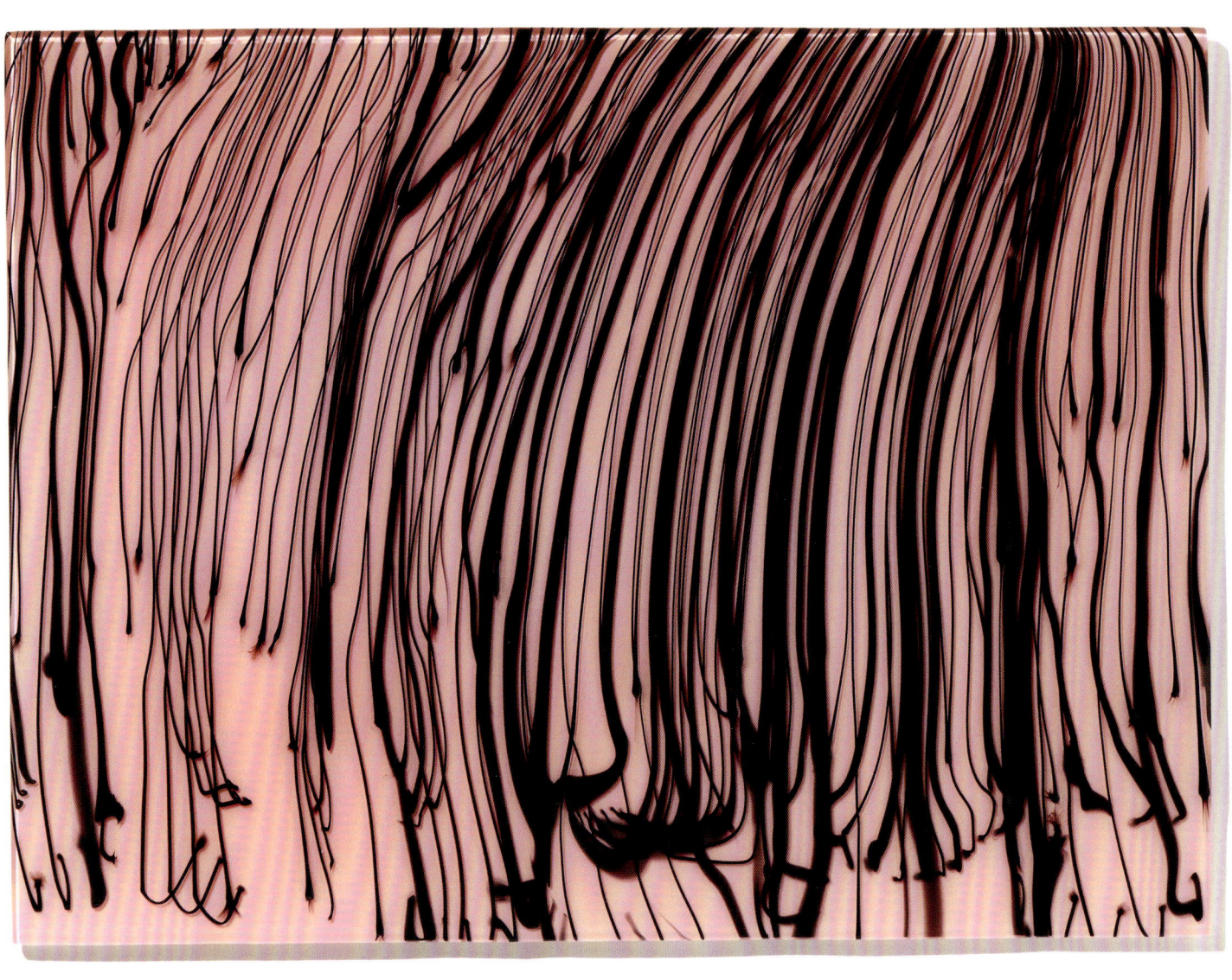

CHK. 37   *Comme les Filles* (detail), 2023

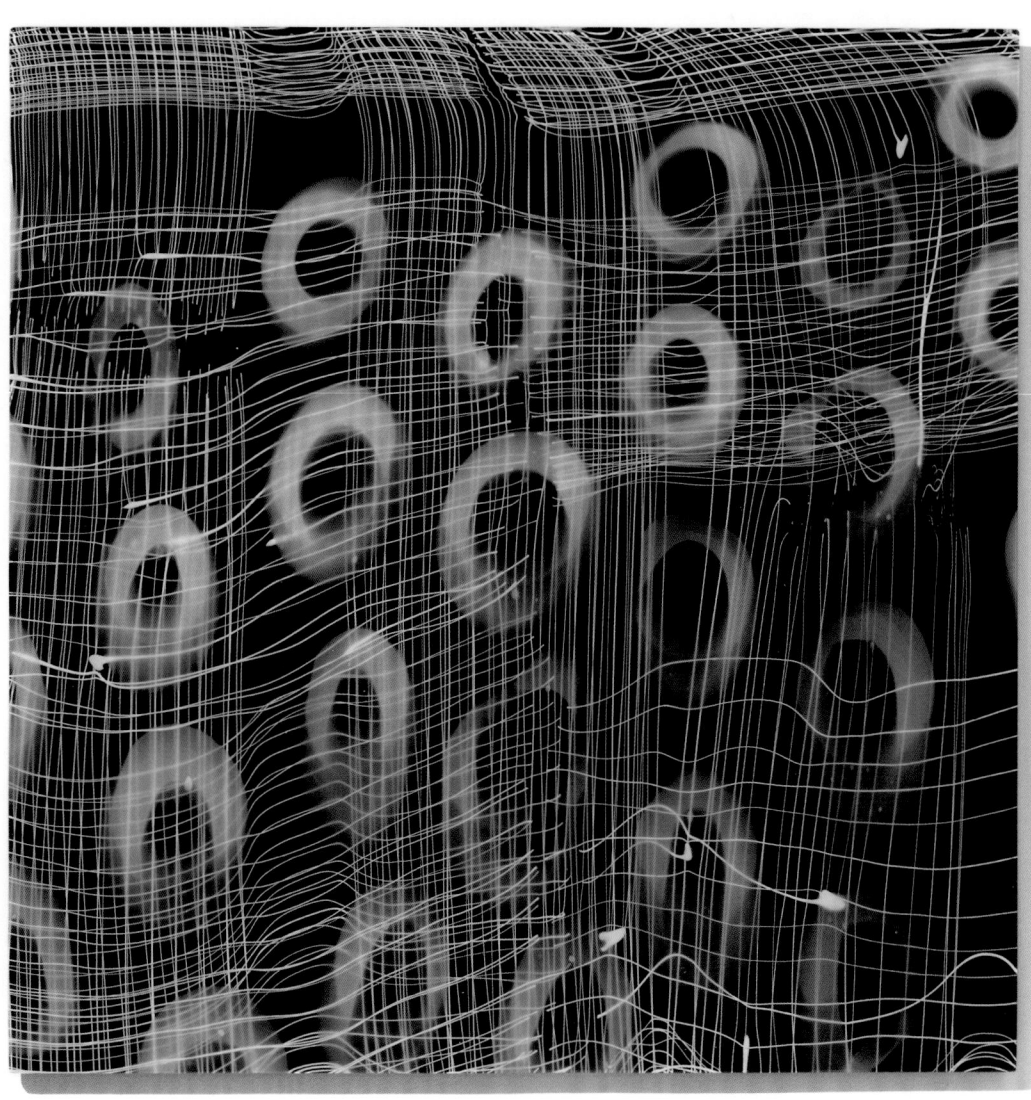

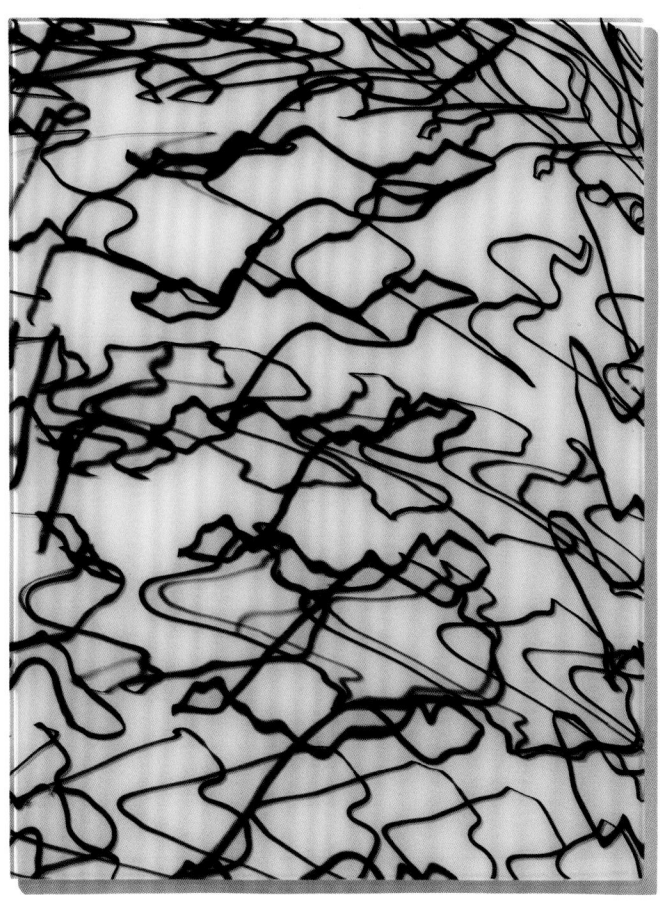
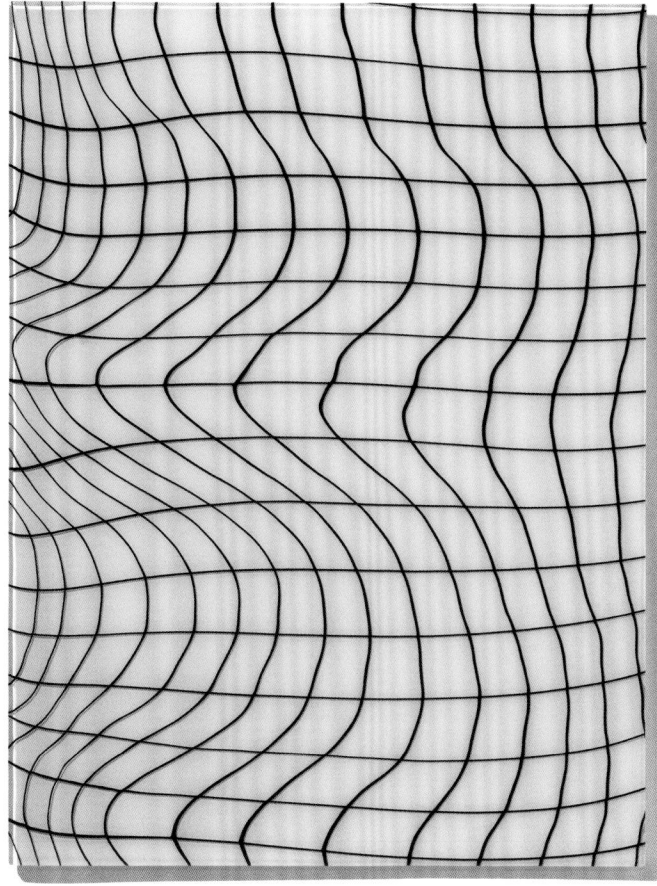

CHK. 37 *Comme les Filles* (detail), 2023

A few years ago, I started thinking about making a book of just my pattern work—a record of my designs in glass. Then I thought—why not put the sketchbook on the wall? This was the beginning of making the blown and slumped glass panels, centering my pattern ideas and presenting them in a new way. The panels feel like drawings because they are two-dimensional, but they still have the qualities of blown glass that I love—movement and unexpected moments.

—Nancy Callan

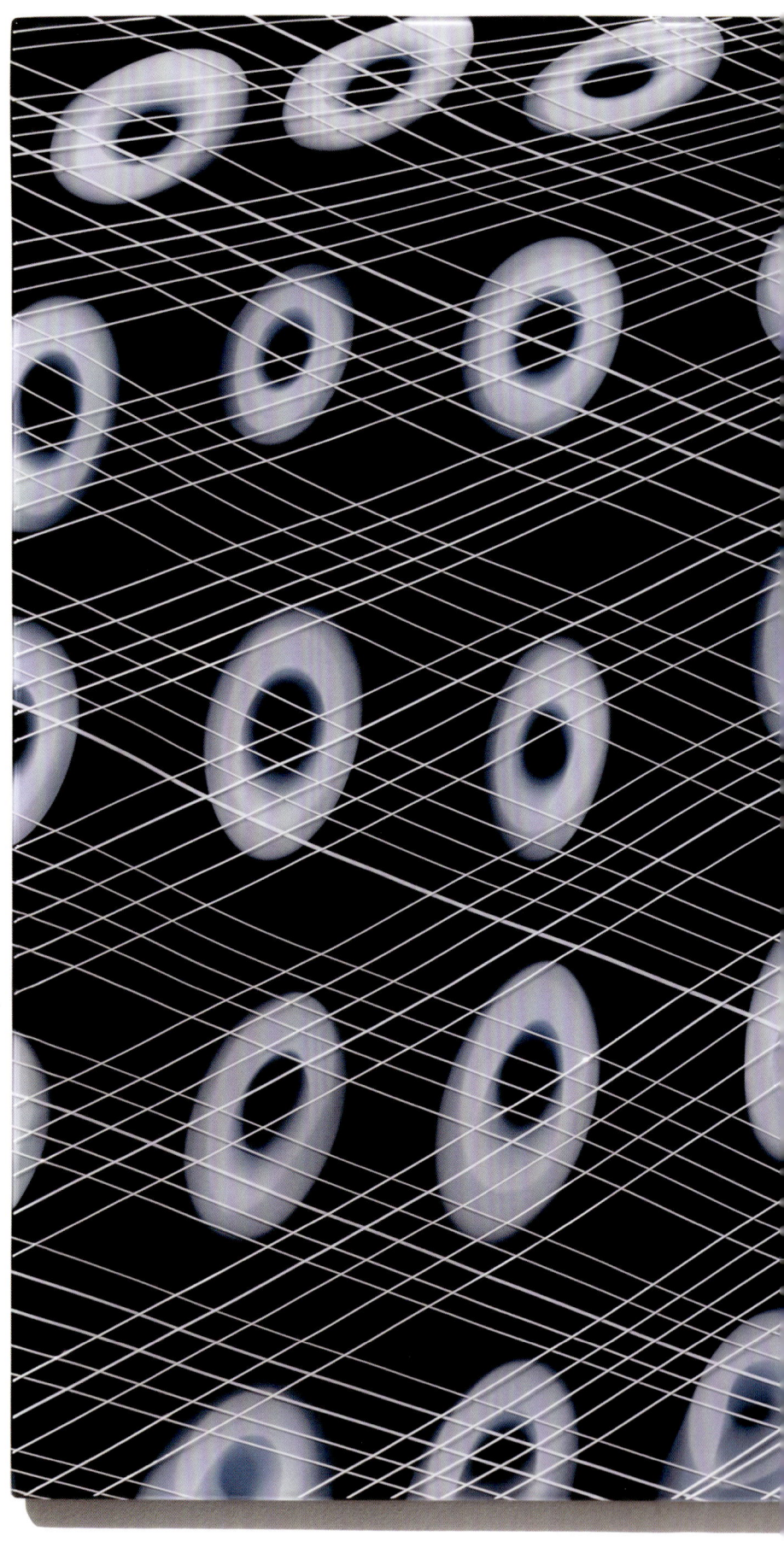

CHK. 37   *Comme les Filles* (detail), 2023

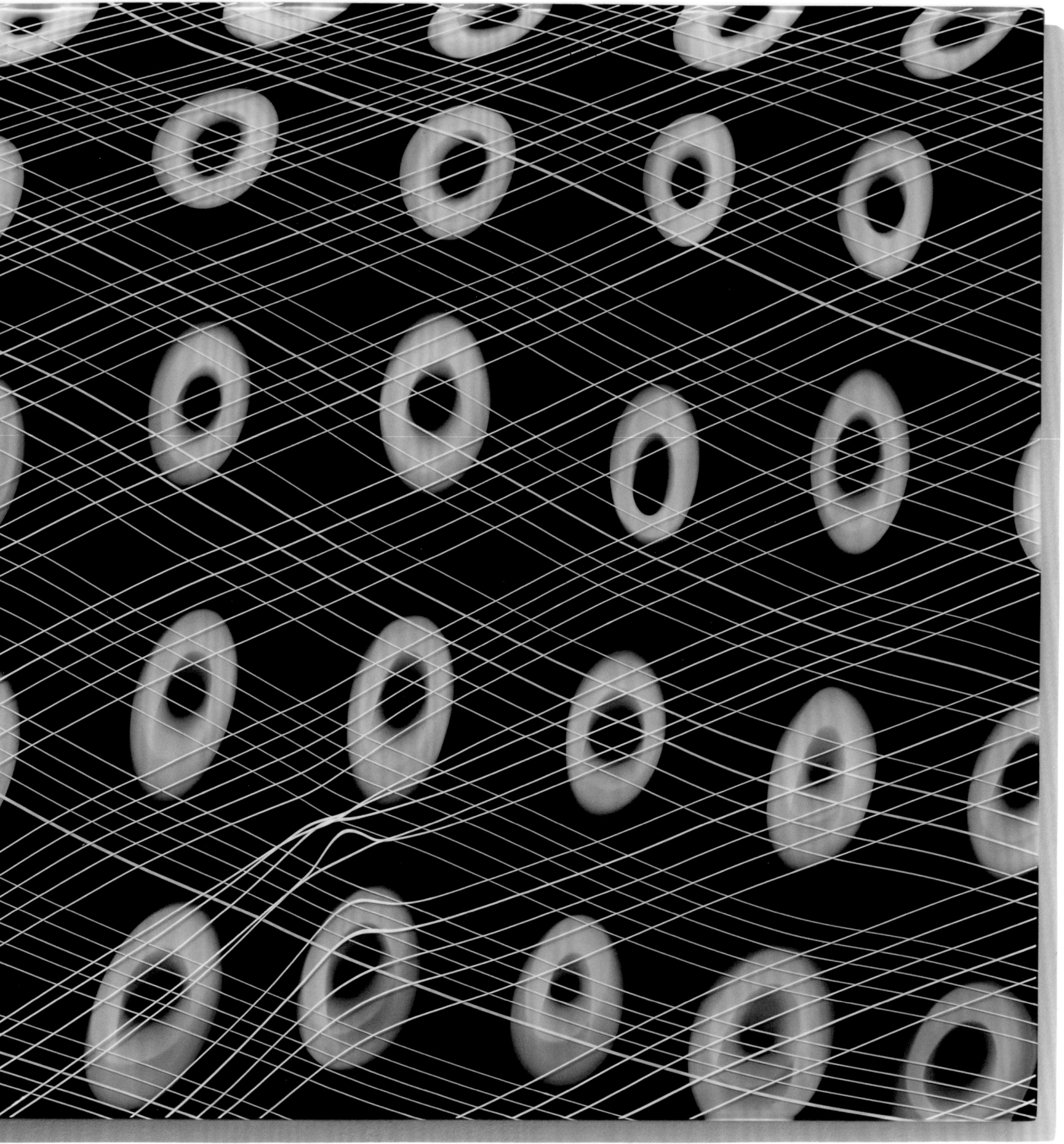

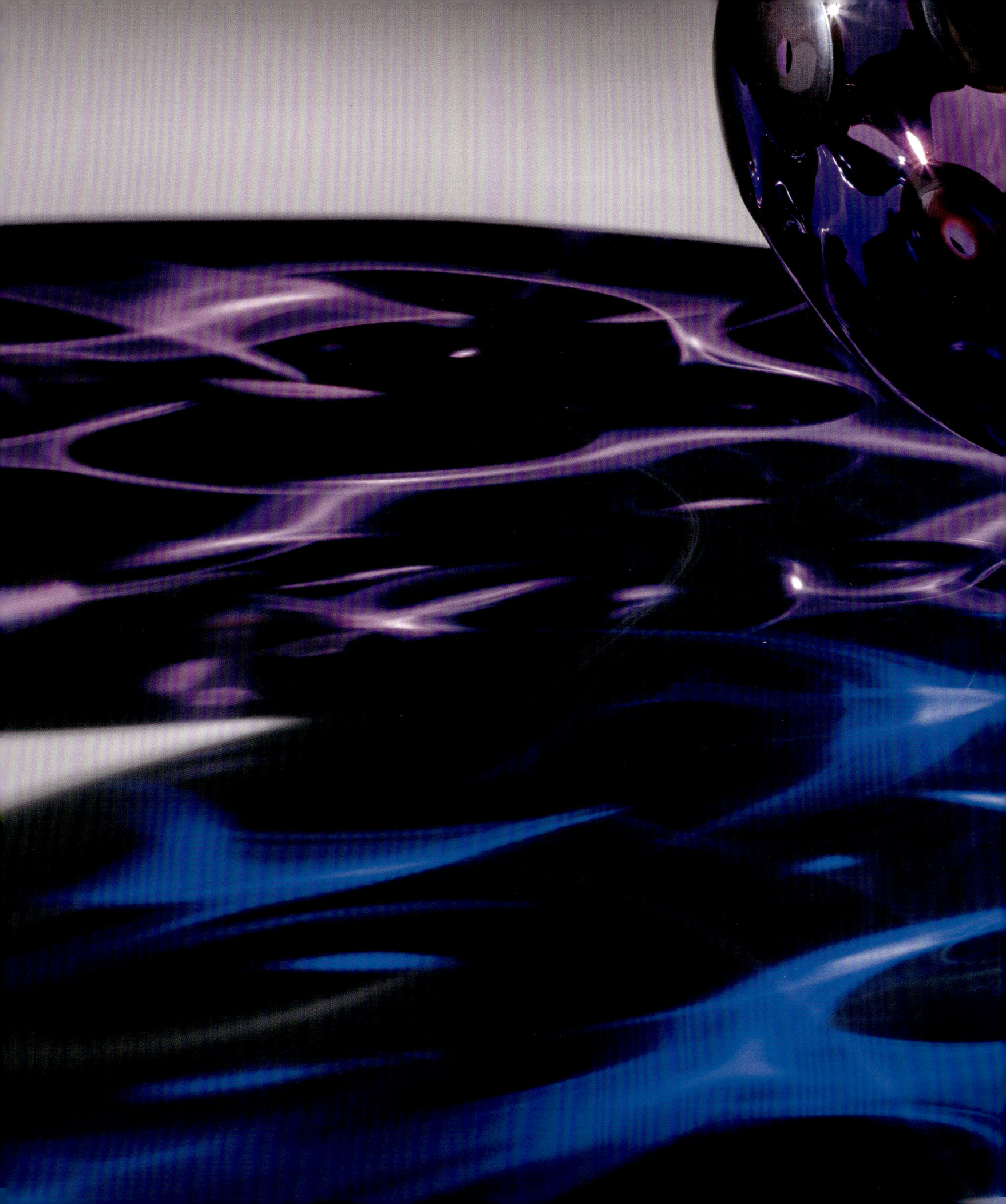

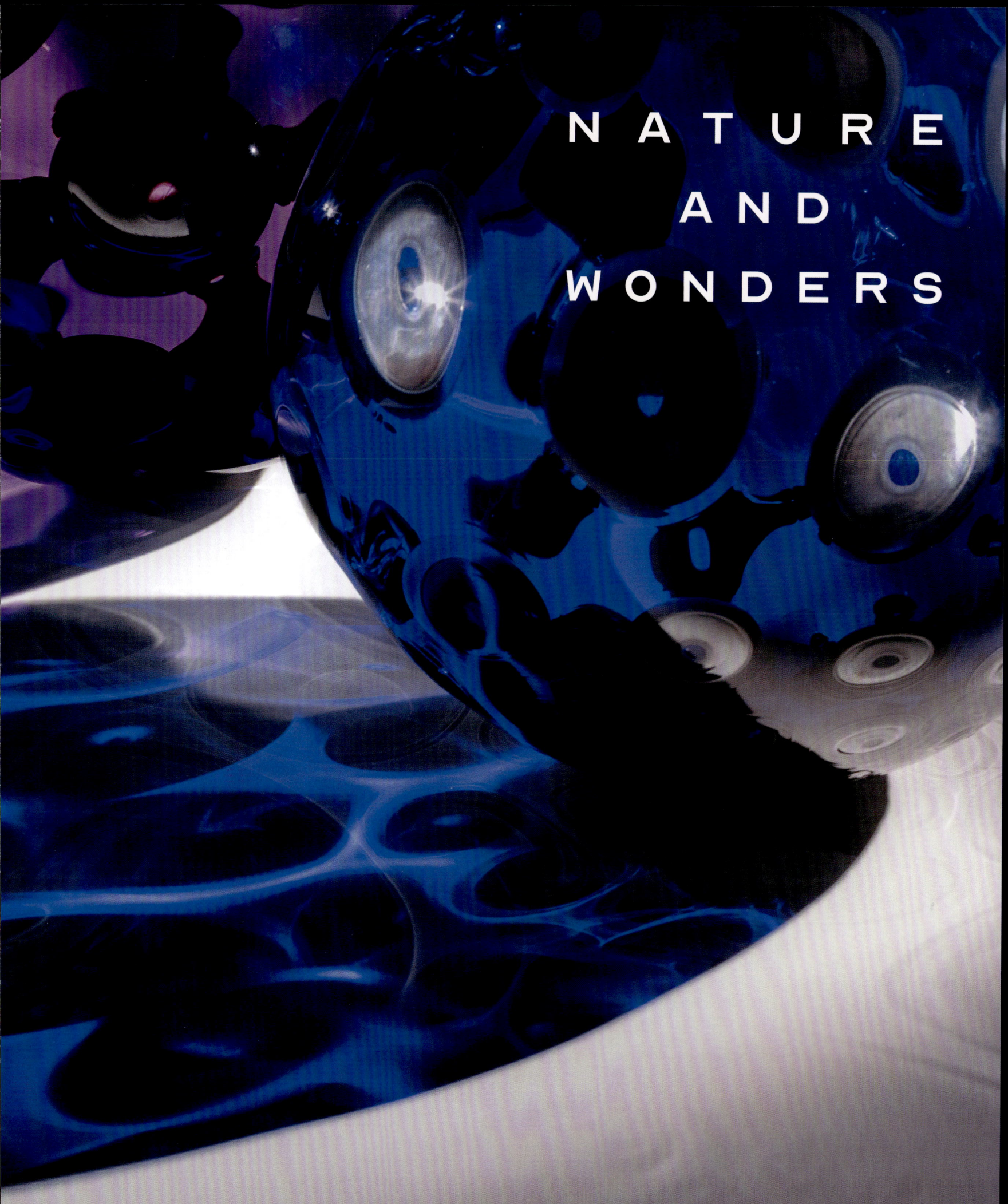

NATURE
AND
WONDERS

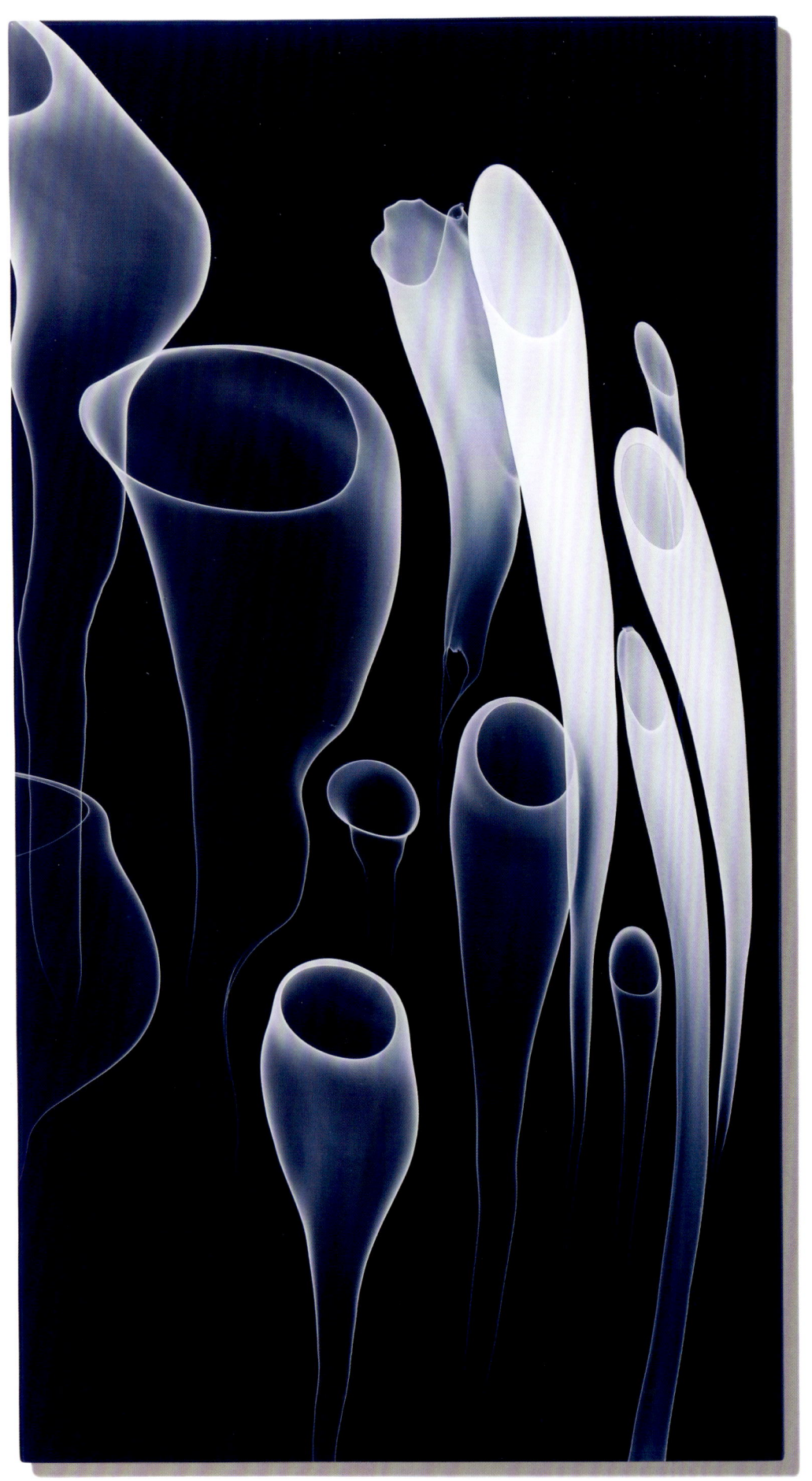

Pages 88–89: *Deep Blue Space Rock* (detail), 2023 (Chk. 40) and *Purple Space Rock I* (detail), 2023 (Chk. 45)

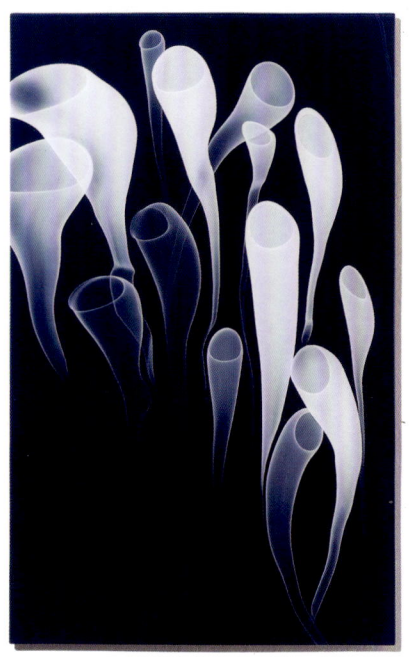 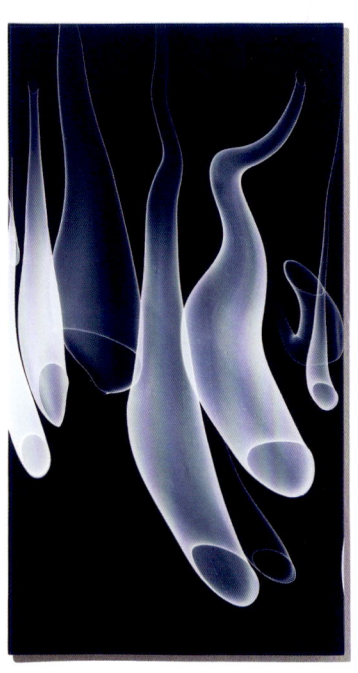 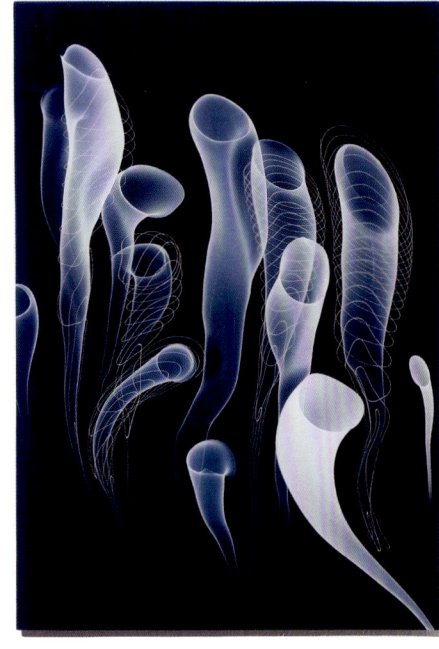 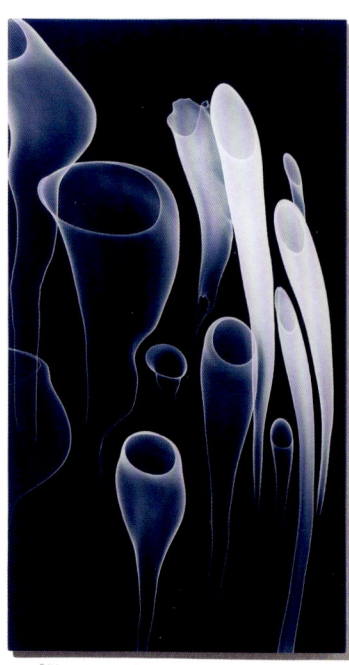

CHK. 31   *Ghost Oasis, 2021*

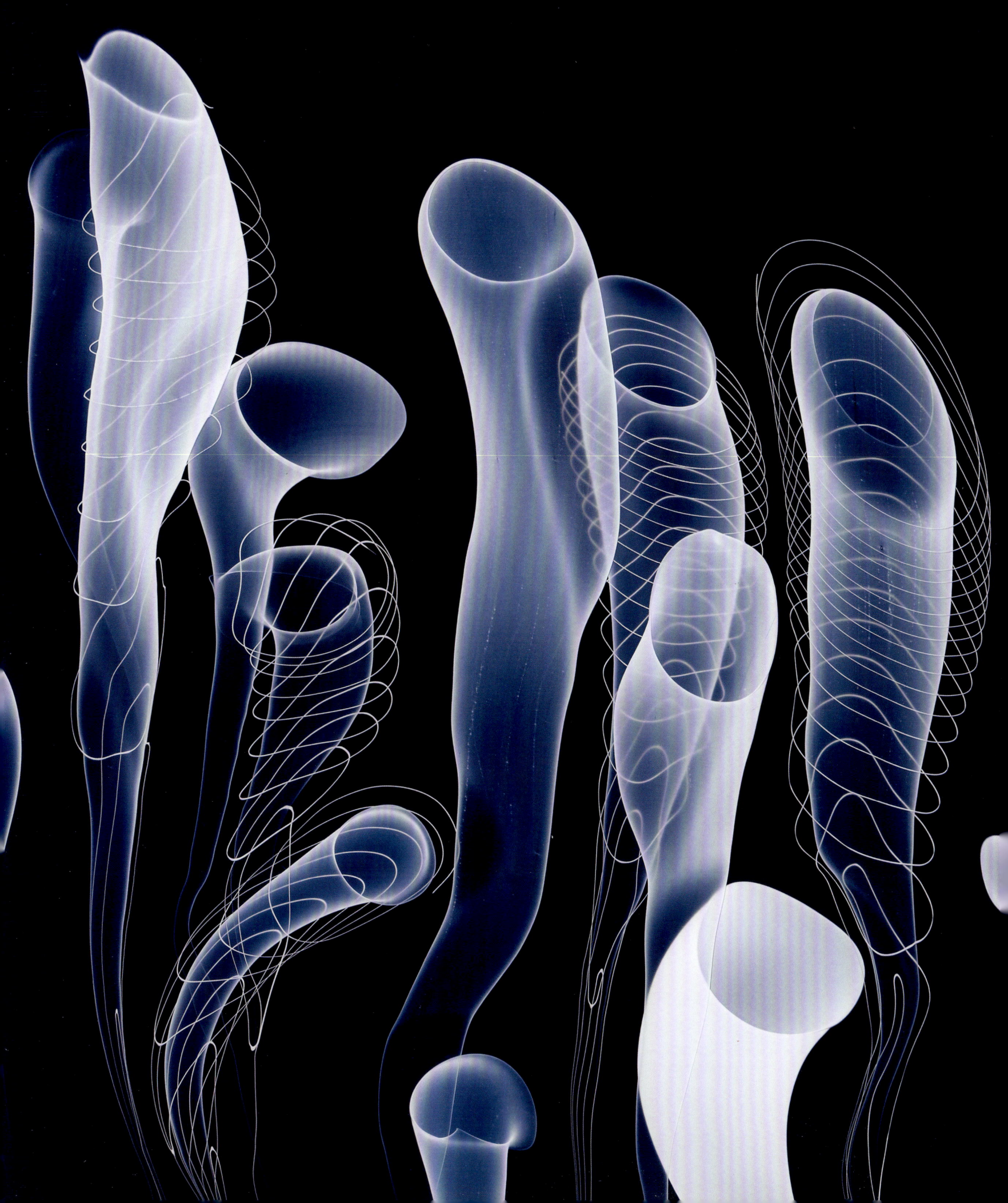

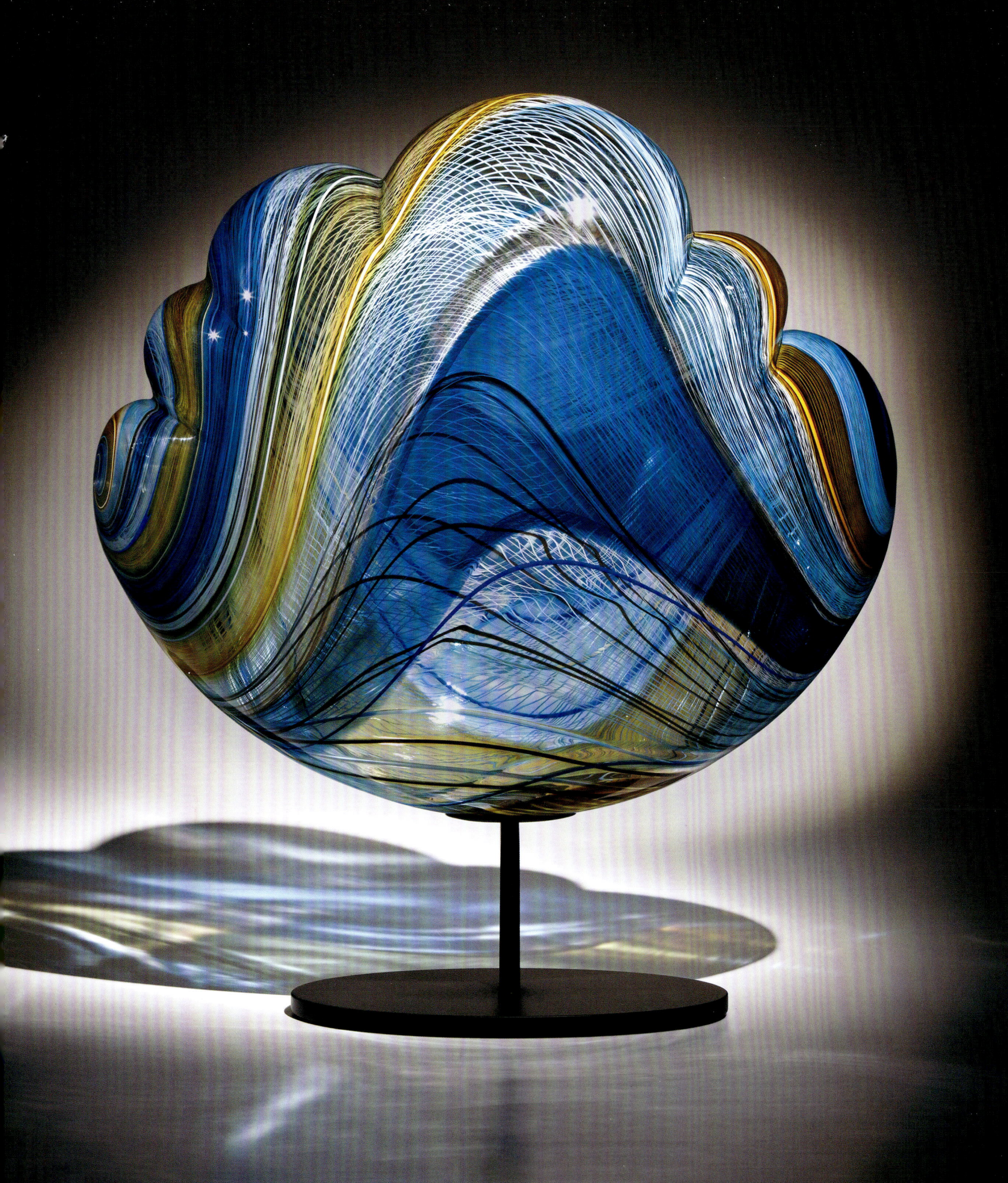

Nature is a great springboard for the imagination. I like to think about creating a world inside a piece of glass, whether it's the swirling movement of color in a *Cloud* or the swimming "anemone canes" in a *Droplet*…if it feels alive, it's more satisfying to me.

—Nancy Callan

CHK. 19 *Silver Anemone,* 2013

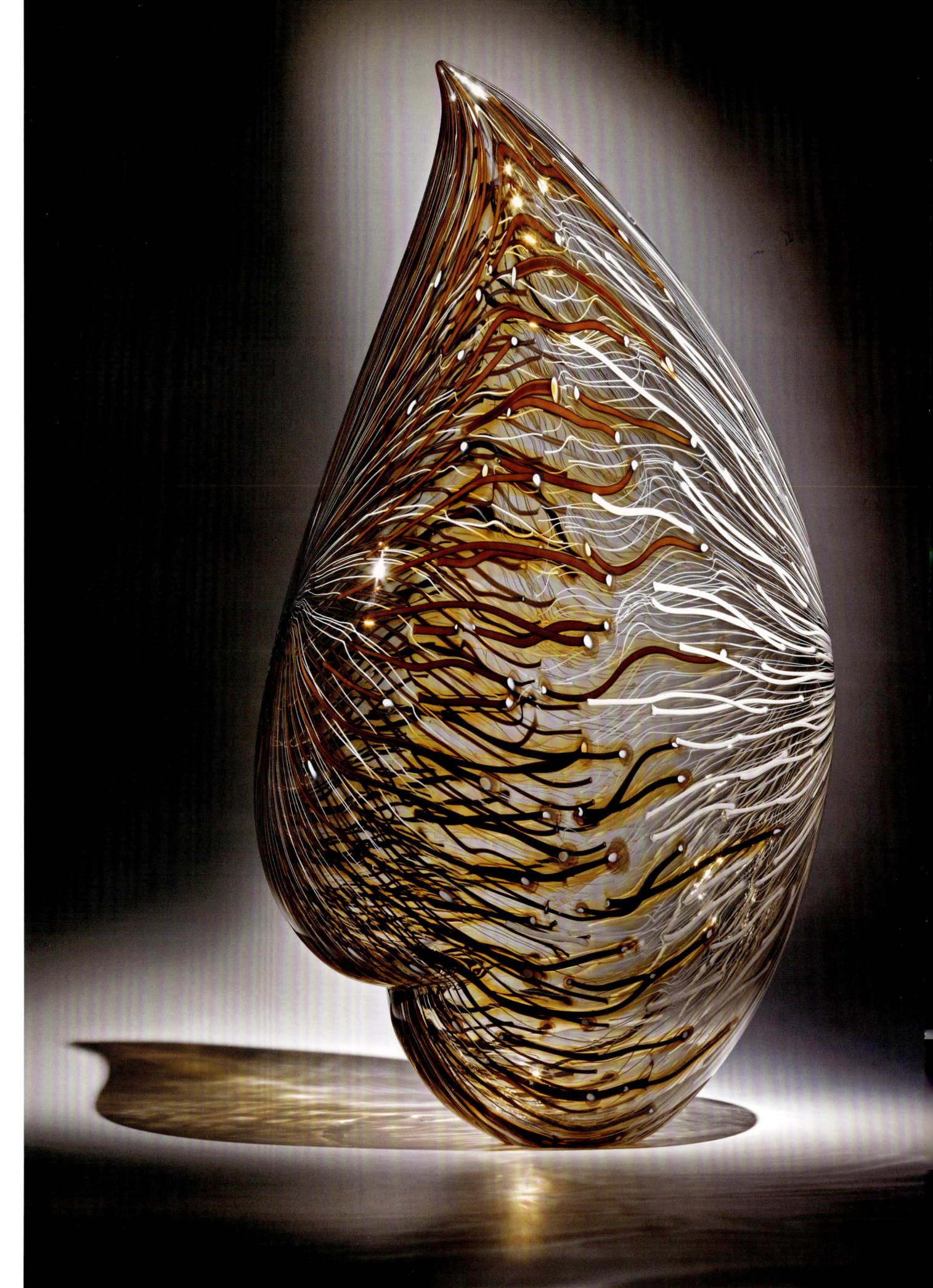

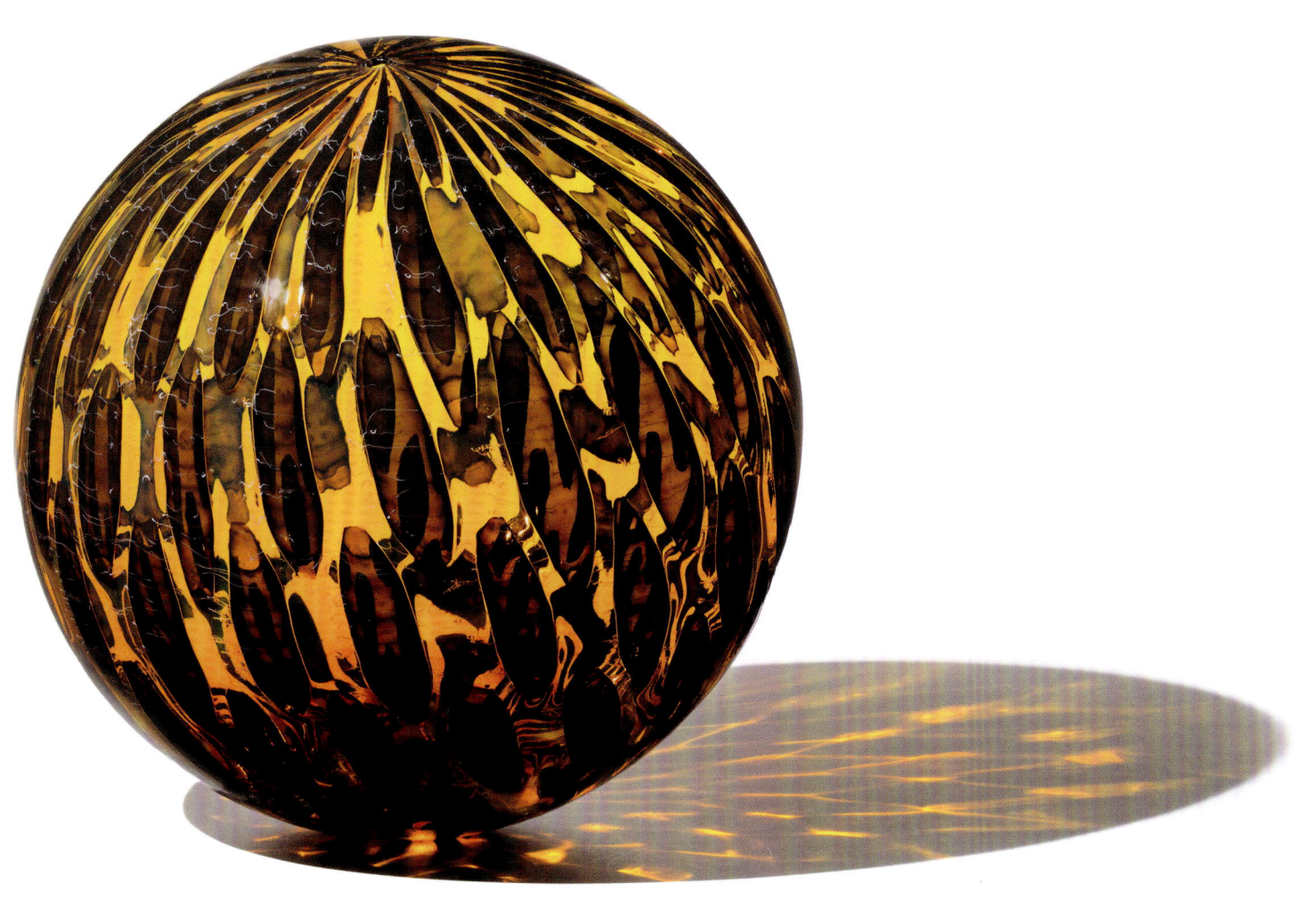

CHK. 27 *Amber Shimmer Orb*, 2018

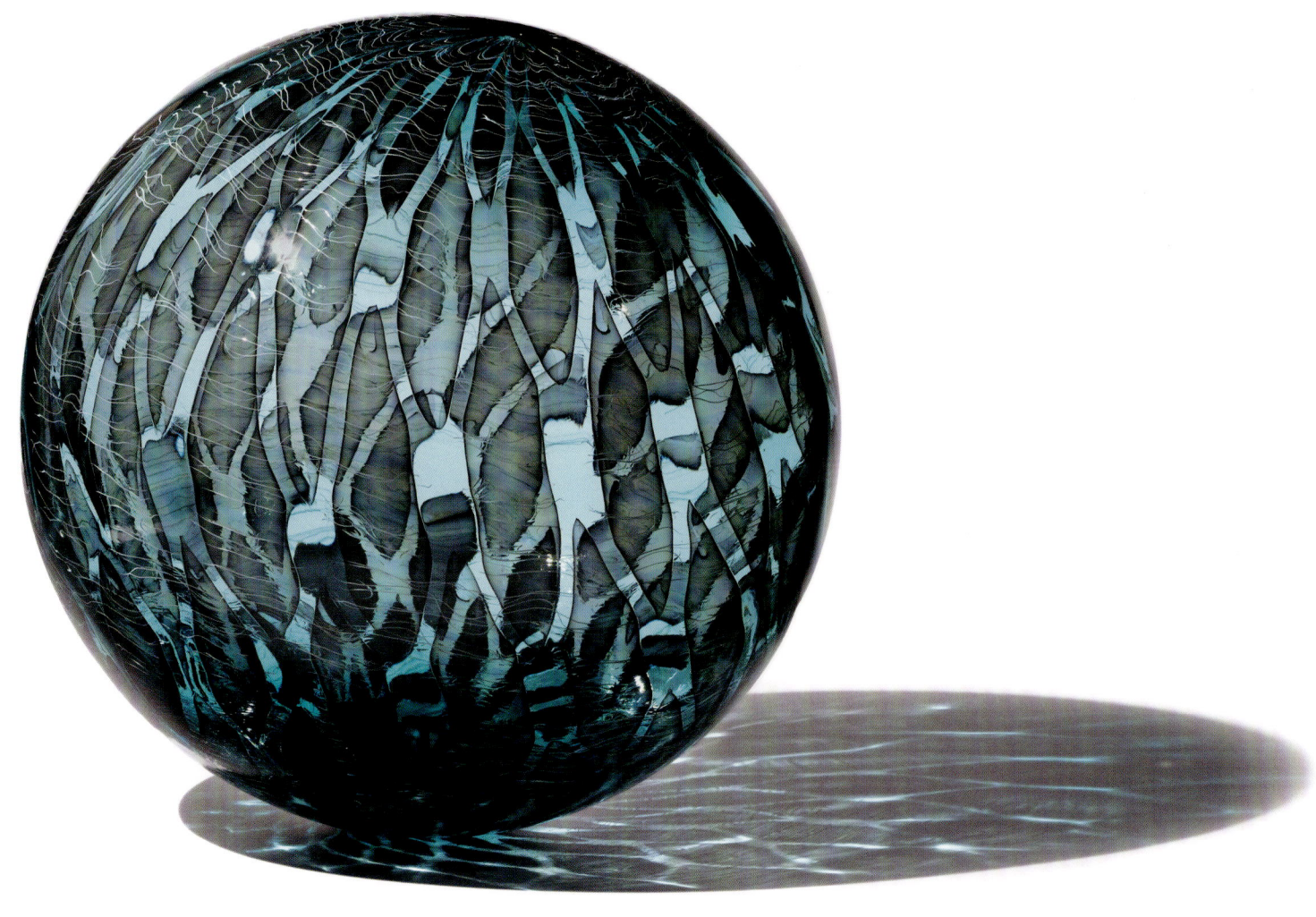

CHK. 28 *Laguna Shimmer Orb, 2018*

CHK. 30 *Witching Hour,* 2020

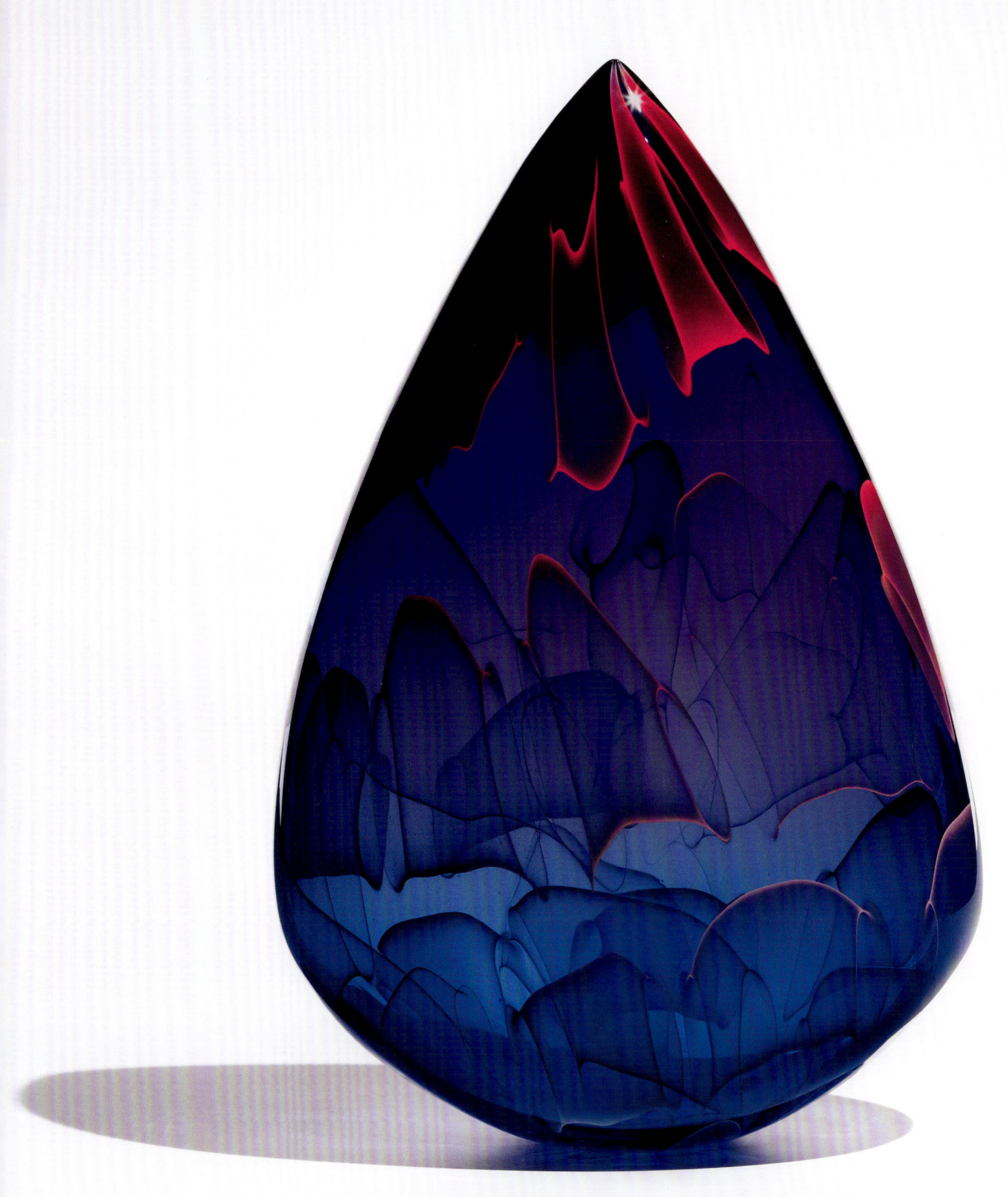

CHK. 48   *Sitka Droplet,* 2023

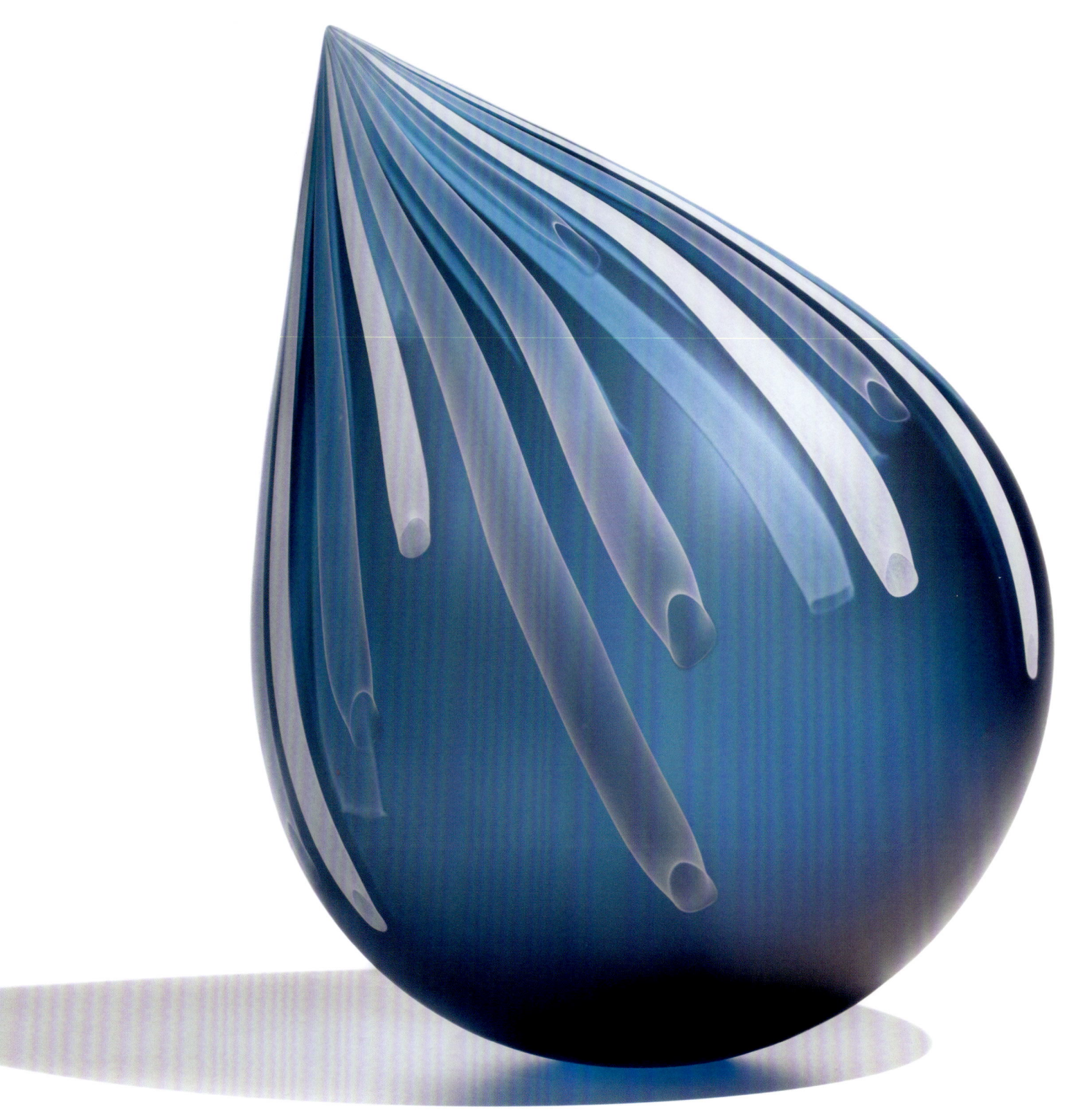

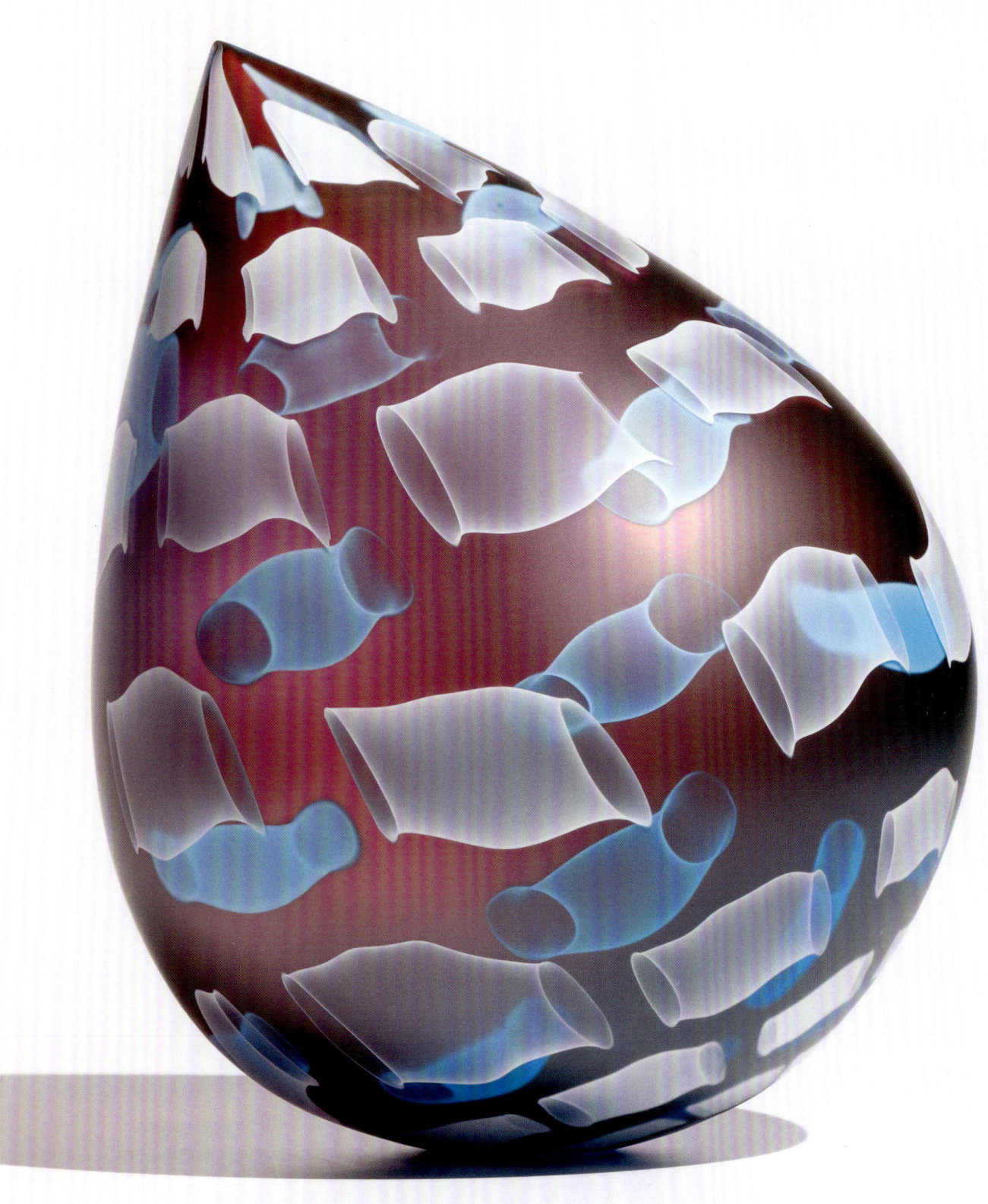

CHK. 32 *Luminescence Droplet, 2021*

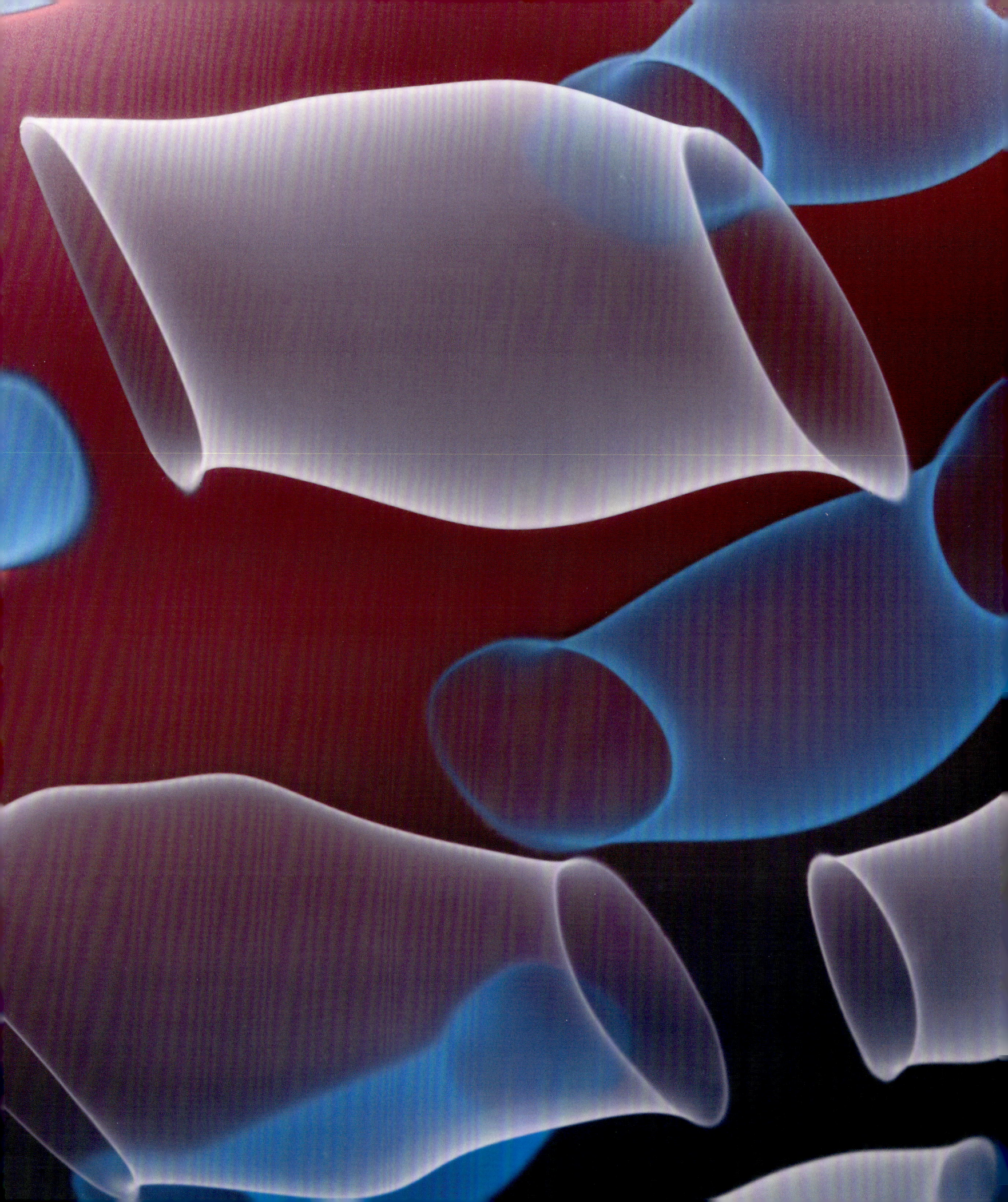

CHK. 44   *Paradise Droplet, 2023*

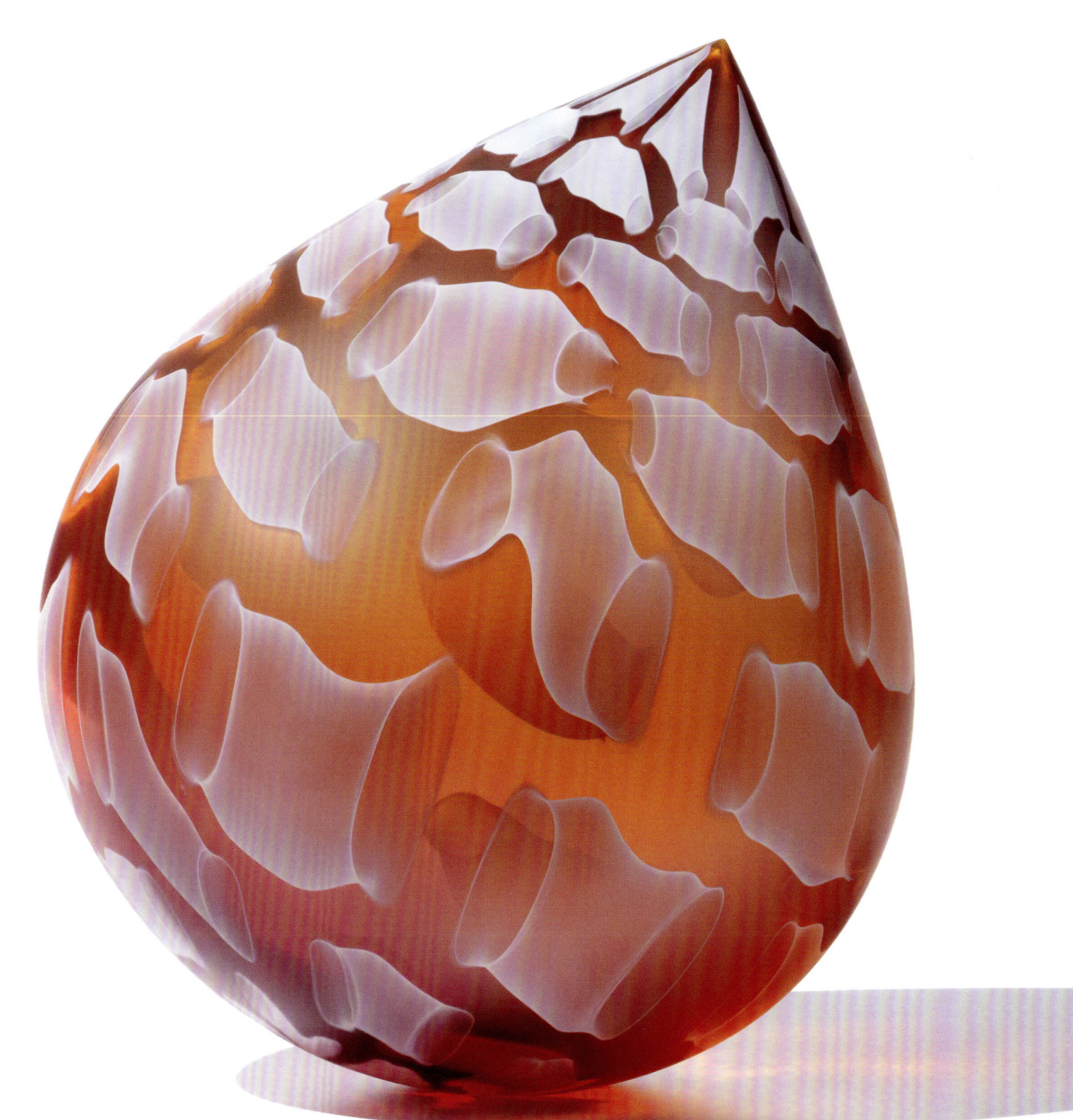

CHK. 43 *Ombre Spire, 2023*   **CHK. 39** *Cypress Spire, 2023*

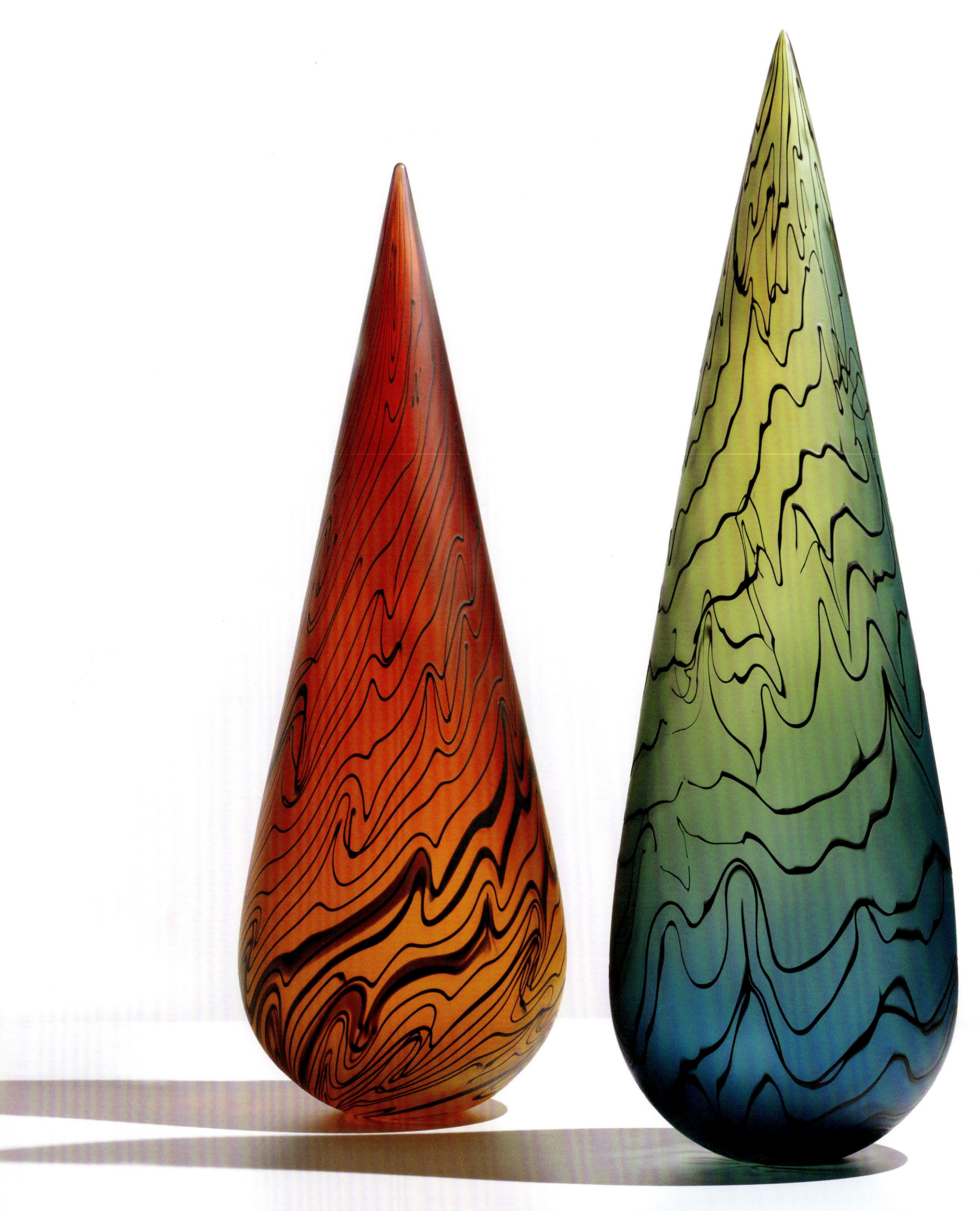

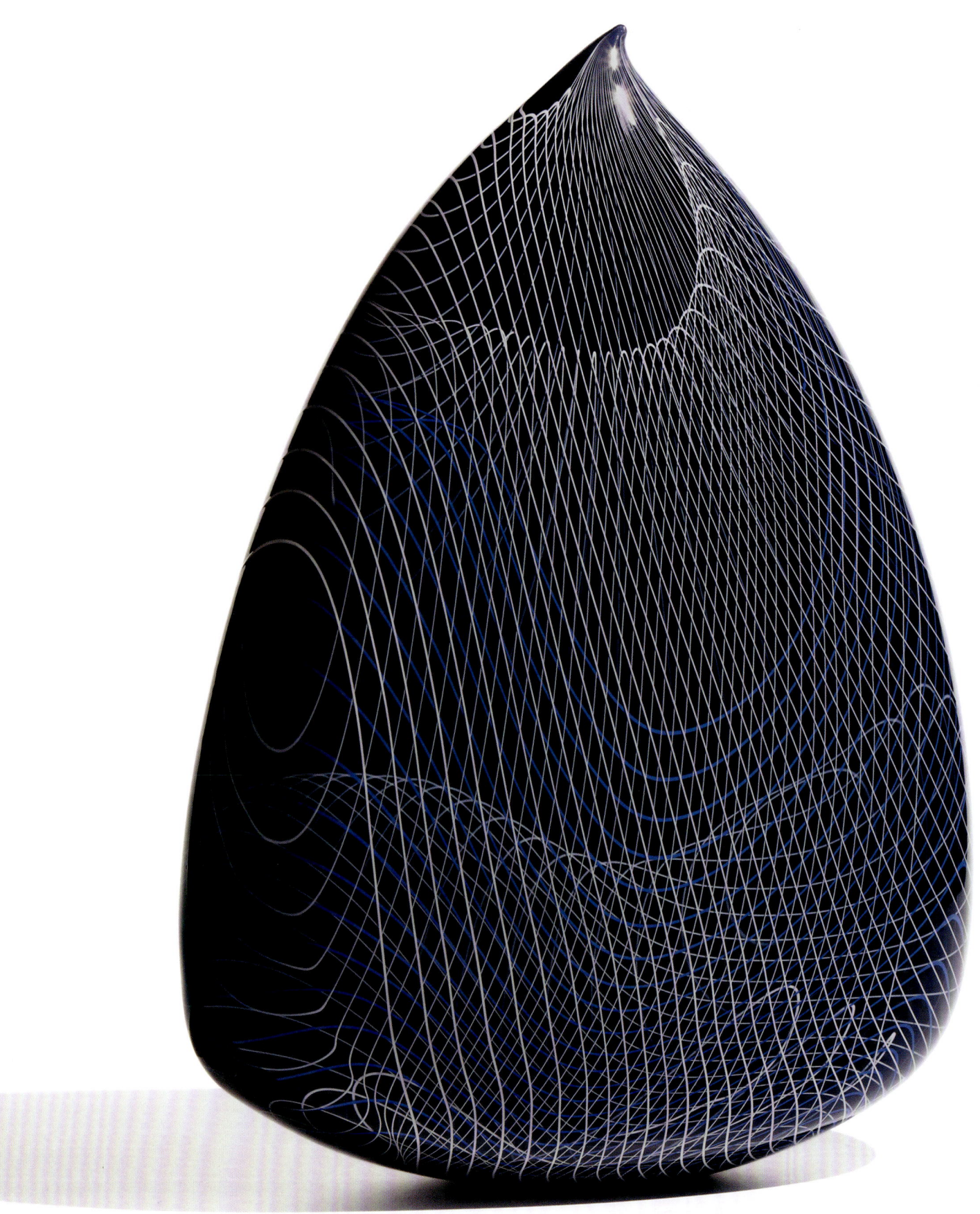

CHK. 25   *String Theory, 2016*

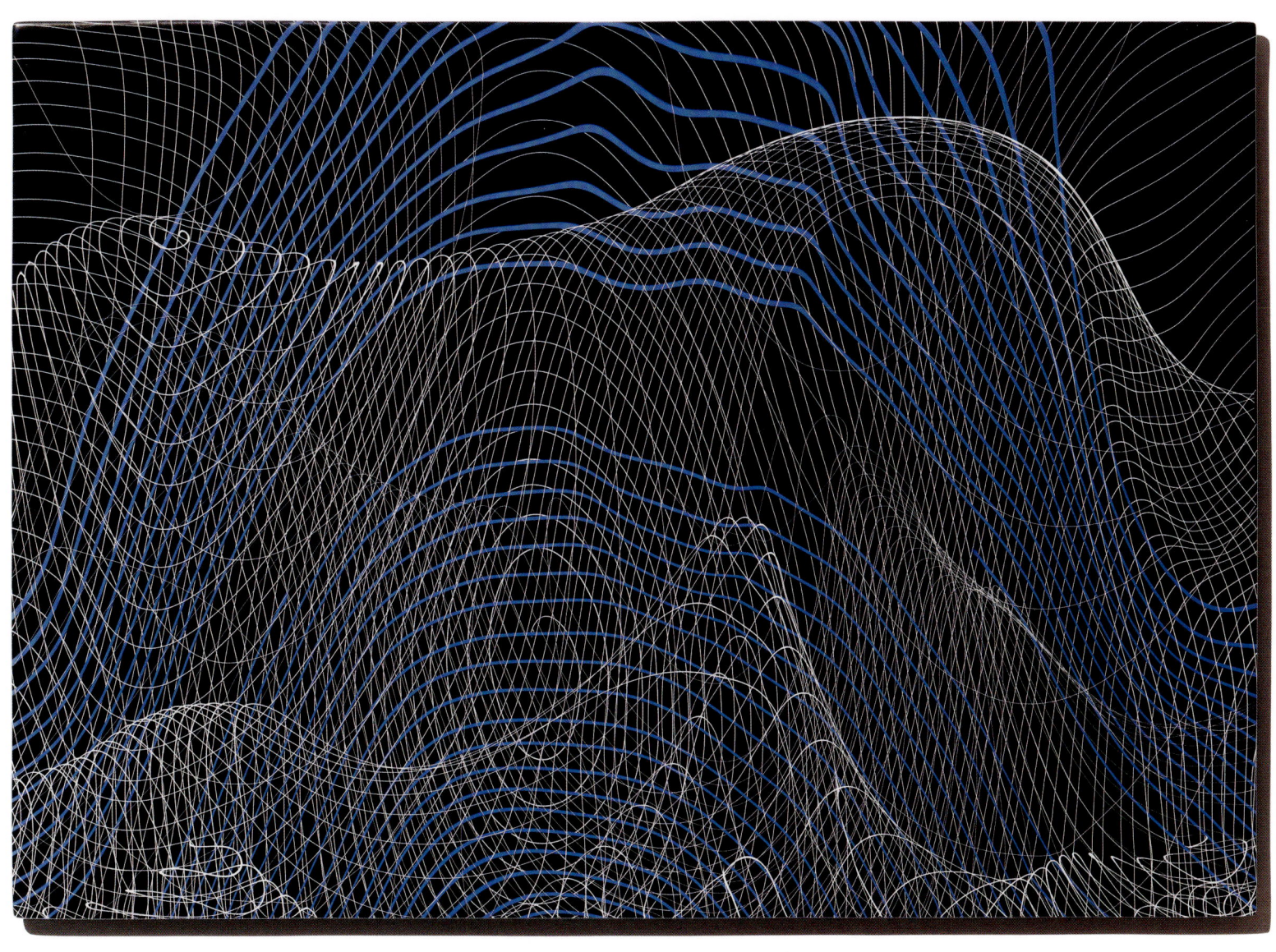

Glass is a fantastic medium for dreaming up new ways to bend space, stretch time, and renew our sense of wonder. Every day in the studio is an exploration, and I love expanding what I think is possible with this magical material.

—Nancy Callan

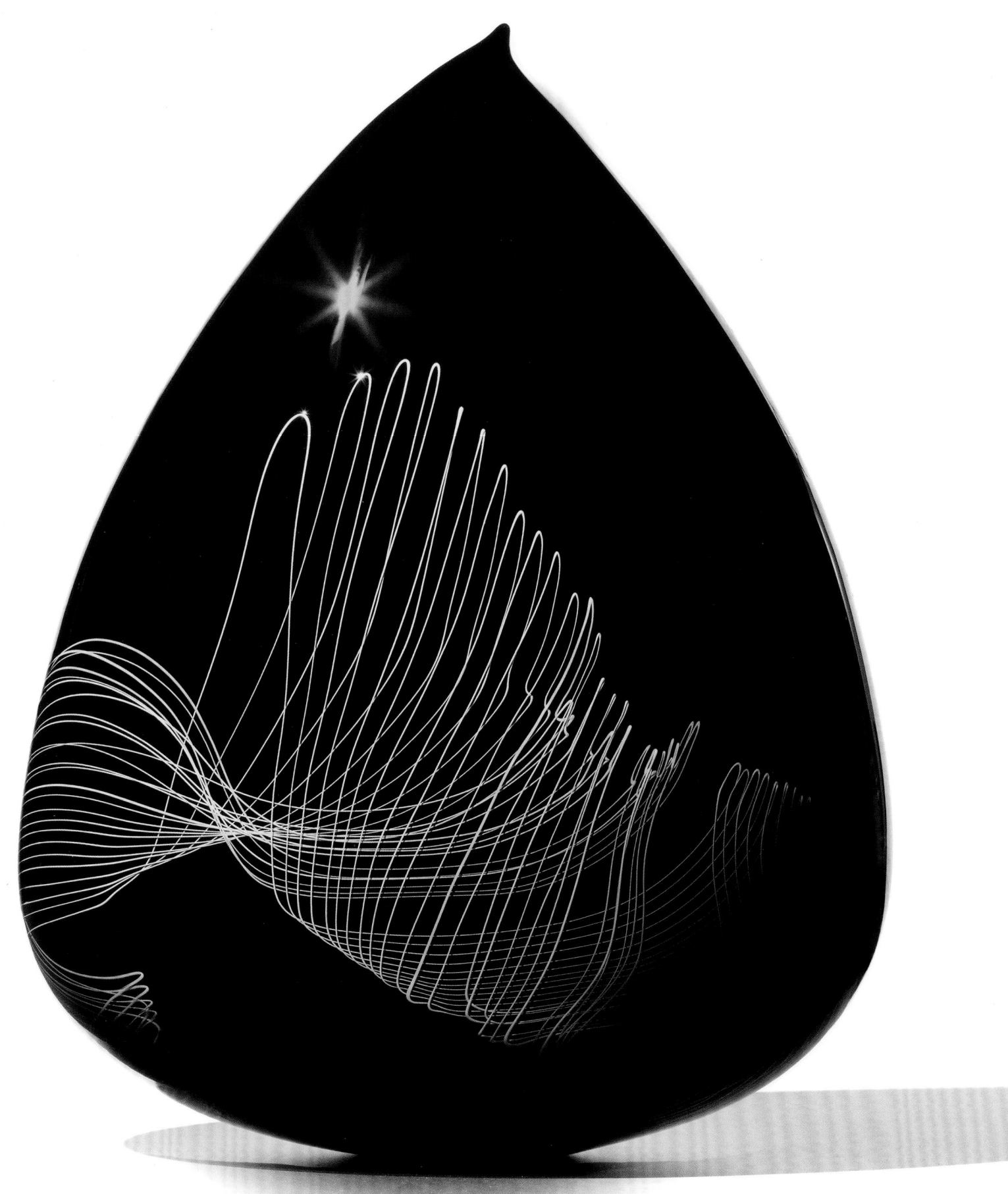

CHK. 35 *Stellar Net,* 2022

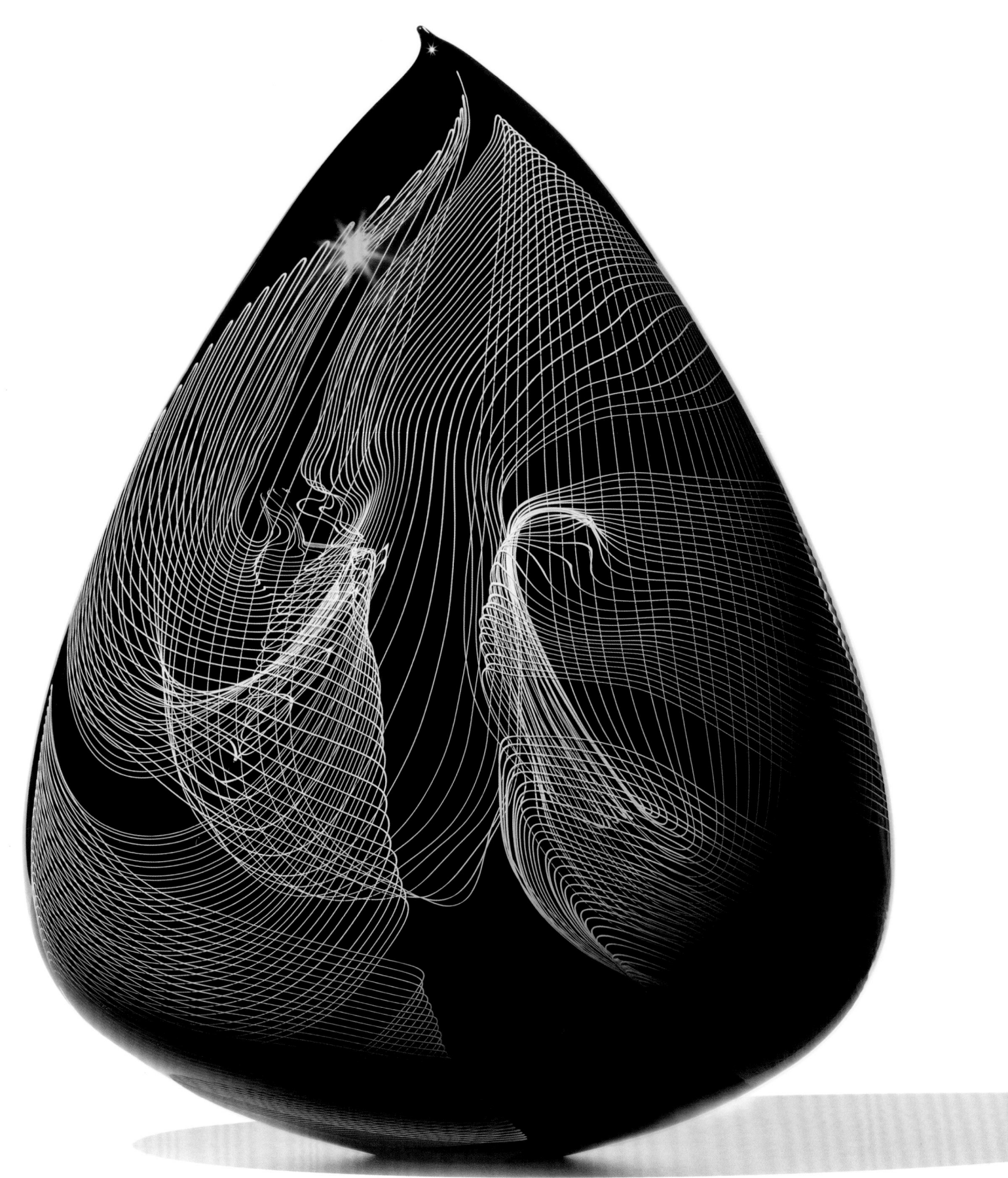

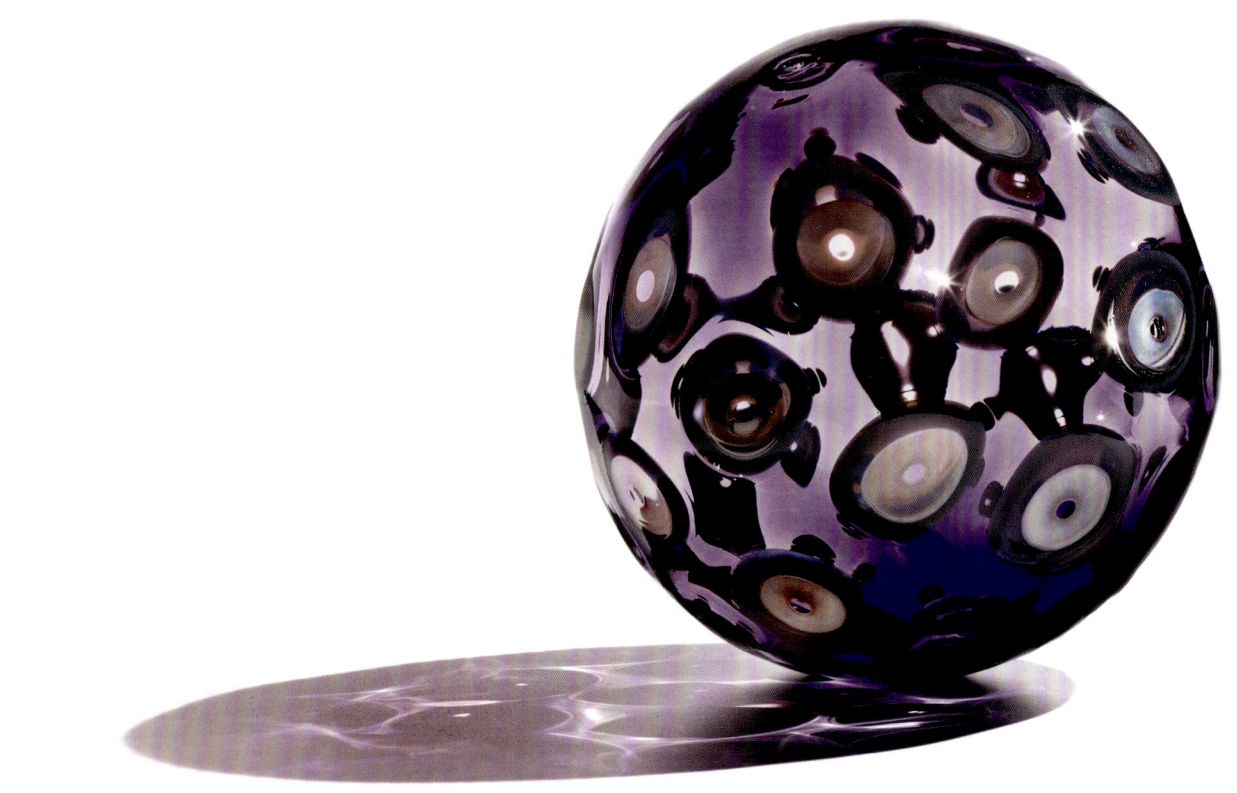

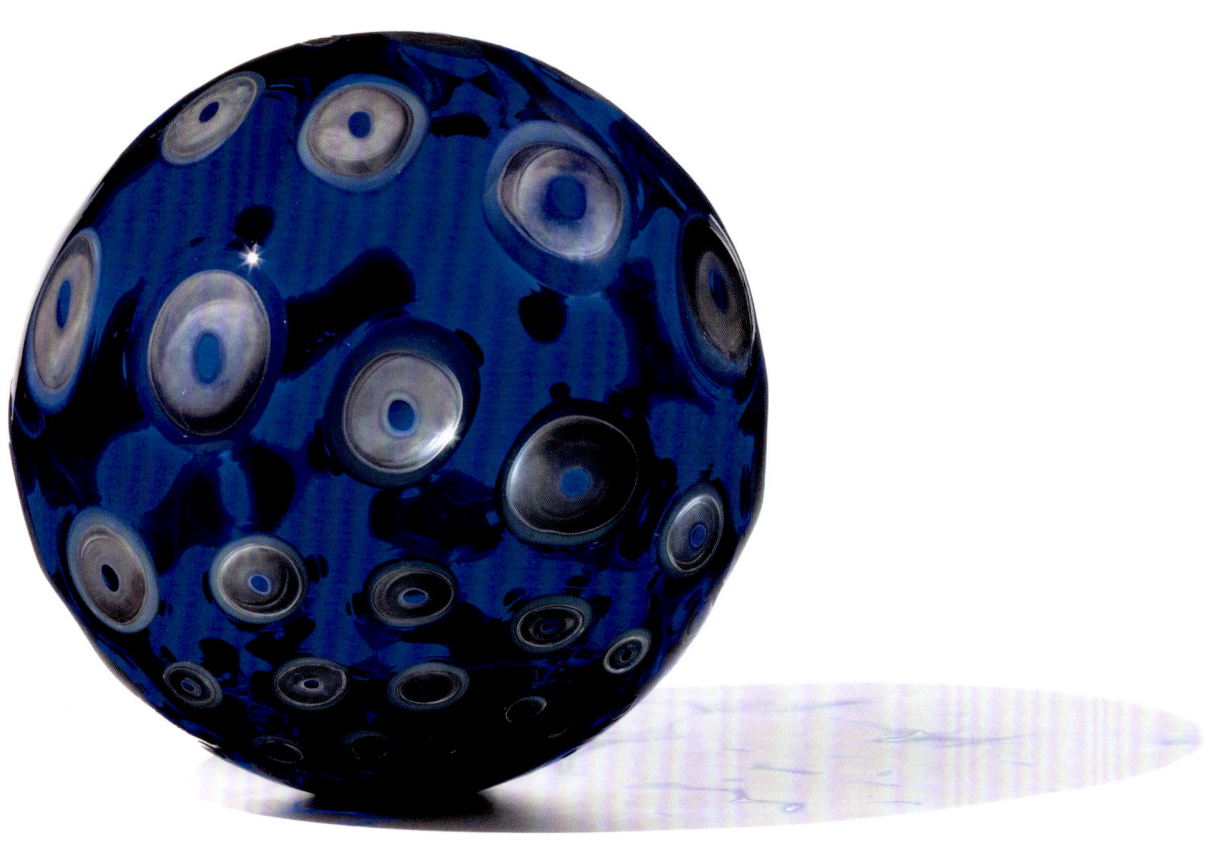

CHK. 40 *Deep Blue Space Rock, 2023*

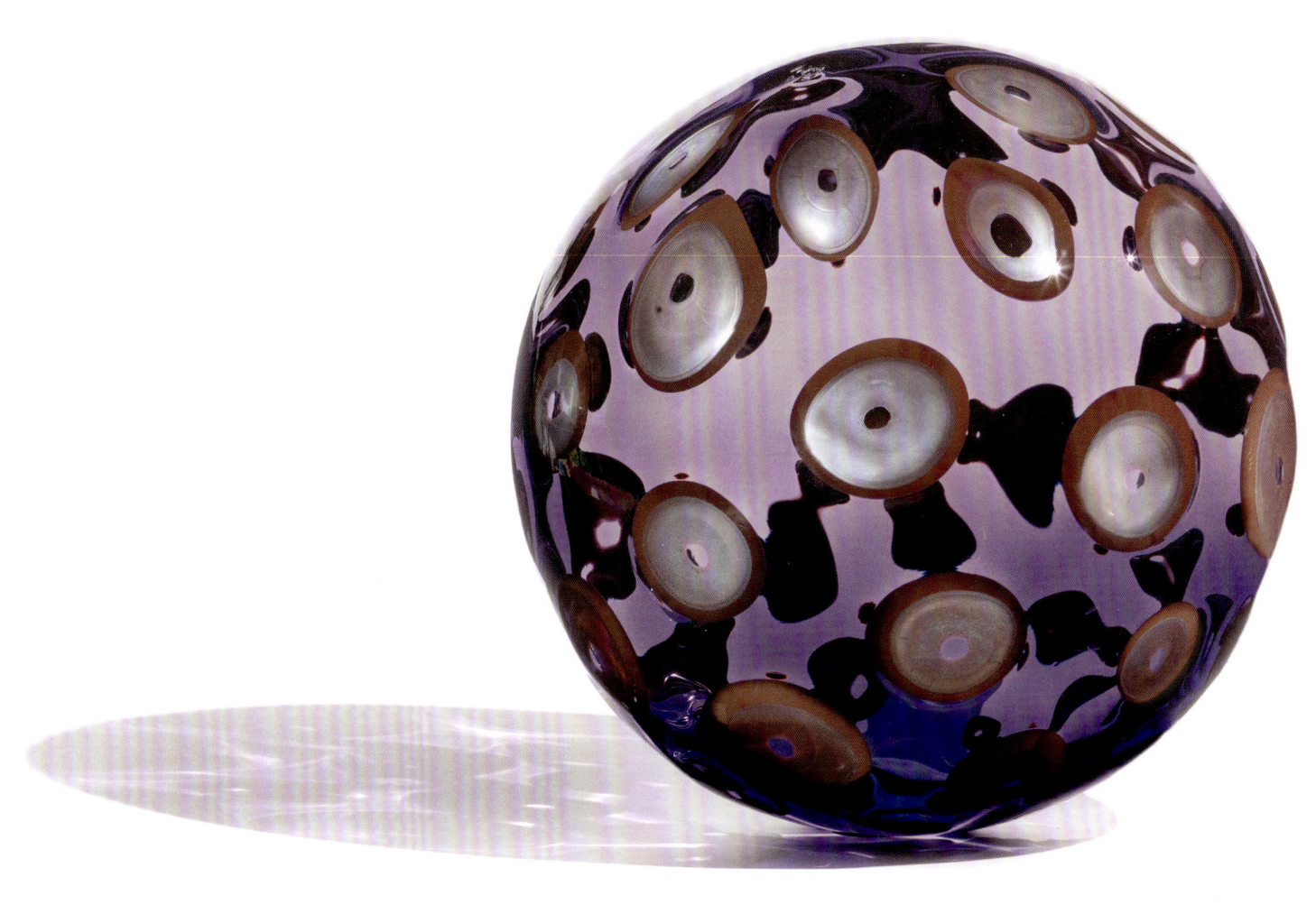

CHK. 45 *Purple Space Rock I, 2023*   **CHK. 46** *Purple Space Rock II, 2023*

Glass comes from the earth, from sand
and metals and fire. It's very primal, but
also cosmic—we know that beads of
glass travel the universe in asteroids and
comets, but don't yet know how they
formed. What forces were at play? . . .
I want to harness some of this energy
in my work, and show more of the raw
beauty of the material.

—Nancy Callan

CHK. 47 *Shadow Realm* (detail), 2023

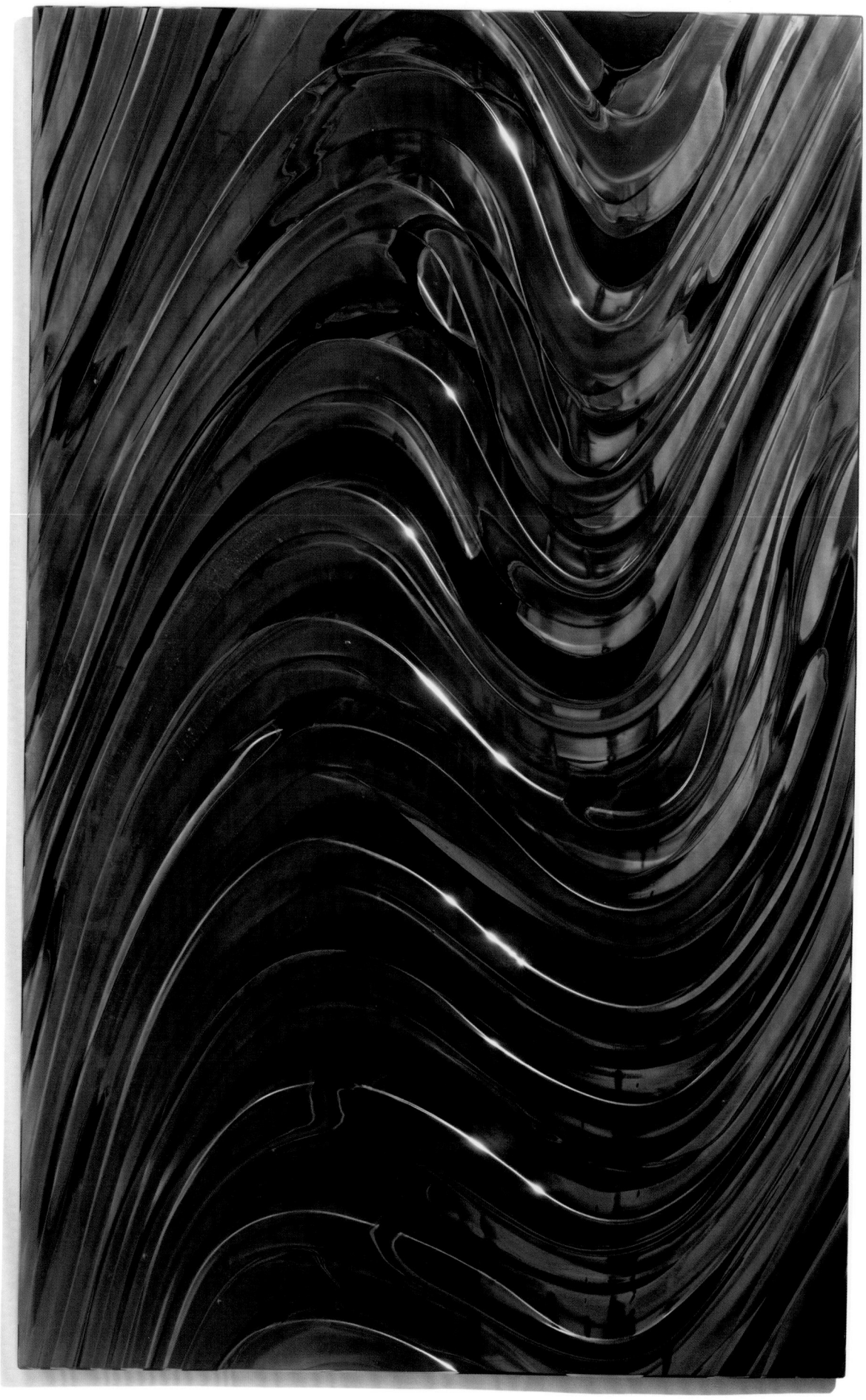

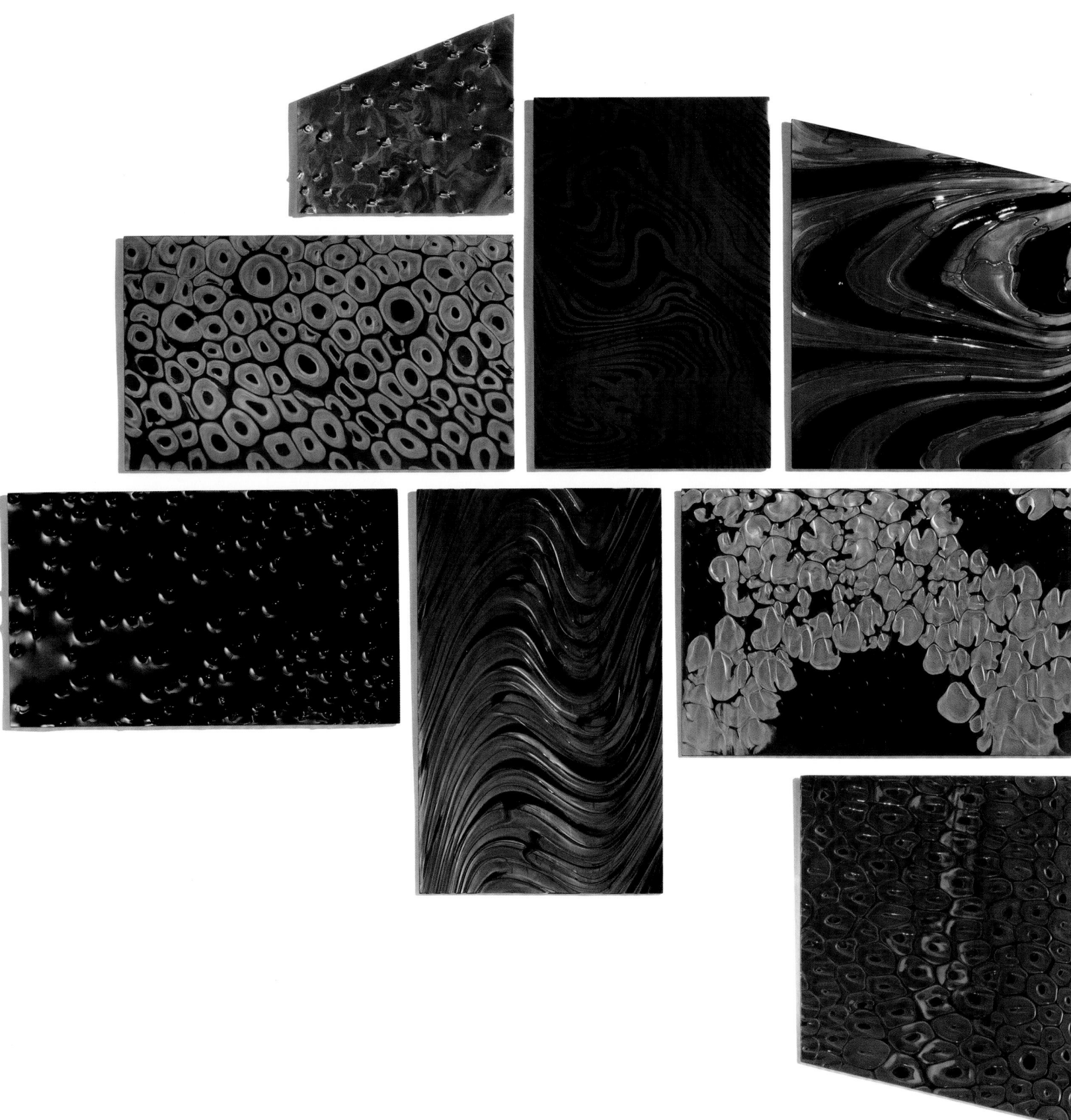

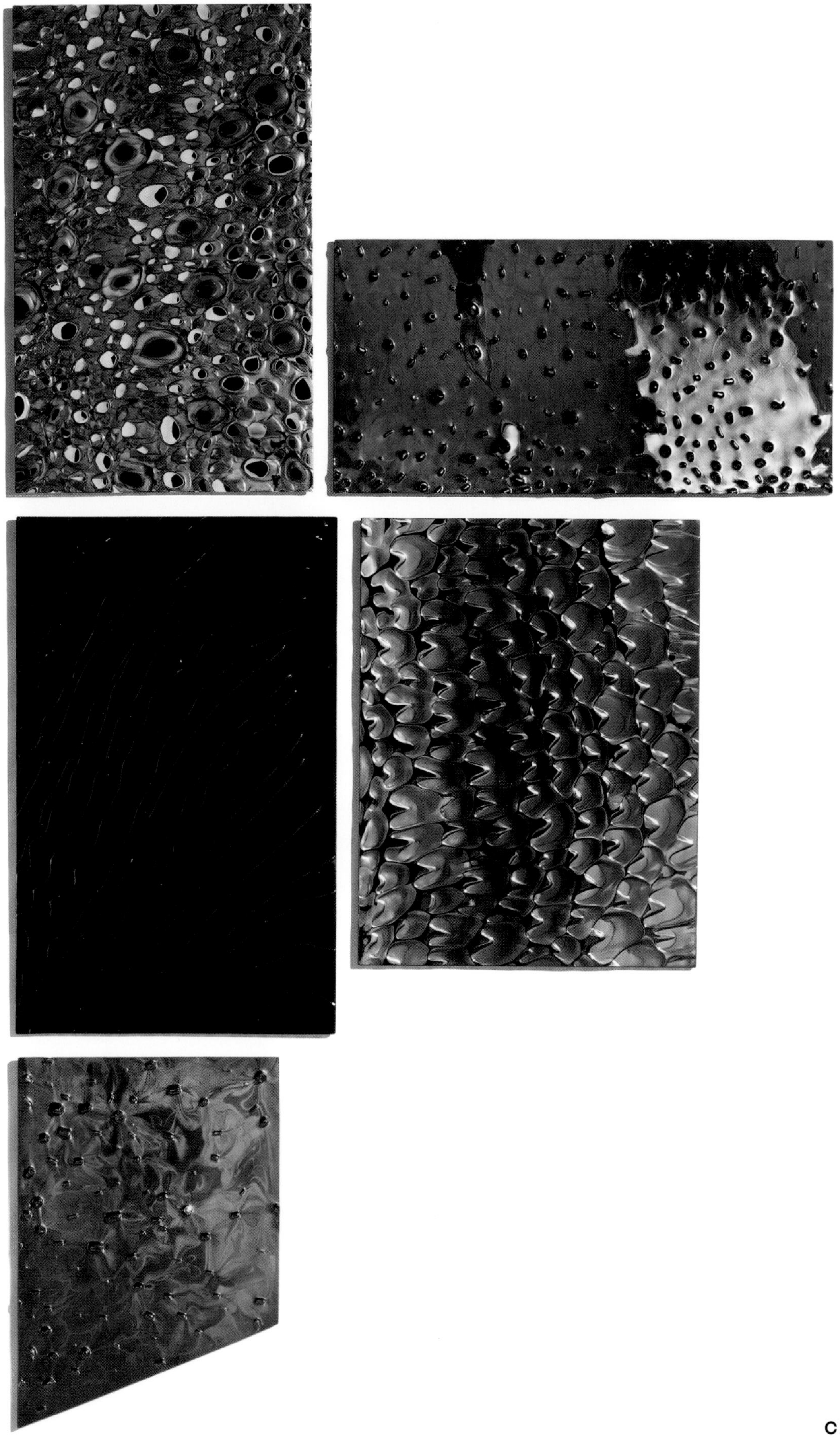

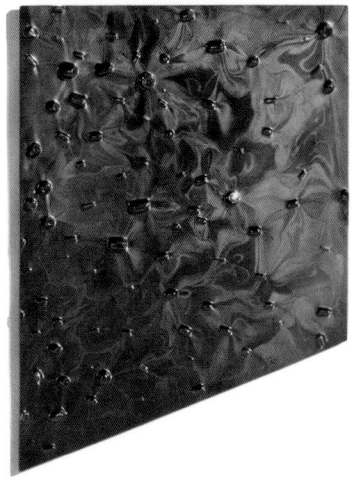

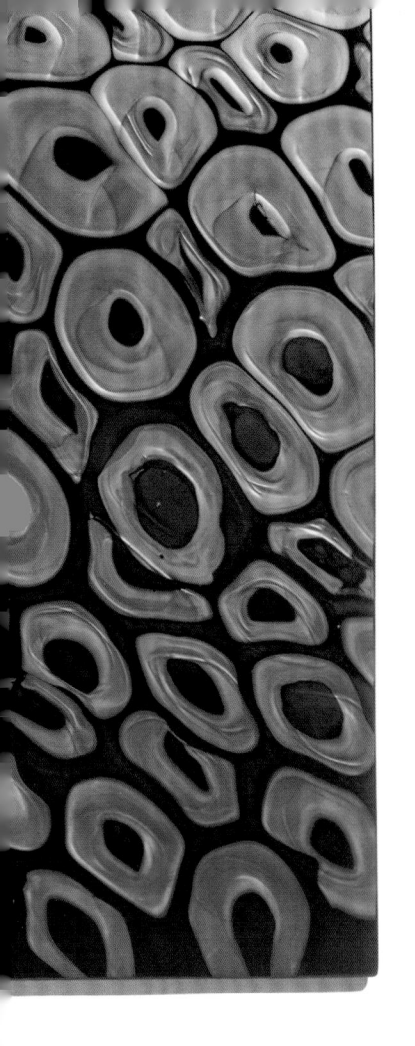
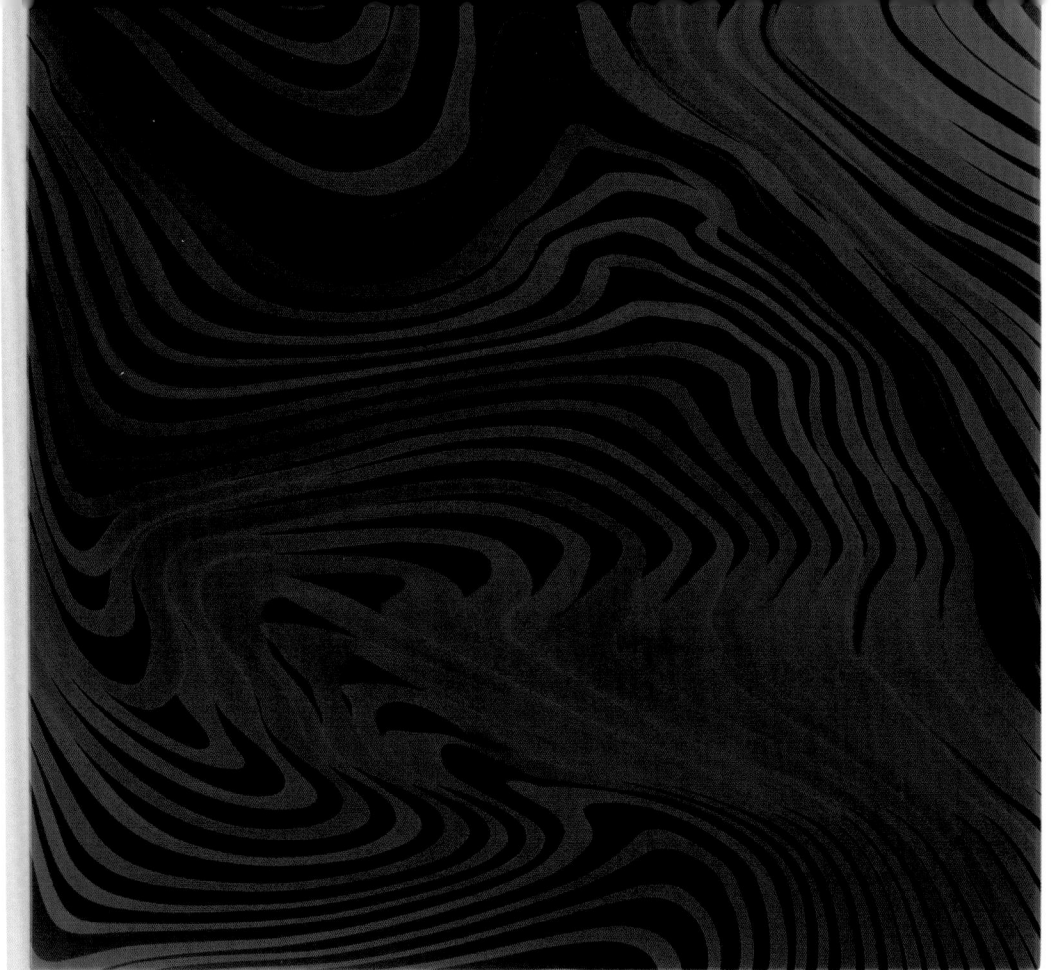
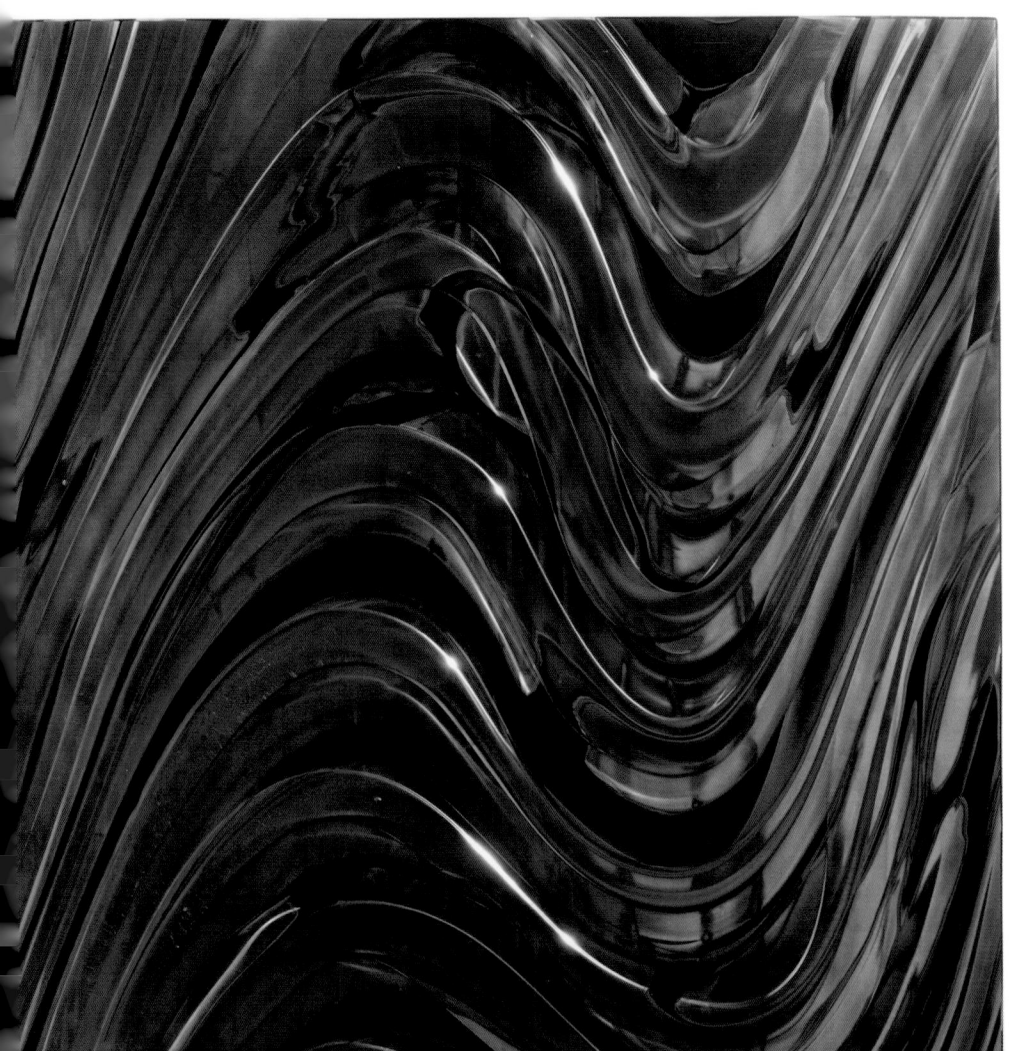
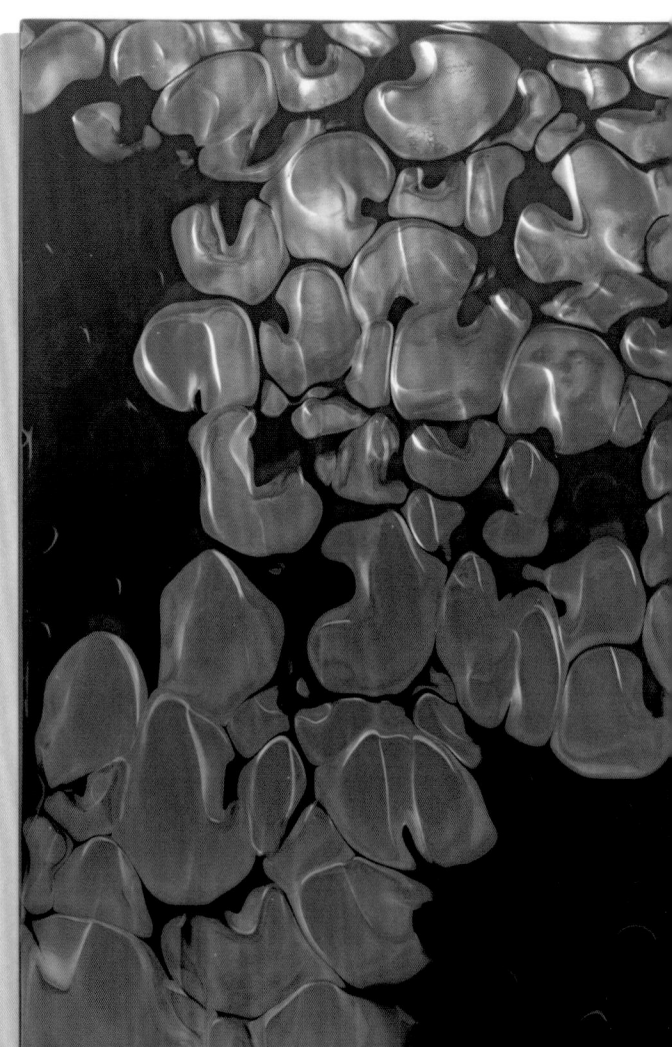

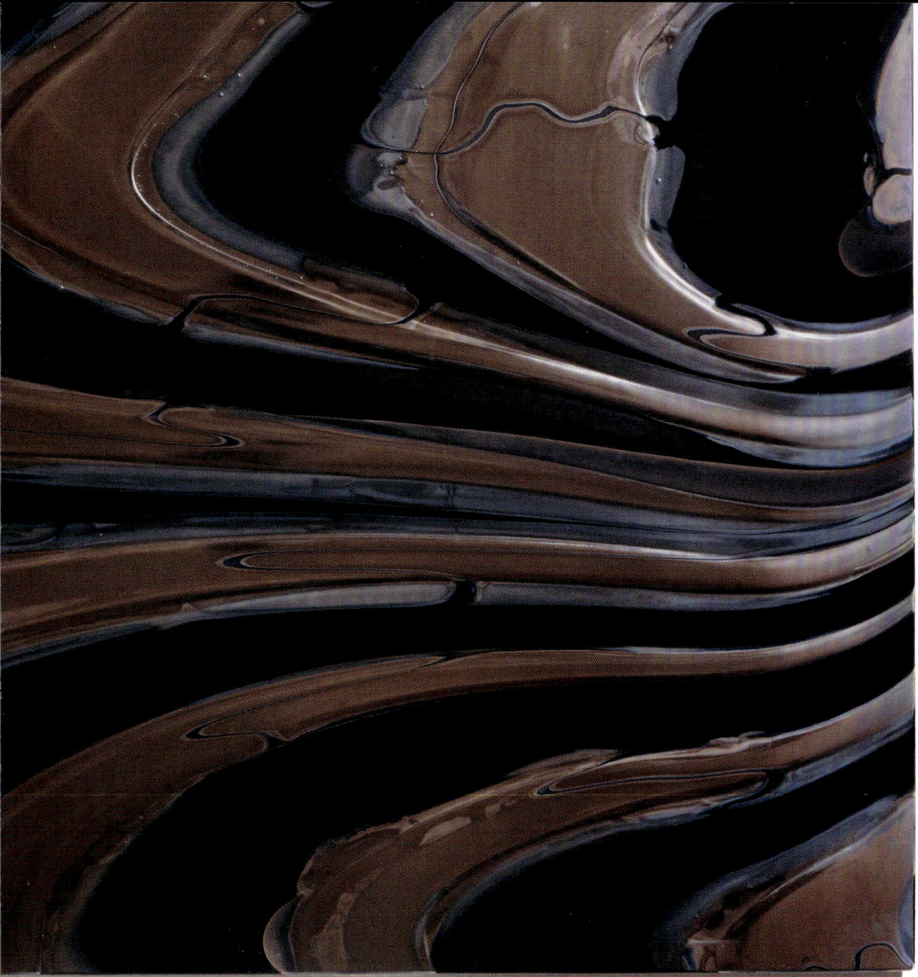

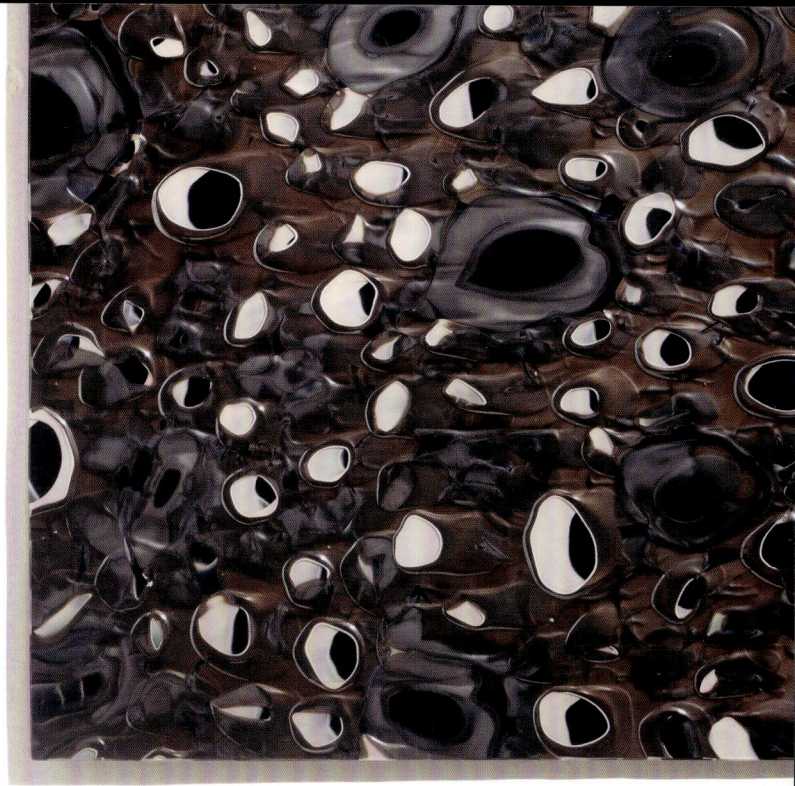
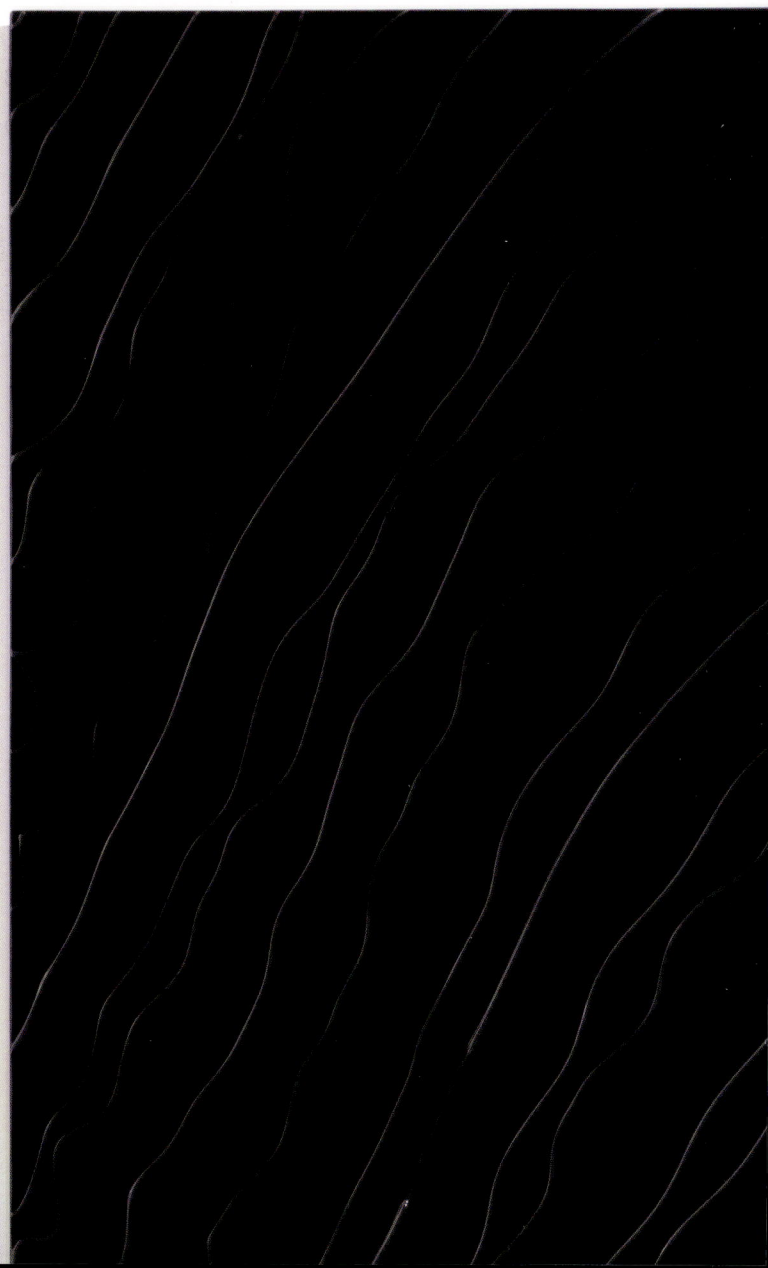

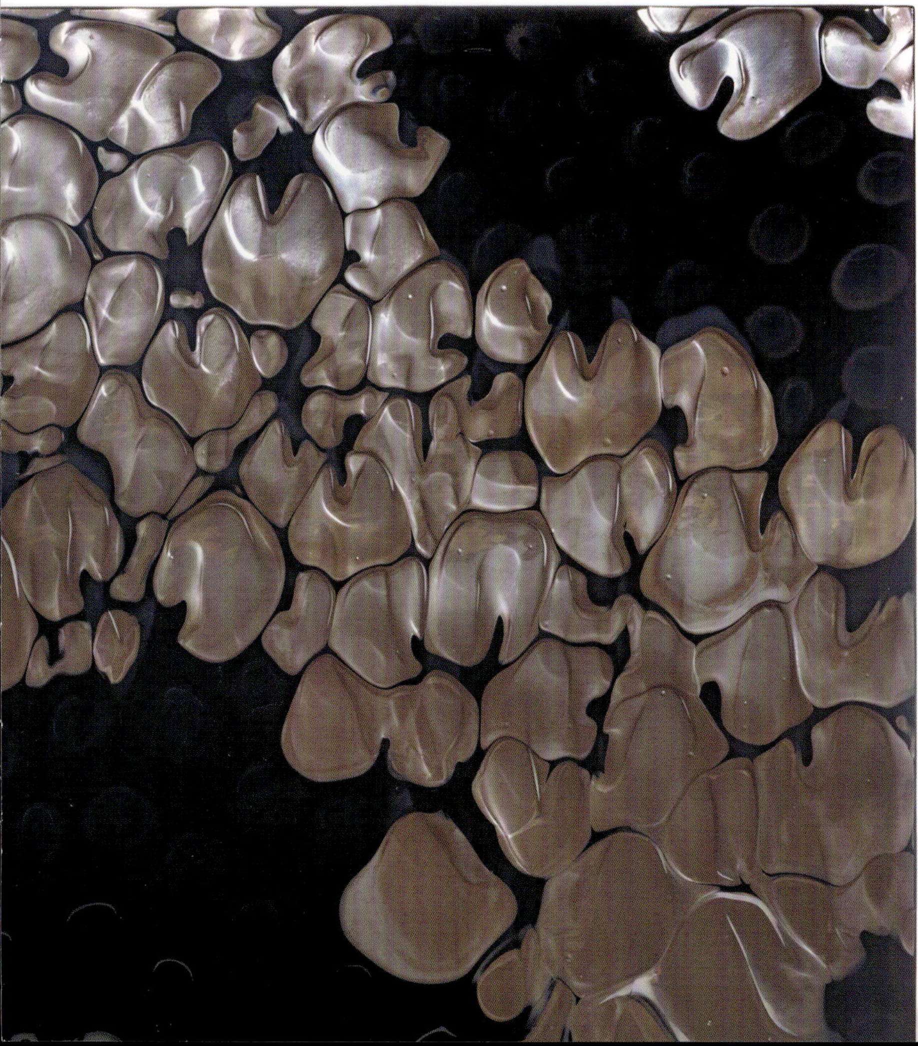

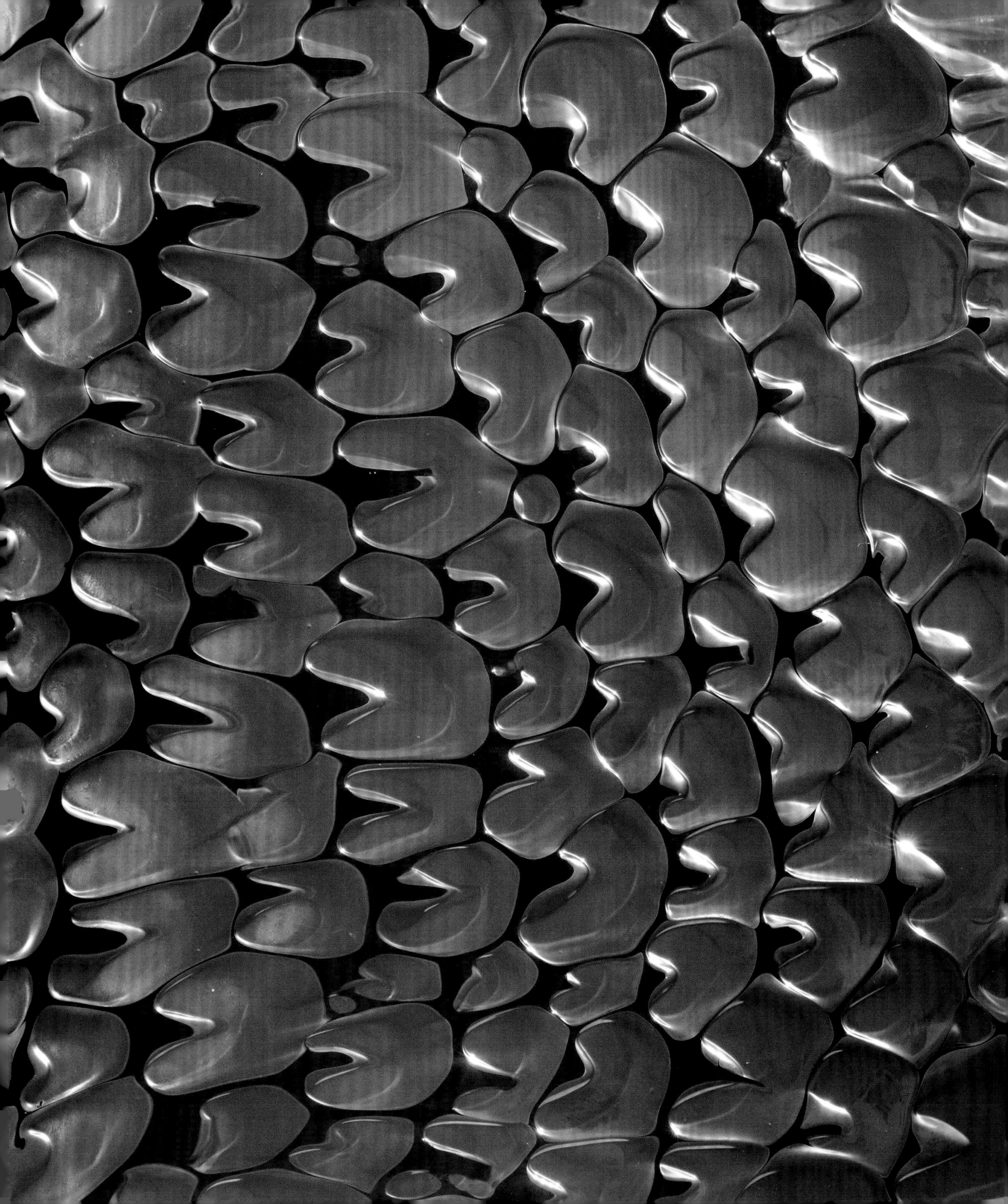

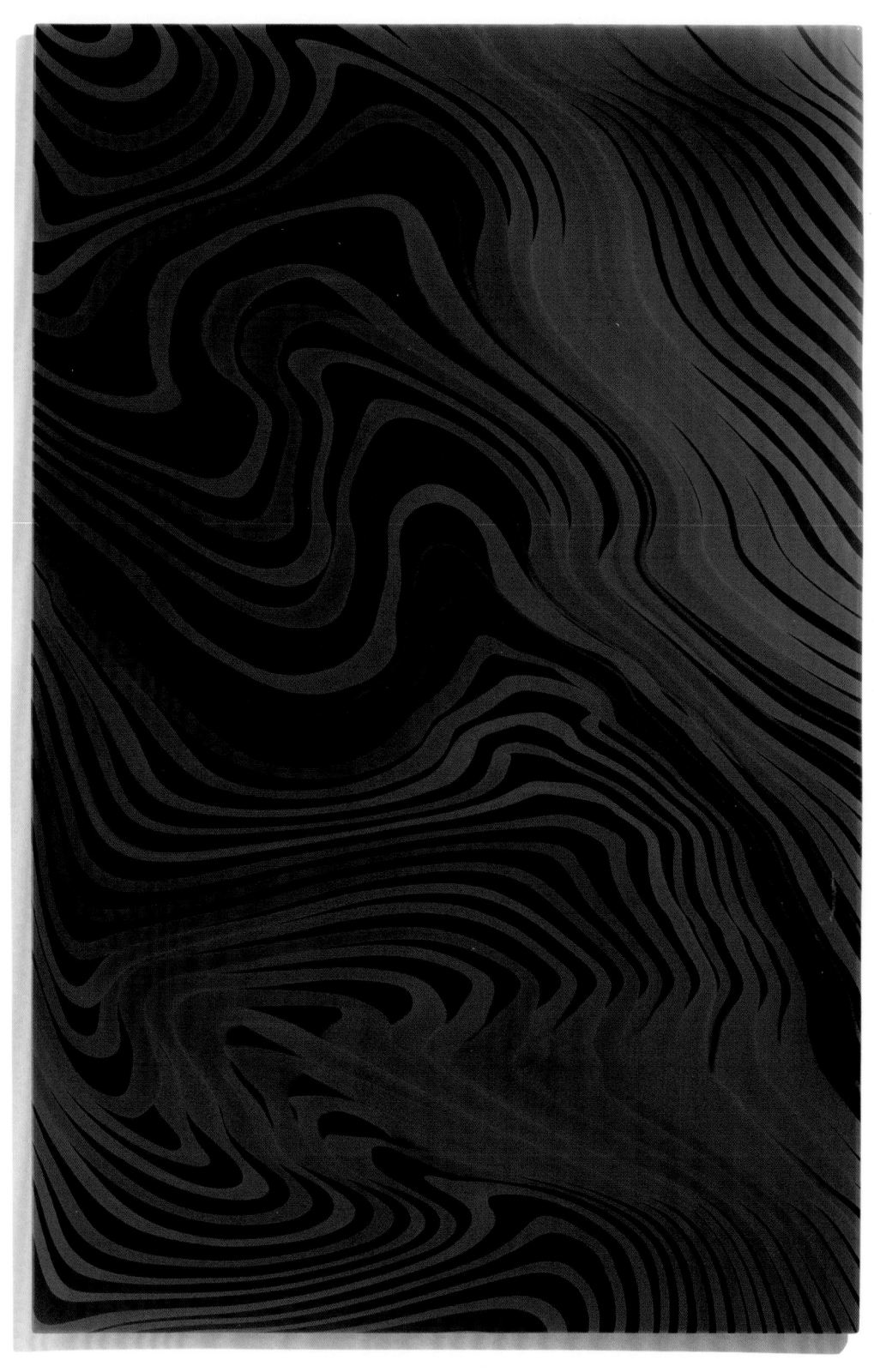

CHK. 47 *Shadow Realm* (detail), 2023 125

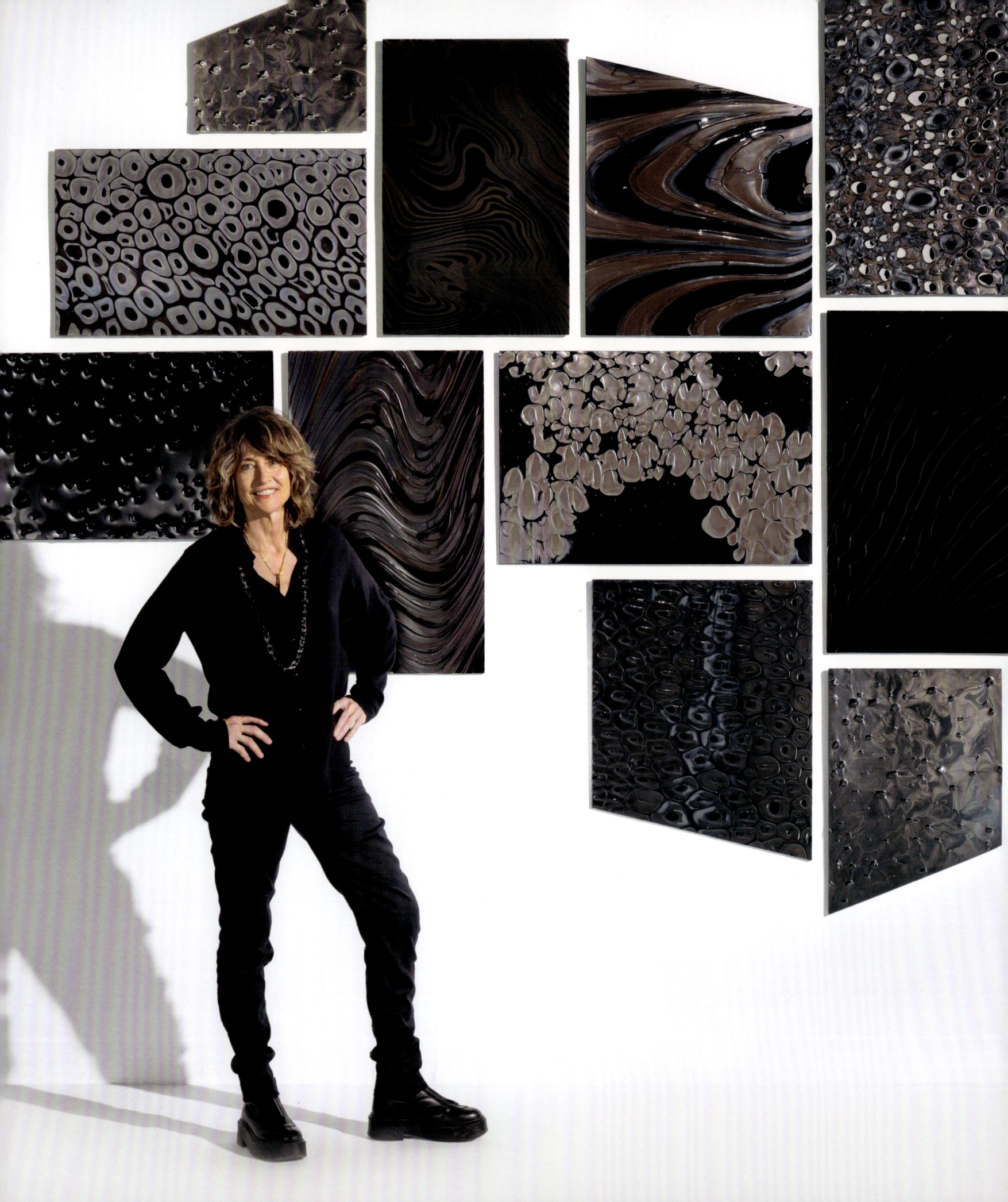

CHECKLIST

All objects are by Nancy Callan (American, born 1964); all objects are courtesy of the artist unless otherwise indicated.

All objects are blown glass unless otherwise indicated.

All measurements are height precedes width precedes depth.

All objects made at Museum of Glass, Tacoma, Washington, are identified with (*).

Checklist sequence is ordered by date.

1.
Pilchuck/Woodchuck, 2002
15 × 6½ × 5½ in. (38.1 × 16.5 × 14 cm)
Page 37

2.
Pinup Girls, 2002
Tallest: 12½ × 3½ in. (31.8 × 8.9 cm)
Collection of Alysia Duckler
Page 38

3.
Ask Alice, 2003
14 × 8½ × 4 in. (35.6 × 21.6 × 10.2 cm)
Collection of Fay Jones
Page 34

4.
Beefcake Boys, 2003
Tallest: 14 × 6 in. (35.6 × 15.2 cm)
Collection of Joey Lizotte
Page 39

5.
Night Cap, 2003
13½ × 8 × 6 in. (34.3 × 20.3 × 15.2 cm)
Collection of Rosalind B. Poll
Page 33

6.
Missoni Winkle, 2007
26 × 10 × 8 in. (66 × 25.4 × 20.3 cm)
Collection of Karen Koehler
Page 66

7.
Red Riding Hood, 2007
Blown and etched glass
17 × 12 × 8 in. (43.2 × 30.5 × 20.3 cm)
Page 64

8.
Bee Butts, 2007–2008
Largest: 10 × 10 × 12 in. (25.4 × 25.4 × 30.5 cm)
Page 46

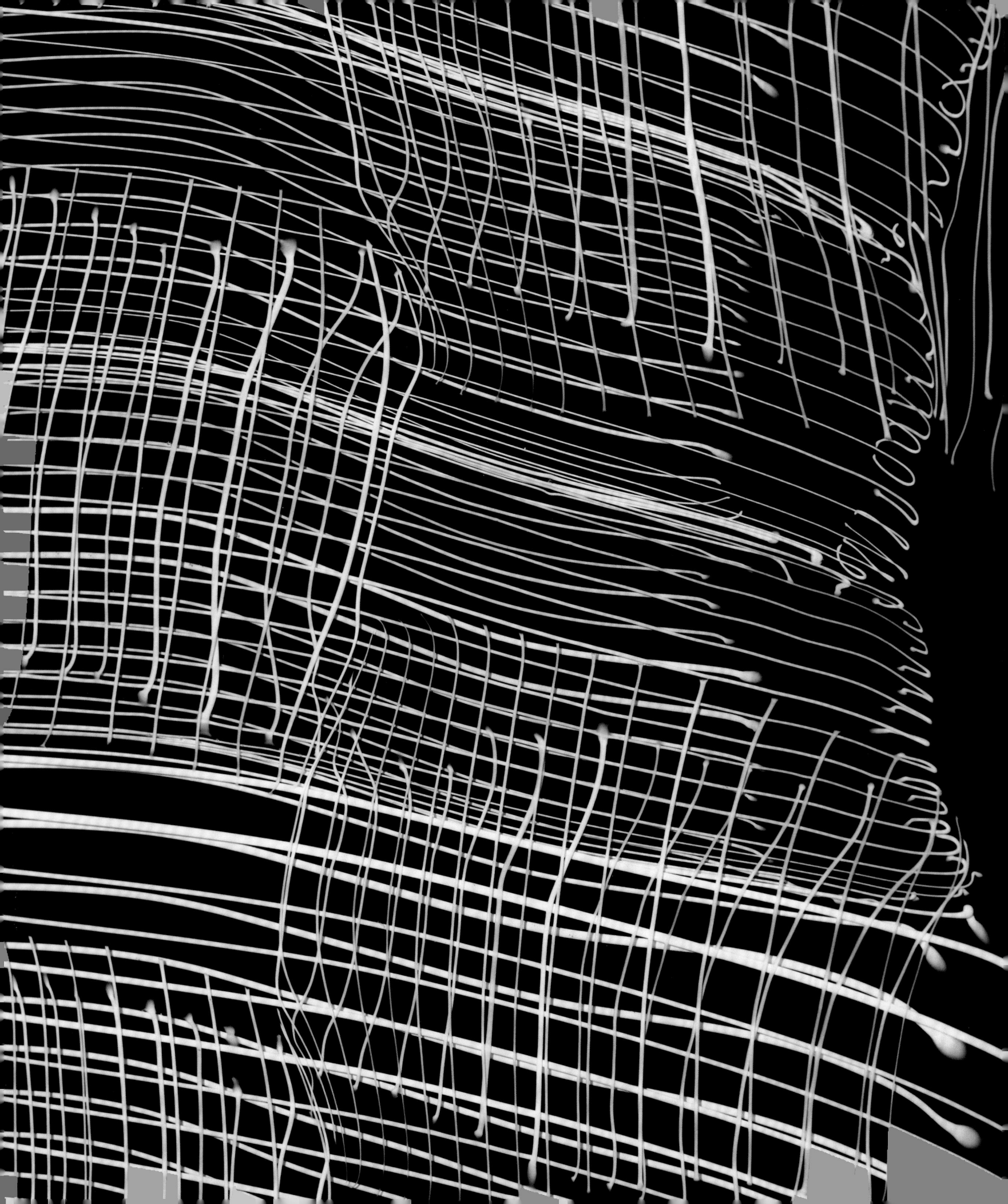

Comme les Filles (detail), 2023
(Chk. 37)

SELECTED BIBLIOGRAPHY

2023

McQuade, Kate. "Alumni Art Show Fetes 150 Years of Mass College of Art – and Those Who Dare to Be Different." *Boston Globe*, October 20, 2023.

2022

Dorfman, John. "Nancy Callan's Art: Pattern-Seeking." *Art & Antiques* (April 2022): 30–35; excerpted online at https://www.artandantiquesmag.com/nancy-callans-glass-art/.

Tasnim, Sadia. "CONVERSATION: Nancy Callan on Capturing Fleeting Moments in New Work Now on View at San Francisco's Montague Gallery." *UrbanGlass Hot Sheet*, March 24, 2022. https://urbanglass.org/glass/detail/nancy-callans-phenomena-at-the-montague.

2021

Childs, Mary. *In Her Voice: Influential Women in Glass.* Sandwich, MA: Sandwich Glass Museum, 2021. Exhibition catalog.

Clemans, Gayle. "Nancy Callan and Katherine Gray," review of *The Clown in Me Loves You. Glass: The UrbanGlass Art Quarterly*, No. 164 (Fall 2021): 54–55.

Melting Point. New York: Heller Gallery, 2021. Exhibition catalog (digital). https://www.hellergallery.com/june242021.

"Nancy Callan." *Talking Out Your Glass* (podcast). Season 6, episode 3 (January 21, 2021), with linked article by Shawn Waggoner: "Nancy Callan: Synthesizing Tradition and Innovation." https://talkingoutyourglass.com/nancy-callan/.

Page, Andrew. "What I Learned From Lino." *Glass: The UrbanGlass Art Quarterly*, No. 165 (Winter 2021): 12–19.

The Clown in Me Loves You: Nancy Callan and Katherine Gray. Bainbridge Island Museum of Art, 2021. Exhibition catalog.

2020

Cesarato, Monica. "Le Stanze del Vetro's New Project: Venice & American Studio Glass." *Monica Cesarato* (blog), October 22, 2020. https://www.monicacesarato.com/blog/le-stanze-del-vetros-new-project-venice-the-american-glass-studio/.

Drury, John. "Nancy Callan." Review of exhibition at Heller Gallery. *Glass: The UrbanGlass Art Quarterly*, No. 160 (Fall 2020): 55–56.

Oldknow, Tina and William Warmus. *Venice and American Studio Glass.* (Milan: Skira editore SpA, 2020): 35–37, 40, 43, 55, 64–65, 71–73, 216, 217, 230–233, 342, 355, 357.

Page, Andrew. "Venice Exhibition that Traces the American-Murano Connection and Its Influence on Studio Glass Pushes Back Opening Date Due to Covid-19 Virus." *UrbanGlass Hot Sheet*, March 3, 2020. https://urbanglass.org/glass/detail/venice-exhibition-that-traces-the-american-murano-connection-and-its-influence-on-studio-glass-pushes-back-opening-date-due-to-covid-19-virus.

Park, Emma. "On the Shoulders of Giants." *Glass: The UrbanGlass Art Quarterly*, No. 161 (Winter 2020): 34.

Smith, Farah Rose. "Her Recent Virtual Artist Talk and Exhibit, as well as the Challenges of Making Glass Art During a Pandemic." *UrbanGlass Hot Sheet*, May 2, 2020. https://urbanglass.org/glass/detail/nancy-callan-virtual-studio-tour-and-artist-talk.

2019

Cabe, Diane Cooper. "Line Meets Form: A Spectacular Collaboration." *James Renwick Alliance Craft Quarterly* (Summer 2019): 8–9. https://www.jra.org/uploads/1/1/6/9/116957809/jra_quarterly_summer2019-final.pdf.

Warmus, William. "Behaving Boldly." *Glass: The UrbanGlass Art Quarterly*, No. 154 (Spring 2019): 48–54.

2018

"Artist of the Month." *Art Alliance for Contemporary Glass*, December 2018 (digital newsletter). https://contempglass.org/artists/entry/nancy-callan2018.

"Demonstrations." *The Glass Art Society Journal* (2018): 57.

Logan, Liz. "Support System: Glass Artists Nancy Callan and Katherine Gray's Kinship – in Art and Life – Has Stood the Test of Time and Distance." *American Craft* (April/May 2018): 66–71. https://www.craftcouncil.org/magazine/article/support-system.

O'Connell, Robert. "Five Highlights from SOFA." *American Craft Council Newsletter* (Nov 8, 2018). https://www.craftcouncil.org/post/five-highlights-sofa-2018.

2017–2010

Logan, Liz. "How One Workshop Became the East Coast Epicenter of Glass Art." *Introspective Magazine*, 2017. https://www.1stdibs.com/introspective-magazine/urbanglass/.

The Corning Museum of Glass. *New Glass Review* 38 (2017): 9, 103.

"New Age Nancy Callan." *Luxe Interiors + Design* (April 2017): 154–55.

Wright, Diane. *From Here to Infinity*. Seattle: Traver Gallery, 2016. Exhibition catalog.

"Different Rays of Light." *Home & Décor Malaysia*, Issue 48 (October 2014): 62.

Shaw, Kurt. "Color Coordinated: Delicate Glass Balanced Machine-Made Sculpture on View in Regent Square." *The Tribune Review*, September 26, 2013.

"Artist of the Month." *Art Alliance for Contemporary Glass*, June 2012 (digital newsletter). https://contempglass.org/artists/entry/nancy-callan.

"Elemental." *American Art Collector* (May 2012): 122–23.

Connell, E. Jane, and Art Martin, eds. *50 × 50: Celebrating the 50th Anniversary of Studio Glass*. Muskegon, WI: Muskegon Museum of Art, 2012. 9, 18.

Stark, Melissa. "Molten Magic: Two Talents Bring Distinctive Approaches to Glass Art." *Columbus Dispatch*, April 18, 2012.

Klanten, Robert, ed. *Lux: Lamps and Lights*. Berlin: Gestalten, 2011. 90.

Flights of Fancy: The Soaring Imagination of Nancy Callan. Stockbridge, MA: Schantz Gallery, 2011. Exhibition catalog.

Josslin, Victoria. "Reviews: Nancy Callan and Julia Ricketts: 'She Said, She Said,' Traver Gallery, Tacoma, Washington, September 18–October 10, 2010." *Glass: The UrbanGlass Art Quarterly*, No. 121 (Winter 2010): 38, ill. 1064–900X.

"Nancy Callan - 21st Century Glassblower." Presentation at 2011 TEDxEast, New York, NY. http://www.youtube.com/watch?v=XpWZlr6yDt0.

Forneret, Alice. "Opening: 'Glass Quake' at Mobilia Gallery in Cambridge, Massachusetts." *UrbanGlass Hot Sheet*, April 5, 2011. https://urbanglass.org/glass/detail/opening-glass-quake-at-mobilia-gallery-in-cambridge-massachusetts.

Page, Andrew. "Opening: Nancy Callan's Collaboration with Painter Julia Ricketts at Traver Tacoma Saturday Evening." *UrbanGlass Hot Sheet*, September 17, 2010. https://urban glass.org/glass/detail/opening-nancy-callans-collaboration -with-painter-julia-ricketts-at-traver-t.

The Corning Museum of Glass. *New Glass Review* 31 (2010): 100.

2009–2003

Clark, Vicki A. Review of *Nancy Callan: Seventh-Inning Stretch. Glass: The UrbanGlass Art Quarterly*, No. 117 (Winter 2009): 38.

Shaw, Kurt. "Artist Brightens Up Pittsburgh Glass Center with Latest Solo Exhibition." *Tribune Review*, July 8, 2009.

"Pop Goes the Glass: PGC to Open Nancy Callan's *Seventh-Inning Stretch* Exhibition." *Pop Filter*, July 2009. http:// www.popcitymedia.com/popfilter/pgc0624.aspx.

Martin, Art. "Nancy Callan: Seventh-Inning Stretch," Muskegon, WI: Muskegon Museum of Art, 2009. Exhibition catalog essay.

Miller, Marla. "Playful, Colorful Tone Infused in Glassblower Nancy Callan's Work." *Muskegon Chronicle*, February 22, 2009.

Kimelman, Molly. "Childhood Recalled in Colorful Blown Glassworks at Muskegon Museum of Art." *Grand Rapids Press*, March 1, 2009.

Page, Andrew. "3 Questions for . . . Nancy Callan." *UrbanGlass Hot Sheet*, October 26, 2009. https://urbanglass.org/glass /detail/3-questions-for-...-nancy-callan.

The Corning Museum of Glass. *New Glass Review* 28 (2007): 9, 73.

Kieffer, Susan, ed. *500 Glass Objects*. New York: Lark Books, 2006. 13, 58–59.

Oldknow, Tina, ed. *25 Years of New Glass Review*. (Corning, NY: Corning Museum of Glass, 2006): 209, 212, 244.

"Public Glass Demos Coming to Centre." *Advocate-Messenger*, May 9, 2005: A3.

"Two Shows on Tap at Clark." *Lincoln Journal*, April 1, 2004.

Hannegan, Barry. "Artists Use Color to Convey Their Message." *Pittsburgh Post-Gazette*, May 6, 2004.

Ruhling, Nancy A. "Glass Acts: Contemporary Glass Artists Shatter the Preconceptions About Their Art Form." *Art & Antiques* 27 (May 2004): 42–49.

Shaw, Kurt. "From Texture to Tension." *Pittsburgh Tribune*, December 23, 2004.

Moran, Lewis, ed. "Portfolio." *American Craft Magazine* (Oct/ Nov 2003): 78.

Kangas, Matthew. "Nancy Callan at Traver Gallery" and "Nancy Callan and Julia Ricketts at Solomon Fine Art." *Glass: The UrbanGlass Art Quarterly*, No. 92 (Fall 2003): 57–58.

Morrison, Scott, producer. "Artists Express." Seattle Community College Public Access Television. 30 minutes: VHS format.

Kangas, Matthew. "Global Glass: 33rd Annual Conference of Glass Art Society." *Crart: Craft & Art* (August 2003): 58–63.

The Corning Museum of Glass. *New Glass Review* 24 (2003): 6, 35.

1994

Carlock, Marty. "Combining Glass and Art." *Wayland and West Town Crier*, June 9, 1994.

Silver, Jeanne. "Sculptures Beyond Beautiful in Mass Glass." *Boston Herald*, June 10, 1994.

Stapen, Nancy. "Art Glass with an Edge." *Boston Globe*, June 9, 1994.

ARTIST BIOGRAPHY AND EXHIBITION HISTORY

Born 1964, Lynn, Massachusetts
Lives and works in Seattle, Washington

Selected Solo and Two-Person Exhibitions

2024   *Nancy Callan: Forces at Play*, Museum of Glass, Tacoma, WA
        Counterpoint, with Mel Douglas, Sandra Ainsley Gallery, Toronto, Canada

2023   *Confluence: Nancy Callan and Mel Douglas*, Centre du Verre Contemporain, Biot, France
        The Clown in Me Loves You: Nancy Callan and Katherine Gray, Robert and Frances Fullerton Museum of Art at California State University, San Bernardino, CA

2022   *Nancy Callan: Phenomena*, Montague Gallery, San Francisco, CA

2021   *The Clown in Me Loves You: Nancy Callan and Katherine Gray*, Bainbridge Island Museum of Art, WA

2020   *Nancy Callan: Dialogues*, Heller Gallery, New York, NY

2019   *Spin, Weave, Gather*, Mint Museum, Charlotte, NC

2018   *Infinite Patterns*, Duane Reed Gallery, St. Louis, MO

2017   *Anemones*, Duncan McClellan Glass, St. Petersburg, FL

2016   *From Here to Infinity*, Traver Gallery, Seattle, WA

2015   *Over the Top*, Duncan McClellan Glass, St. Petersburg, FL

        Nancy Callan/Steve Jensen, Hawk Galleries, Columbus, OH

2014   *Totem*, with Lindsey Adelman, The Future Perfect, San Francisco, CA

2013   *Robert Lepper & Nancy Callan*, Concept Gallery, Pittsburgh, PA

2012   *Nancy Callan: Elemental*, Blue Rain Gallery, Santa Fe, NM
        Duality: Nancy Callan and Ethan Stern, Hawk Galleries, Columbus, OH

2011   *Clouds*, Davis and Cline Gallery, Ashland, OR

2010   *Nancy Callan: Glass Fantastic*, Museum of Northwest Art, La Conner, WA
        Nancy Callan: Blown Glass Sculpture, Dane Gallery, Nantucket, MA
        The Secret Garden, with Lindsey Adelman, The Future Perfect, New York, NY
        She Said, She Said, with Julia Ricketts, Traver Gallery, Tacoma, WA

2009   *New Work by Nancy Callan*, Hawk Galleries, SOFA, Chicago, IL
        Nancy Callan: Seventh-Inning Stretch, The Muskegon Museum of Art, MI, and Pittsburgh Glass Center, PA
        Come On, Get Happy!, Hawk Galleries, Columbus, OH

2008   *NeoNature*, Traver Gallery, Seattle, WA
        Nancy Callan, Davis and Cline Gallery, Ashland, OR

2007	*Wobble and Bob*, Daniel Kany Gallery, Portland, ME
2006	*Woolgathering*, William Traver Gallery, Seattle, WA
	New Work, Alysia Duckler Gallery, Portland, OR
2005	*Bee Butts*, Museum of Glass, Tacoma, WA
	New Work, Alysia Duckler Gallery, Portland, OR
	Topsy Turvy, Hawk Galleries, Columbus, OH
2004	*Objects of Diversion*, William Traver Gallery, Seattle, WA
2003	*New Work*, Alysia Duckler Gallery, Portland, OR
	Chroma, with Julia Ricketts, Friesen Gallery, Sun Valley, ID
	Moxie, William Traver Gallery, Seattle, WA
	Echoes, with Julia Ricketts, Solomon Fine Art, Seattle, WA
2002	*Toyland*, Alysia Duckler Gallery, Portland, OR
2001	*Nancy Callan*, Vetri International Glass, Seattle, WA

Selected Group Exhibitions

2024	*The Pforzheimer Collection of Studio Glass*, Peabody Essex Museum, Salem, MA
	For the Love of Glass: From the Collection of Chris Rifkin, Sandwich Glass Museum, MA
	LA Art Show, Montague Gallery, Los Angeles, CA
2023	*This is Becoming a Pattern*, Pittsburgh Glass Center, PA

	Craft Across Continents, Mint Museum, Charlotte, NC
	Connections, Schack Art Center, Everett, WA
2022	*Beyond The Ceiling*, Sarasota Art Museum of Ringling College of Art and Design, FL
	Fired Up: Glass Today, Wadsworth Atheneum Museum of Art, Hartford, CT
2021	*In Her Voice: Influential Women in Glass*, Sandwich Glass Museum, MA
	Melting Point, Heller Gallery, New York, NY and Ferrin Contemporary Gallery, North Adams, MA
	Fluid Formations: The Legacy of Glass in the Pacific Northwest, Whatcom Museum, Bellingham, WA
2020	*Venice and American Studio Glass*, Le Stanze del Vetro, Venice, Italy
2019	*Transparency: An LGBTQ+ Glass Art Exhibition*, Museum of Glass, Tacoma, WA
	Secret Admirer, Pilchuck Glass Gallery, Seattle, WA
	SOFA Chicago, Duane Reed Gallery, IL
2018	*Inner Visions*, Hawk Galleries, Columbus, OH
	TEFAF (The European Fine Art Fair), Michele Beiny Gallery, Maastricht, The Netherlands
	Masterpiece London Art Fair, Michele Beiny Gallery, New York, NY
2017	*No Glass Ceiling: Women Working in Glass Part 1*, Palm Springs Art Museum, CA

2016 *Nancy Callan: Snowmen*, Museum of Glass, Tacoma, WA
Hotspot: Contemporary Glass from Private Collections, Toledo Museum of Art, OH

2015 *Group Show*, Chihuly Collection, St. Petersburg, FL
Glass Works, Museo, Langley, WA

2014 Schantz Galleries, Stockbridge, MA
Masters of Glass, Napua Gallery, Waimea, HI
Traver Gallery, Seattle, WA

2013 *Curiosity Vessels*, Carwan Gallery, Katara Art Center, Doha, Qatar
eXpose, Habatat Galleries, Royal Oaks, MI
Nancy Callan: Snowmen, Museum of Glass, Tacoma, WA
Glass Today, Blue Rain Gallery, Santa Fe, NM
Contemporary Glass from the Kaplan/Ostergaard Collection, Palm Springs Art Museum, CA

2012 *Strong Presence*, Hodgell Gallery, Sarasota, FL
50 x 50: Celebrating the 50th Anniversary of Studio Glass, Muskegon Museum of Art, MI

2011 *Homage to Bornholm*, Grønbechs Gård, Hasle, Denmark
Schantz Gallery Glass Tour, Seattle, WA
Glass Quake, Mobilia Gallery, Cambridge, MA
Convergence Zone, Bellevue Arts Museum, WA

2010 *Nancy Callan: Summer Series*, Schantz Galleries, Stockbridge, MA
Glass Arts Society Group Exhibition, Zephyr Gallery, Louisville, KY

2009 *Blue Rain Gallery and the New Glass Art Movement of the Southwest*, Blue Rain Gallery, Santa Fe, NM
The Blue Room, New Glass Art and Photography, Berlin, Germany

2008 *Clear Your Mind: Contemporary Glass Invitational*, Figge Museum, Davenport, IA
Homage to a Maestro, Museum of Glass, Tacoma, WA

2007 *Ongoing Invention*, Robert V. Fullerton Art Museum, California State University, San Bernadino, CA
Behind Glass: Creativity and Collaboration, The Arts Center, St. Petersburg, FL
Summer Exhibition, Holsten Gallery, Stockbridge, MA

2006 *Seattle Artists Exhibition*, D&A Fine Arts, Los Angeles, CA
Burning Ideas: Contemporary Visions in Glass, River Tree Center for the Arts, Kennebunk, ME
Made at the Museum, Museum of Glass, Tacoma, WA

2005 *Contemporary Glass*, Missoula Art Museum, MT

2004 *The Italian Influence in Contemporary Glass*, Corning Museum of Glass, NY
Fall for Glass '04, Morgan Contemporary Glass, Pittsburgh, PA

A New Vanguard, Chappell Gallery, New York, NY
Long Live the Lamplighters, Priceless Works Gallery, Seattle, WA
Fiery Influences, Hanson Gallery, New Orleans, LA
The Language of Color, Morgan Contemporary Glass, Pittsburgh, PA
Glass Invitational, Clark Gallery, Lincoln, MA

2003 *Artists of My Area/Era Working Drawings*, Bubba-Mavis Presentation, Seattle, WA

2002 *New Artists*, William Traver Gallery, Seattle, WA
Introductions, Alysia Duckler Gallery, Portland, OR

2001 *The White Exhibition*, Portfolio Gallery, Vancouver, BC

2000 *Pratt Instructors Show*, CoCA Gallery, Seattle WA

1996 *Glass: The Cutting Edge*, Clark Gallery, Lincoln, MA
Master and Students, Grohe Gallery, Boston, MA
Mass Glass, Bakalar Gallery, Boston, MA

Professional Experience

2023 Co-Instructor with Mel Douglas, Penland School of Craft, Bakersville, NC

2022 Co-Instructor with Mel Douglas, The Studio, Corning, NY
Demonstrating Artist, Glass Arts Society Conference, Murano, Italy
Co-Instructor with Mel Douglas, Pilchuck Glass School, Stanwood, WA
Demonstrating Artist with Shelley Muzylowski-Allen, REFRACT at Seattle Glassblowing Studio, Seattle, WA

2021 Visiting Artist, Rochester Institute of Technology, NY, via Zoom
Gallery Talk with Katherine Gray, Bainbridge Island Museum of Art, WA

2020 Guest Artist, Panel Discussion, "Venice and American Studio Glass," via Zoom

2019 Master Class, Fluid, Belle Île, France
Artist Lecture, Seven Bridges Foundation, Greenwich, CT
Guest Artist Lecture, James Renwick Alliance, Washington, DC
Guest Speaker, American Craft Council 2019 Conference, Philadelphia, PA

2018 Demonstrating Artist, Glass Art Society Conference, Murano, Italy
Co-Instructor with Mel Douglas, Pittsburgh Glass Center, PA
Instructor, The Studio, Corning, NY

2017 Instructor, Pilchuck Glass School, Stanwood, WA
Instructor, UrbanGlass, Brooklyn, NY
Visiting Artist with Katherine Gray, UrbanGlass, Brooklyn, NY

2016 Instructor, Pittsburgh Glass Center, PA

Instructor, The Studio, Corning, NY
Demonstrating Artist, Ignite Glass Studios, Chicago
Demonstrating Artist with Rich Royal, Schantz
Galleries Glass Weekend, Canaan, NY

2015 Instructor, Haystack Mountain School, Deer Isle, ME
Artist Lecture, Museum of Fine Arts,
St. Petersburg, FL
Demonstrating Artist, 2015 GAS Conference,
San Jose, CA
Instructor, Penland School of Crafts, Bakersville, NC

2014 Instructor, Pilchuck Glass School, Stanwood, WA

2013 Visiting Artist, Berlin Glas, Germany
Visiting Artist, Aalto University of the Arts,
Helsinki, Finland
Presenter, Kawasaki City Glass Conference,
Kanagawa, Japan

2012 Visiting Artist, Aalto University of the Arts,
Helsinki, Finland

2011 Presenter, TEDxEast, New York, NY

2010 Instructor, Pilchuck Glass School, Stanwood, WA

2009 Instructor, Pittsburgh Glass Center, PA

2008 Instructor, Haystack Mountain School of Crafts,
Deer Isle, ME

2006 Gaffer for artist Anne Wilson, Museum of Glass,
Tacoma, WA
Featured Artist, Museum of Glass, Tacoma, WA

2005 Gaffer, Pilchuck Glass School, Stanwood, WA
Visiting Artist, Center College, Danville, KY
Featured Artist, Museum of Glass, Tacoma, WA

2003 Instructor, Haystack Mountain School of Crafts,
Deer Isle, ME
Gaffer, Pilchuck Glass School, Stanwood, WA

2001 Instructor, Beginning Glassblowing, The Studio,
Corning, NY
Gaffer, Pilchuck Glass School, Stanwood, WA

1998–2006 Gaffer for Ginny Ruffner, Seattle, WA

1998–2003 Assistant to Josiah McElheny, Seattle, WA

1998–2001 Instructor, Pratt Fine Arts Center, Seattle, WA

1998 Teaching Assistant to Josiah McElheny, Pilchuck Glass
School, Stanwood, WA
Hot Shop Manager and Gaffer, Manifesto Corporation,
Seattle, WA

1996–2016 Assistant to Lino Tagliapietra, Seattle, WA

Selected Grants, Awards, Fellowships, and Residencies

2023 Museum of Glass, Tacoma, WA
Centre du Verre Contemporain, Biot, France

2022 The Studio, Corning, NY
Museum of Glass, Tacoma, WA

2019 Chrysler Museum of Art, Norfolk, VA
Museum of Glass, Tacoma, WA

2018 Pittsburgh Glass Center, PA
STARworks, Star, NC

2017 Museum of Glass, Tacoma, WA

2016 Visiting Artist, University of Wisconsin–Stevens Point
STARworks, Star, NC

2015 Gaffer Olympian, Pilchuck Glass School,
Stanwood, WA
Museum of Glass, Tacoma, WA

2014 University of Texas at Arlington
Chrysler Museum of Art, Norfolk, VA

2013 Pittsburgh Glass Center, PA

2012 Toledo Museum of Art, OH
Museum of Glass, Tacoma, WA

2011 Museum of Glass, Tacoma, WA

2010 Museum of Glass, Tacoma, WA
University of Louisville, KY

2005 Center College, Danville, KY

2004 Museum of Glass, Tacoma, WA

2003 Featured Artist, Museum of Glass, Tacoma, WA
King County Special Projects Grant, King County, WA

2001 Creative Glass Center of America Fellowship,
Wheaton Village, Millville, NJ

1996 Corning Glass Studio Scholarship, NY

Selected Collections

Bainbridge Island Museum of Art, WA
Barry Art Museum, Norfolk, VA
Chrysler Museum of Art, Norfolk, VA
The Corning Museum of Glass, NY
Fort Worth Museum of Art, TX
Foundation for the Carolinas, Charlotte, NC
Imagine Museum, St. Petersburg, FL
Microsoft Collection, Redmond, WA
Mint Museum, Charlotte, NC
Museum of Glass, Tacoma, WA
Museum of Northwest Art, La Conner, WA
Muskegon Museum of Art, MI
Peabody Essex Museum, Salem, MA
Racine Art Museum, WI
Seven Bridges Foundation, Greenwich, CT
Shanghai Museum of Art, China
Sir Elton John and David Furnish, Atlanta, GA
Toledo Art Museum, OH
Wheaton Village Museum of Glass, Millville, NJ

Education

1996 Bachelor of Fine Arts, Massachusetts College of
Art, Boston
Advanced Glassblowing Workshop, Lino Tagliapietra,
The Studio, Corning, NY

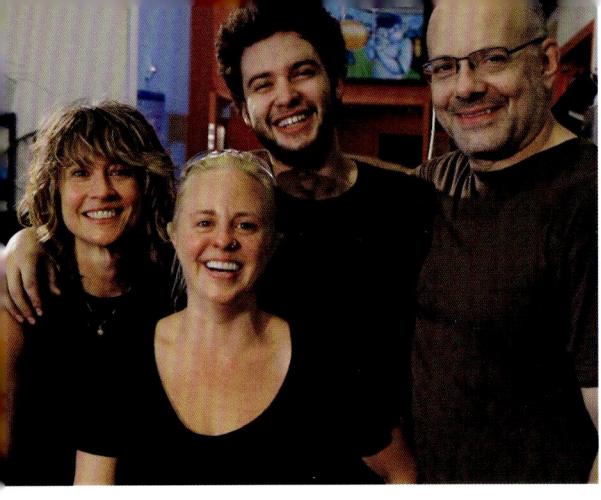
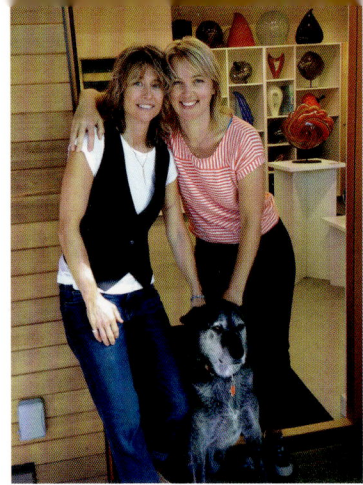
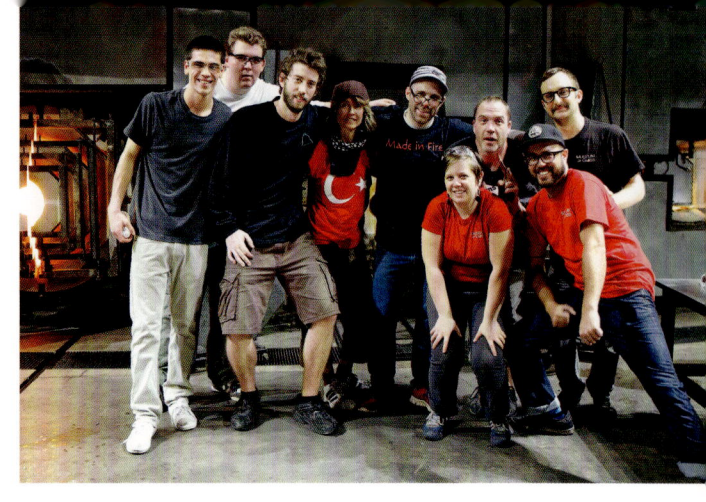
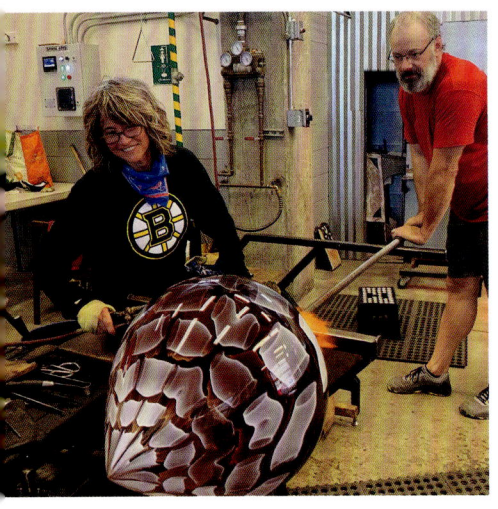
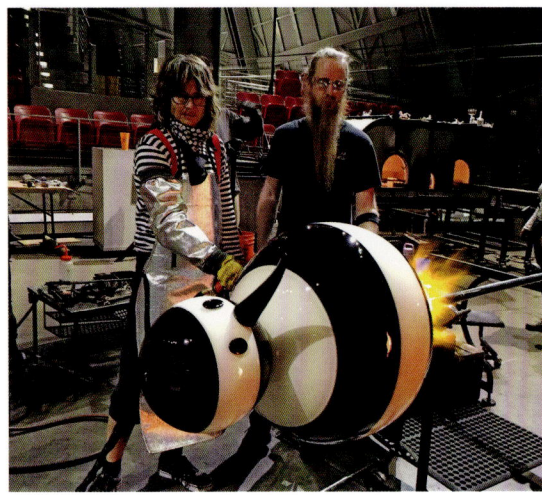
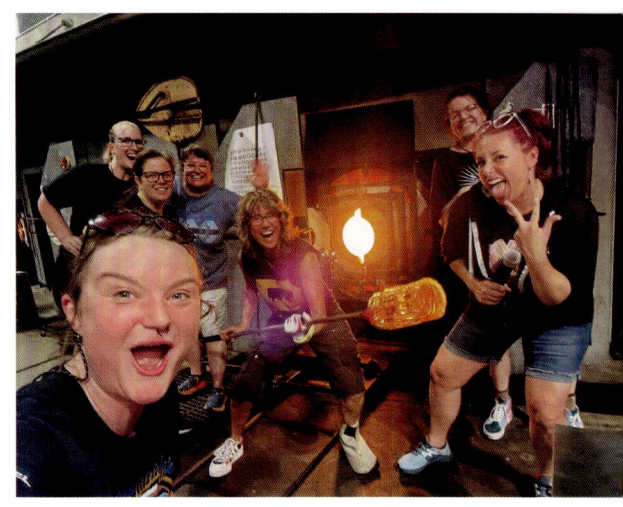
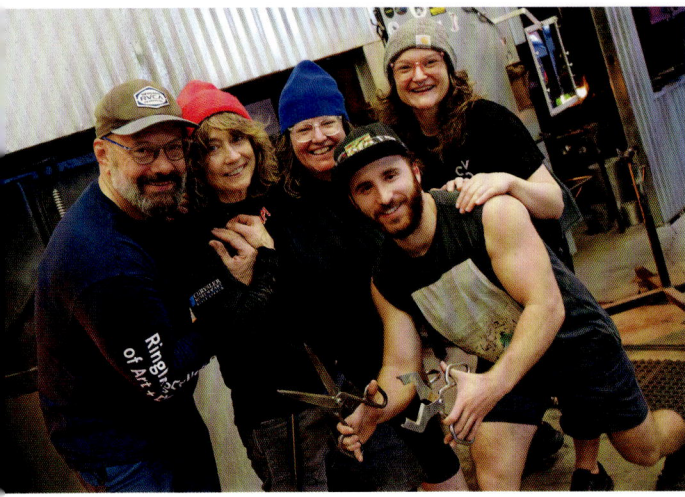
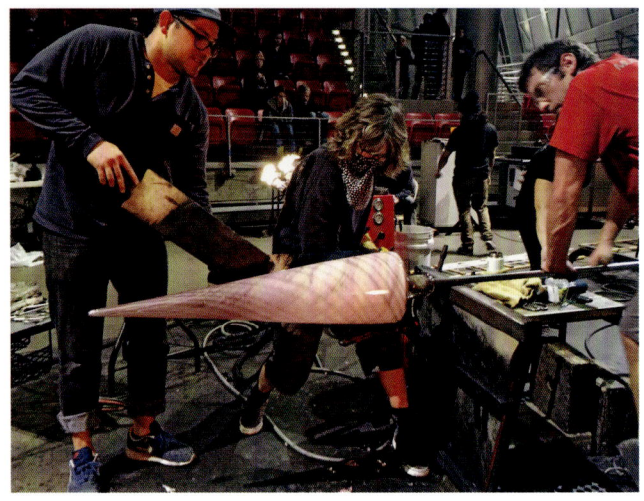
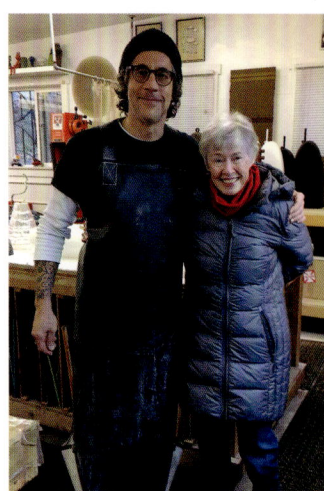
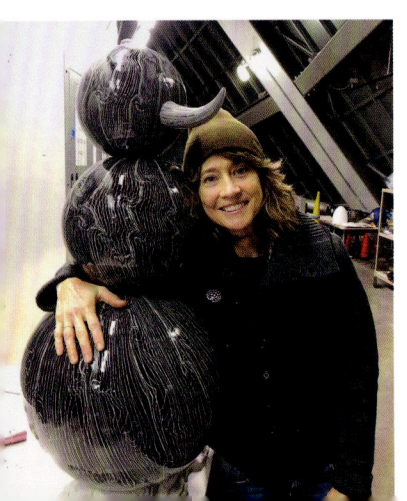
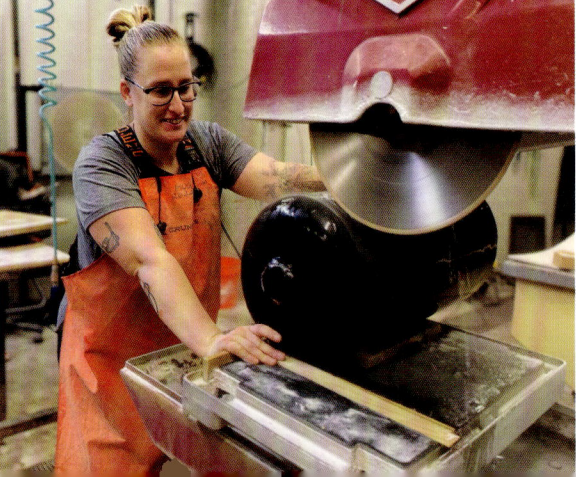
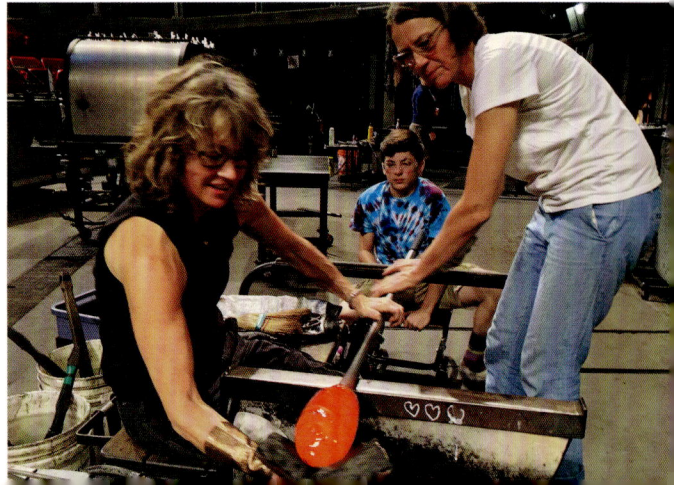

Members of the artist's team,
family, and community

ACKNOWLEDGMENTS FROM THE ARTIST

Thank you to Julia Ricketts for your unconditional love, talent, and wisdom. The hours and hours of time spent imagining, writing, creating, brainstorming, and helping me to realize my vision are incalculable. You make life so much better!

I am grateful to the community of glass workers and artists who helped me make the work for this exhibition, especially my current team—David Walters, Jen Elek, Kristin Elliot, Tanner Weiss, and Mariah Cavanagh: thank you for supporting me and for truly making me feel like you want me to succeed. Huge thanks to the Museum of Glass team: Ben Cobb, whose inability to say "no" and whose incredible dedication and skills I value deeply, Courtney Branam, Nick Davis, Sarah Gilbert, and Gabe Feenan. Thanks also to Granite Calimpong, Alix Cannon, Jason Christian, Nico Dimitrijevic, Darin Denison, Isaac Feuerman, Karsten Oaks, Greg Owen (RIP), Jack Spitzer, Austin Stern, Ethan Stern, and Alex Stisser for their contributions. Special thanks in memory of Joseph BenVenuto.

Deep appreciation to the amazing Russell Johnson for putting my work in the best light with his photography, and to Lisa Liedgren Alexandersson, Ken Emly, Suzanne Head, Derek Klein, and KCJ Szwedzinski for their creative and technical contributions.

To my lifelong friends and collaborators—Lindsey Adelman, Mel Douglas, and Katherine Gray—thank you for your love and inspiration!

To my *Maestro* Lino Tagliapietra, a profound thank you for showing me the way. You are my greatest teacher; thank you for sharing your life and legacy with me.

To my parents, Rita Callan and in memory of Bob Callan: thank you for nurturing my creativity and always making me feel confident in who I am. I love you. To my inspiring big brother, Joey Lizotte: thank you for always being there!

To the Museum, for the many opportunities to work in the Hot Shop with outstanding people and significant resources. The artistic growth that came from these residencies is a profound gift.

Thank you to all of my gallerists and dealers, particularly Jim Schantz and Kim Saul of Schantz Galleries. To the many collectors, mentors, and friends who have helped me along the way: this exhibition would not be possible without you.

In memory of Millie Warren, whose love and support meant the world to me.

CREDITS

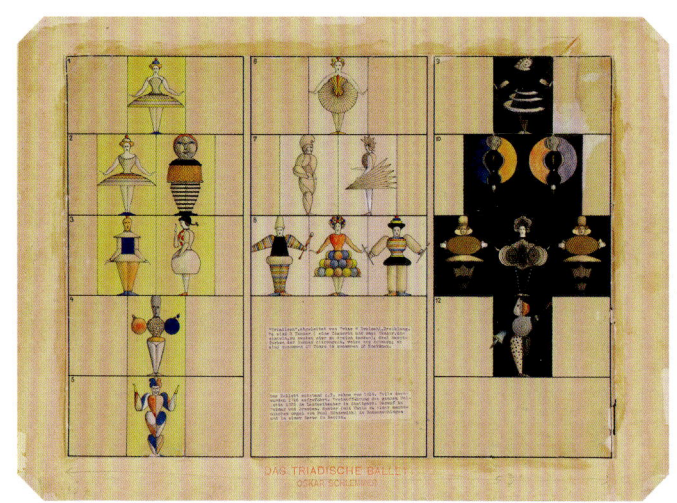

All objects are by Nancy Callan (American, born 1964), unless otherwise indicated

All photography © Russell Johnson, unless otherwise indicated

Introduction by Katie Buckingham

Fig. 1
Artist assisting Lino Tagliapietra in Mukilteo, Washington, 2013

Fig. 2
Artist making *Stellar Net* (Chk. 35) at Museum of Glass assisted by Jen Elek and Hot Shop team member Sarah Gilbert, 2022
Photo by Kristin Elliot

Fig. 3
Artist and Hot Shop Director Benjamin Cobb at Museum of Glass Snowman Blow, making *Blueprint for a Snowman I*, 2012 (Chk. 16), in 2011
Photo by Ken Emly

Interplay: Identity and Influence in the Art of Nancy Callan by Gayle Clemans

Fig. 1
Artist assisting Lino Tagliapietra in Mukilteo, Washington, 2012
Photo by Ken Emly

Fig. 2
Pop Top, 2014 (Chk. 21)

Fig. 3
Artist, assisted by Jen Elek, shaping large cylinder at Museum of Glass, 2023

Fig. 4
Walter Lieberman (American, born 1954)
How Nancy Callan makes her flat panels, 2019
Chalk on the Museum of Glass Hot Shop concrete floor
Approx. 60 × 60 in. (152.4 × 152.4 cm)
Photo by Walter Lieberman

Fig. 5 (entire image above)
Oskar Schlemmer (German, 1888–1943)
Costume Designs for *Das Triadische Ballet* [The Triadic Ballet] (detail), 1926
Black ink, opaque and transparent watercolor, metallic paint, and graphite on cream wove paper mounted to cream card
15³⁄₁₆ × 21⅛ in. (53.7 × 38.6 cm)
Harvard Art Museums/Busch-Reisinger Museum, Museum Purchase
Photo © President and Fellows of Harvard College

Fig. 6
The Robber, 2016
Blown glass
31 × 18½ in. (78.7 × 47 cm)
Collection of Doug and Pat Perry

Fig. 7
Road Trip with Keith, 2022 (Chk. 34)

Fig. 8
Shadow Realm (detail), 2023 (Chk. 47)

Nancy Callan: Playing to Her Strengths by Kim Harty

Fig. 1
Toy Wallpaper (detail), 2023
Photos on vinyl
Courtesy of the artist

Fig. 2
Artist with *Catwoman Stinger*, 2022 (Chk. 33)

Fig. 3
Aqua Silk Crinkle Winkle, 2006
Blown glass
33 × 7 × 9 in. (83.82 × 17.78 × 22.86 cm)
Collection of Jeremy Harrison

Fig. 4
Comme les Filles, 2023 (Chk. 37)

Fig. 5
Azure Droplet, 2016
Blown and etched glass
13 × 14½ in. diam. (33 × 36.8 cm)
Courtesy of the artist

Fig. 6
Shadow Realm (detail), 2023 (Chk. 47)

CONTRIBUTORS

Katie Buckingham

Katie Buckingham is the curator at Museum of Glass, where she develops exhibitions, researches collections, and coordinates MOG's vibrant Visiting Artist Residency program. Through her research, Buckingham aims to establish dynamic connections between glass past and present, including most recently in her essay "Hindsight is 1920: Reflecting on Glass a Century after René Lalique," for the Museum of Glass exhibition publication *René Lalique: Art Deco Gems from the Steven and Roslyn Shulman Collection* (2020).

Buckingham is active within her local museum community, currently serving as past president of the Washington Museum Association. Prior to Museum of Glass, she worked at the Museum of History and Industry in Seattle. Buckingham received an MA in museology from the University of Washington and a BA with Honors in art history from Whitman College.

Gayle Clemans

Gayle Clemans is an art historian, critic, and writer with frequent contributions of art criticism and journalism to the *Seattle Times* and *Glass: The UrbanGlass Art Quarterly*. Her essays appear in a variety of publications, including journals, exhibition catalogs, *Smarthistory*, and the award-winning book *The Map as Art* (2010). Having received a PhD in modern and contemporary art from the University of Washington, Clemans works on deconstructing the canon (which was always a fabrication) to shed light on a variety of art practices and the diverse positionalities of artists.

Clemans is professor of critical + contextual studies and current co-chair of the Art Department at Cornish College of the Arts in Seattle, where she teaches art history and critical arts writing. Clemans has also engaged in material research and artmaking, which grounds her in the creative practices she researches and writes about. In the realms of speculative fiction and creative non-fiction, Clemans writes short stories and novels that gravitate toward symbolism, institutional critique, and the importance of locating deeply personal experiences within larger socio-historical contexts.

Kim Harty

Kim Harty is an artist and scholar whose work investigates the connection between craft and performance through sculpture, installation, video, and performance. She is heavily informed by her training as a glassblower and is interested in undoing traditional methods of making and investigating how materials can confound their expected function. Harty is section lead and associate professor of glass at the College for Creative Studies in Detroit.

SPONSORS

Doug and Nanci Allen

Art Alliance for Contemporary Glass (AACG)

Brenda and Jeffrey Atkin

Richard and Judith Baerg

Dr. Laurie Baxter and Charles Cannon

Alix Cannon

Howard Cohen and Myra Musicant

Laurie and Jerry Feinberg

Katherine Gray

James Renwick Alliance for Craft

Lorne Lassiter and Gary Ferraro

Joey Lizotte

Nancy and Roger MacPherson

Jill and Steve Miller

Roger Myers and Trudi Rowbury

The Norcliffe Foundation

Jacob Price

Chris Rifkin

Kim Saul and Jim Schantz

Dorothy Saxe

Scott Schade and Lisa Kjaer-Schade

Ann and John Underwood

Kenneth Winter

Jonathan and Nancy Wolf

Barbara and Richard Wortley

Nancy Callan: Forces at Play accompanies the exhibition of the same name organized by Museum of Glass, Tacoma, Washington, on view October 5, 2024–August 2025.

Library of Congress Control Number: 2024934234
ISBN: 978-0-9726649-9-8

Museum of Glass
1801 Dock Street
Tacoma, Washington 98402
www.museumofglass.org

Distributed by University of Washington Press
www.uwapress.uw.edu

Produced by Marquand Books, Seattle
www.marquandbooks.com

Designed by Ryan Polich
Edited by Kathleen Garrett
Proofread by Ivy Long
Typeset in Quarion and Optician Sans by Brynn Warriner
Project managed by Rebecca J. Engelhardt
Printed and bound in China by C&C Offset Printing Co.

Cover: *Cosmic Waves*, 2023 (Chk. 38)

Title spread: Artist with *Comme les Filles*, 2023 (Chk. 37)

Page 4: Callan's pattern and form begin to take shape as molten glass is reheated in the Museum of Glass Hot Shop, 2023

Page 6: Museum of Glass' iconic Hot Shop Cone, located on Tacoma's Thea Foss Waterway, 2017. Photo courtesy of Museum of Glass

Page 8: Artist using jacks to shape a large glass bubble in the Museum's Hot Shop, 2023

Page 22: Artist making *incalmo* in the Museum of Glass Hot Shop, 2012. Photo by Ken Emly

Pages 42–43: Artist with Museum of Glass Hot Shop team making *Blueprint for a Snowman I*, 2012 (Chk. 16), at Museum of Glass Snowman Blow, in 2011. Photos by Ken Emly

Page 55: A *Stinger* takes shape from molten glass in the Museum's Hot Shop, 2013. Photo by Ken Emly

Page 56: Artist making *Mystique Stinger* (Chk. 42) at the Museum of Glass Hot Shop, assisted by Tanner Weiss, David Walters, and Benjamin Cobb, 2023. Photo by Kristin Elliot

Page 67: Artist making *Missoni Winkle* (Chk. 6) at Pilchuck Glass School, assisted by Anne Rushing, Kait Rhoads, and Kelly O'Dell. Also pictured: iLan Epstein and Michael Hernandez, 2007.

Page 126: Artist with *Shadow Realm* (detail), 2023 (Chk. 47)

Page 138: Members of the artist's team, family, and community. Top left photo by Derek Klein; top right photo by Ken Emly; all other photos courtesy of the artist